ORGANIZATIONAL EPISTEM

Organizational Epistemology

George von Krogh
Professor of Management
Institute of Management
University of St Gallen
Switzerland

and

Johan Roos
Professor of Strategy
International Institute for
Management Development (IMD)
Switzerland

St. Martin's Press

First published in Great Britain 1995 by
MACMILLAN PRESS LTD
Houndmills, Basingstoke, Hampshire RG21 6XS
and London
Companies and representatives
throughout the world

A catalogue record for this book is available
from the British Library.

ISBN 0-333-60987-5

10   9   8   7   6   5   4   3   2   1
04   03   02   01   00   99   98   97   96   95

Printed and bound in Great Britain by
Antony Rowe Ltd
Chippenham, Wiltshire

First published in the United States of America 1995 by
Scholarly and Reference Division,
ST. MARTIN'S PRESS, INC.,
175 Fifth Avenue,
New York, N.Y. 10010

ISBN 0-312-12498-8

Library of Congress Cataloging-in-Publication Data
von Krogh, Georg.
Organizational epistemology / by Georg von Krogh and Johan Roos.
p.   cm.
Includes bibliographical references and index.
ISBN 0-312-12498-8 (cloth)
1. Organizational effectiveness.   2. Learning strategies.
3. Continuing education.   4. Knowledge, Sociology of.   I. Roos
Johan.   II. Title.
HD58.9.V66   1995
302.3'5—dc20   95-17926
                                                         CIP

Contents

List of Figures

Foreword

Dear Reader,   Santa Fe, New Mexico
                                      November 11, 1994

The purpose of this letter is to provide some background and perspective to this book. This book is about how we learn to know things.

At the time of this writing, Georg and Johan (the authors) and I are at the Santa Fe Institute, New Mexico, for a meeting that brings together business people and researchers. The subjects being discussed range across a spectrum of scales from microbiology to macroeconomics and all the complexity inbetween.

Each of us expects to learn something of value as a result of our being here. None of us knows exactly what we are going to learn or which path we will take in pursuit of this knowledge. We are confident, however, that the process works.

The process is well-developed and understood among the three of us. We never know what will come from the process ahead of time. We listen carefully, then we talk to each other about what we thought we heard.

Each successive iteration builds a new unplanned branch of thought to our past understandings, as we each contribute our personal views about what we have absorbed.

This book should be considered as part of the same process at a different scale. It is a carefully considered output (from Georg and Johan) to be offered into the mix of what the rest of us are routinely thinking and talking about. Absorb it, think about it, then talk about it.

Sincerely
KENNETH R. SLOCUM

1 Devising a Concept of Organizational Knowledge

INTRODUCTION

By expounding, discussing and illustrating organizational knowledge the objective of this book is to give the reader an observational scheme to better understand organizational knowledge development on the individual and the social scale. This observational scheme is intended for the knowledge development of the reader. It does *not* represent any pre-given 'truth' of organizational knowledge development whatsoever. The book is our first attempt to develop such a scheme and, as such, the book is only a brief report from an ongoing knowledge development process.

Our conceptual system distinguishes between individual knowledge and social knowledge, and describes properties of both. It also makes two further attempts: first, to innovate a language that can describe the properties of knowledge, without resorting to conventional nomenclature; and second, to innovate a language that can describe the messy, complex, and iterative processes that give rise to organizational knowledge. It is not until we have made the proper conceptual innovations, in our opinion, that we can be said to begin to conceive of a notion of organizational knowledge. This conceptual innovation will be derived from autopoiesis theory and a theory of scaling. From this book we hope to give input to the reader so that he can self-construct his own images of organizational knowledge. Of course, each reader decides which of these inputs are meaningful to him/her.

Any study of knowledge runs up against problems of definitions. This is not only a modern puzzle. In one of his many dialogues, Socrates discussed with a young mathematician, Theaetetus, what he thought knowledge was. After clearing up the confusion between knowledge and application of

1

knowledge, the dialogue centres on knowledge as (1) sensible perception, (2) knowledge as true opinion, and (3) knowledge as true opinion with reasoned explanations. All these definitions, claimed as true by Theaetetus during the dialogue with Socrates, are refuted at the end.[1]

Moving back to our own century, some 50 years ago Ludwig Wittgenstein pointed out that 'knowledge' is not easily defined in an exact manner. Wittgenstein further warns us that this lack of definition may lead us to believe that since we do not know what it means we have no right to use it. His reply would be that: '*There is no exact usage of the word knowledge; but we can make up several such usages, which will more or less agree with the ways the word is actually used.*'[2]

Acknowledging the accumulated wisdom in existing literature, this text does not attempt to define precisely the phrase 'organizational knowledge'. Rather it attempts to create a *context* for it by showing its usage in our text. Of course, this text in turn aims at describing how knowledge comes about in organizations.

Although we, like Socrates, Theaetetus, and Wittgenstein, lack a precise definition of knowledge we are at content with the idea that human beings 'know', mainly because knowledge is intimately associated with life and experience.[3] So, as long as we are alive (at least if we are conscious) we come to know new experiences. (So, in spite of its circularity: we know that we experience – that we know…).

WHAT DO WE KNOW?

The idea of the 'knowing human being' is relatively unproblematic at this general level. We will however not inquire further into why we know, nor why organizations know. This is not to say that such questions are uninteresting, nor central to the understanding of knowledge in organizations. Nevertheless, a full discussion would require a substantial investigation of existential and philosophical issues (i.e. what is man, body, soul or mind), and this would extend beyond the studies that have gone into preparing this book.

Recognizing that we know may lead us to ask questions like: *What* do we know, or even, *How* do we know? If we follow a representationistic information processing model, as will be outlined in Chapter 2, the two questions seem relatively straightforward. In the most simplistic model, you know what you are able to convey in terms of information,[4] and you come to know through processing information about an external pre-given environment.[5] The world functions as a 'fixed point' around which you can develop and improve representations.

However, if we relax the very strict assumptions of the cognitivist school, the two questions no longer seem so easy. Reflecting on the first question gives some people a sense of dizziness: What do I know? For example, I know about Switzerland, I know about Lugano, a city in Switzerland, I know about some nice cafes in Lugano, I know about the history of the city, I know about the depth of the lake outside the city and I also know my way through the city. etc. Like Theaetetus, I might initially think of my perception of Lugano as my knowledge of this city; I can see and touch the buildings, the lake, its people, and even the surrounding mountains. But, is this knowledge of Lugano? All in all I will have trouble in compiling a list of all the 'items of knowledge' that are actually in my possession. In fact, it seems that the more I think about what I know, the more uncertain I become with respect to what I actually know. Indeed, the same tantalizing feeling occurs that Theaetetus probably experienced in his dialogue with Socrates about what is knowledge.

The dizziness arises, perhaps, due to a problem of identifying the boundaries of knowledge, like depths and breadths (in Euclidean terms). We lose the fixed point (that is so tremendously important to many of us, not least if we intend to mirror a pre-given reality).

The second question, 'How do I know?', is no less troublesome and may also evoke a sense of vertigo: How *do* I know? Is it just my opinion? Did I read these things in a book? Did I feel them? Did I see them myself? Did somebody tell me? (or worse) did I make things up? Can I ever know if I got it 'right' or 'wrong'? (According to what?). A simple idea produces difficult questions and the answers evoke a strong sense of vertigo.[6] Like in Ancient Greece, so many questions, so few answers, or at least, so few exact definitions. In this book we focus on this, the second question: processes by which organizational knowledge develops on the individual and the social scales.

ORGANIZATIONAL KNOWLEDGE

Suggesting a notion of 'organizational knowledge' is no longer a simple idea, and should produce even more difficult questions giving rise to even deeper bewilderment. Given that knowledgeable individuals come together, does the *organization* know? And what does it actually know? More or less than the individuals engaged in it know? How does it know? When does it know? Are the experiences of the individual similar to or different from the experiences of the organization? Why? Why not?

By now, perhaps, some readers are ready to put this book aside, possibly ask for a refund, concluding that a book on organizational knowledge is impossible by definition. That, we feel, would be unwise. Why? Because we should not try to avoid a study of organizational knowledge extending *beyond a conventional perspective*, just because we expect it to lead us into tautological and paradoxical questions and answers.

Rather than abandoning the issue due to its 'wickedness',[7] we should embark on the task of studying organizational knowledge. We believe that the major task for such a study is to invent concepts that allow us to describe organizational knowledge as an existing, but undiscovered, and hence under-mapped realm. In doing this we very much rest on Nietzsche's recognition that many souls are never discovered unless one invents them first. Conceptual inventions open new avenues for further exploration, allow new phenomena to be discovered, allow existing definitions to be rethought, and allow for pleasant, stimulating and interesting conversations.[8] Nevertheless, our task remains an essentially speculative enterprise.

OUTLINE OF THE BOOK

We will begin this journey by discussing conventional epistemologies in Chapter 2, cognitivism and connectionism, which is what we distinguish ourselves from in the remaining part of the book. The theoretical lens through which we develop the organizational epistemology is autopoiesis theory; this is discussed in Chapter 3. Making use of this lens to conceive organizational knowledge, Chapter 4 focuses on individualized organizational knowledge. To understand the dynamics of individualized and socialized organizational knowledge, we develop a theoretical understanding of scaling in Chapter 5. By now the groundwork is laid for discussing how organizational knowledge is brought forth on all scales, by means of languaging. Therefore, the following two chapters deal with organizational knowledge and languaging (Chapters 6 and 7). Impediments to organizational knowledge are discussed in Chapter 8. To fuel the dialogue we try to invite further research in Chapter 9. Chapter 10, finally, is a discussion of management models and, in particular, an illustration of the new epistemology in use: The SENCORP Management Model.

Notes

1. Plato/North Fowler (1987). In this particular dialogue Socrates underscores several times that his role is to to bring other scholars' (self-conceived) ideas into light; to act as midwife to young and noble men and for all who are fair. At the end Theaetetus admits that although he is still pregnant in terms of not having exactly defined knowledge, with the help of Socrates, he has brought forth that he does not think he knows that which he does not know, in this case, knowledge.
2. Wittgenstein (1958: 27).
3. Of course, life and experience, like knowledge, are also concepts that may have little exact usage. In the present text we attempt to use them consistently hoping to convey some meaning to the reader.
4. This was very much the idea pursued by the Artificial Intelligence research programs.
5. Newell and Simon (1956).
6. This vertigo has also been alluded to and discussed under the label of 'carthesian anxiety' in Bernstein (1983).
7. See Rittel (1972) for the properties of wicked problems. In his view, wicked problems need an exploratory and partly experimental approach which is precisely what we attempt to follow in this book.
8. As will be seen later in this book, conversations are essential to the development of knowledge.

2 Conventional Organizational Epistemologies

EPISTEMOLOGY WITHIN PHILOSOPHY

The word 'epistemology' comes from the Greek words *episteme* (knowledge) and *logos* (theory). Epistemology has traditionally been conceived of as a branch of one of the grand divisions of philosophy,[1] methodology, or ways we as human beings come to know the world. As such, epistemology has been dealing with the extent '...*the things and qualities of the world are dependent upon their being related as objects to a knower or subject*'.[2] From this perspective, methodology encompasses both the ways of attaining and the ways of interpreting knowledge, thus encompassing both logic *and* epistemology. Logic is concerned with understanding propositions and their use in argumentation addressing, for instance, sources of beliefs and ideas, what constitutes valid arguments, theories of language, theories of modalities, paradoxes and logical fallacies. Epistemology is concerned with understanding the origin, nature and validity of knowledge: it seeks to provide knowledge about knowledge, and hence some refer to epistemology as theory of knowledge. Epistemology typically addresses issues like the role of reasoning in knowledge development, the role of sensory perception in knowledge development, types of knowledge, the difference between knowing and believing, the degree of certainty in knowledge, and so on.

Because the branches of philosophy are partly interrelated, any organizational epistemology is *partly* interrelated with other philosophical questions. Organizational epistemology connects to 'organizational metaphysics', that is, our understanding of 'being' and the 'unified whole' as well as our understanding of the basic characteristics of management and organizational studies, i.e., 'organizational ontology' and 'organizational cosmology'. It follows that a new organizational

7

epistemology implies that a number of phenomena and processes studied in strategic managment and organizational studies are seen in a different light. For instance, the meaning of 'industry', the boundaries of 'organizational change processes', or the themes of 'organizational behaviour', the form of 'leadership', the categories of 'strategic issues', the role of thoughts and actions in 'management of service firms', or the organising principles of global firms.

Organizational epistemology is also interrelated with theory of value in organizations. This concerns the moral values and principles, that is, how we understand what is good and bad, right and wrong, i.e., organizational ethics.[3] A new organizational epistemology may result in rethinking, for instance, the nature and role of moral concepts and judgements in writing an annual report, ethical norms in media firms, or cost and benefits of applied ethics in the Ukraine. Also, theory of value includes our understanding of beauty and taste manifested in management and organizational studies, and with its evaluation, i.e. organizational aesthetics. Thus, aesthetic issues might also be rethought: for instance, aesthetic qualities in organizational design, or dress codes in the city of London.

In this book epistemology is an assemblage of theories or ideas about knowledge, the world, and the relationship between the two. It speculates on the nature of mind; in that it '*deals with the affairs of the intellect*'.[4] Of course, such a conception could make epistemology somewhat remote from daily experience and from the everyday thinking of laymen. Intellect, mind, world and knowledge are in themselves highly experience-distant concepts[5] that do not invite an understanding of everyday life. Here, Goldman warns us against adopting a too narrow definition. Epistemology, he says, encompasses:[6]

> *the whole range of efforts to know and to understand the world, including unrefined, workaday practices of the layman as well as the refined, specialized methods of the scientist or scholar. It (epistemology) includes the entire canvas of topics the mind can address: the nature of cosmos, the mathematics of set theory or tensors, the fabric of man-made symbols and culture, and even the simple layout of objects in the immediate environment. The ways that minds do or*

should deal with these topics, individually or in concert, comprise the province of epistemology.

Thus the central question asked in epistemology is how do individuals or social entities know,[7] or in other words, by which processes do individuals or social entities come to know of the world? But this is not enough. No epistemological investigation could leave the question of the nature of knowledge unanswered.

What should count for knowledge? Is it enough to say I know for something to count as knowledge, or does knowledge have to be socially acceptable as 'knowledge'? Is knowledge of a 'thing' a good representation of that 'thing', like a scaled-down image in a human brain? As seen from Goldman's statement, epistemology deals also with the ways the mind should treat knowledge, in a prescriptive, normative manner.

This set of questions, comprising the starting point of any epistemology, has raised considerable debate in philosophy and the social sciences. Philosophers, psychologists, sociologists, linguists, anthropologists, and others have paid attention to the nature of knowledge for the twofold purpose of providing a field for scientific enquiry, as well as that of better understanding the knowledge development of a specific discipline. Any study of knowledge has a self-referential character;[8] whatever is said about knowledge must have some consequences for the one who makes the statement.

ORGANIZATIONAL EPISTEMOLOGY

The field of management and organization studies has thus far not paid considerable attention to the fundamental issues of epistemology. Knowledge has mostly been taken for granted, often as a decomposable, fuzzy, and substitutable concept. It has been used interchangeably with the concept of information.[9] Nevertheless previous works on organizations carried some basic assumptions about knowledge, sometimes made explicit, but often remaining hidden. In such cases, subsequent studies, building on these previous studies, often did not present any further reflections on the basic assumptions. The organizational epistemology that has gradually emerged carries some assumptions that are worthwhile investigating further in this current volume.

The first task is to give meaning to the term 'organizational epistemology'. Our interpretation of organizational epistemology is, a collection of perspectives, theories and concepts related to the following set of issues:

(1) How and why individuals within organizations come to know.
(2) How and why organizations, as social entities, come to know.
(3) What counts for knowledge of the individual and the organization.
(4) What are the impediments to organizational knowledge development.

These issues, are by far, the only possible ones that can be conceieved of within an organizational epistemology. For example, the question of what organizations or individual organizational members know or when they know is beyond the scope of the above list. Knowledge contents holds an important place in many studies of organizational and managerial knowledge,[10] however, and will continue to do so. Management educators need references for designing training and development programmes (e.g., management knowledge, finance knowledge, human resource development knowledge), managers need references for task design (e.g., knowledge of technical design, knowledge of materials testing, knowledge of financial markets, knowledge of customer needs), personnel departments need references for human resource management (e.g., recruiting of new personnel with task oriented knowledge). Even the emergence of the concept of a knowledge worker, intensifies the focus on the contents of knowledge.[11]

The book might also have been about contents of knowledge not necessarily restricted to categories of subject matter or task orientation, like 'dictionary knowledge', 'directory knowledge', 'recipe knowledge', or 'axiomatic knowledge'.[12] Knowledge contents may also be defined relativistically. Some of our previous work illustrates how categories of knowledge contents may be defined by the functions of knowledge. For example, an organizational member may be aware that he lacks knowledge to perform a certain task ('knowledge about lack of knowledge'). He may also have knowledge that others in the organization possess certain elements of the knowledge that he lacks ('knowledge about other's knowledge').[13] The contents, scope, depth or breadth of a particular type of knowledge can only be understood in relation to other types of knowledge. A similar approach is given by Dorothy Leonard-Barton who suggests that some capabilities or knowledge types of an organization are more core to the operations of that organization than others. She argues that the core capabilities become increasingly apparent to the organization as it attempts to implement product development initiatives that requires capabilities outside this core.[14] Felt lack of knowledge has a sensitizing effect on the organization.

Our attempt will be to go beyond the contents of knowledge and rather, to ask the more fundamental questions of why and how. But we also recognize that pure investigation of processes, abandoning every concern for content, are perhaps overly restrictive and may lead to many pitfalls.[15] In discussing fundamental questions related to processes of knowledge in organizations, many times we find it unavoidable to touch on the contents of knowledge.[16] *What* organizations and individual organizational members know, however, is not our primary concern.

In focusing on epistemological issues of 'why' and 'how', we would like to start with a brief review of some of the more conventional epistemologies that are represented in the organization and management studies. In general, these previous theory developments are based on several assumptions about:

- the nature and functions of the human brain;
- the nature of knowledge and information;
- the nature and functions of computers; and
- the functions of communication and information in organizations

Cognitive science[17] has perhaps been the chief supplier of these epistemological assumptions, founding in its wake a body of literature that applies this insight to the specific domain of organizational and managerial cognition. We have found that many of these previous works seem to support themselves on what Fransisco Varela calls the 'cognitivist perspective'. This perspective has been brought forth by distinguished scholars like Herbert Simon and Marvin Minsky. Its cardinal claim is that a cognitive system, be it a human brain or a computer, creates representations of reality, and that it gradually learns through manipulating these representations.

We have also identified a body of management and organization studies that bases its theorizing on what Varela would call the 'emergence perspective', also alluded to as 'connectionism'.[18] Of a more recent date, this perspective includes advances in 'neural network computing' where cognition is seen as the emergence of global states in a network of simple components. Typically, ideas about self-organization belong to this perspective. We do not claim that our discussions of these two perspectives and of the corresponding literature are extensive or encompassing. Rather we will try to provide 'snapshots'; examples of literature that connect to each of the two perspectives.

THE COGNITIVIST EPISTEMOLOGY

Since the mid-1950s the ideas of Herbert Simon, Noam Chomsky, Marvin Minsky, John McCarthy and others have enabled the growth of cognitive science where the notion of 'human knowledge' holds a particular position.[19] Varela groups the assumptions held by these scholars under what he calls the 'cognitivist epistemology', a perspective that has come to influence the development of many disciplines, including computer science, neuroscience, linguistics, psychology, anthropology, philosophy, biology, and organization theory. We will start by showing the most fundamental (in terms of being shared) idea of the cognitivist epistemology, namely that of 'representationism'. Then we will proceed by discussing some of the assumptions that accompany representationism. Next we will discuss some of the applications of the cognitivist epistemology. Finally, we will discuss the application of cognitivism in organization theory.

At the heart of the cognitivist epistemology is the idea that the mind has the ability to represent reality in various ways, that is, creating inner representation that partly or fully corresponds to the outer world, be it objects, events, or states. This is also frequently referred to as the 'intentionality of the mind'.[20] 'Reality' and 'truth' hold privileged positions, reality being the point of reference for inner representations and truth being the degree to which inner representation corresponds to the outer world. For example, you may look at an apple in front of you on the table, and subsequently represent this apple in your mind. You build an 'image' or a 'concept' of an apple. The degree of 'truth' in your knowledge of the apple depends on whether your mental representation (say shape, colour, relative position, type of apple etc.) fits with the actual apple on the table. Your judgement involves some kind of probability assessment as you cannot be absolutely sure whether you are hallucinating or the apple in front of you is a well-made model in plastic.

Learning in the cognitivist epistemology means to improve representations of the world through assimilating new experiences.[21] As suggested by Bruner, '*A person actively constructs knowledge…by relating incoming information to a previously acquired frame of reference.*'[22] In the example of the apple, a child would for example learn the word for apple and how to associate this word with particular perceptual experiences. As time goes by, an individual may for example learn about many types of apples, how they smell, what colour they are, how large they are, etc.

The cognitivist epistemology does not confine the idea of representationism to concrete phenomena (objects, events or states with phenomenal properties). Richard Rorty traces the historical and epistemological roots of the idea of the mind as having some kind of representational competence.[23] 'Mental images', he suggests, occur for objects, events, and states with and without phenomenal properties.[24] For example, you may recall having seen an apple on a table in the sitting room of your brother's house. In this case an adequate memory seems to be necessary for representations to occur.

What are the assumptions that must be held by the cognitivists if the mind is to have representational competence? From the discussion above, it seems that an epistemology based on representationism must make assumptions as to visual-object recognition, that is perception and memory and processes of reasoning, that is logic and probability judgements.

First, cognitivism views the human being very much as what Rorty calls a 'Glassy Essence'.[25] Human beings are transparent to information from the outside. Through our senses we take in information: we look, feel, taste, smell, and hear,[26] and we subsequently use that information to build mental images that we store in our minds. These mental images may be more precisely described as 'category representations' (chair, table, car, ball, etc.) that classify objects according to their physical characteristics. Visual object recognition is reduced to the following:[27] *'When perceiving an object, an observer compares its perceptual representation to the category representations, and when a 'match' is found, the perceived object is judged to be an instance of that category.'* Typically, the literature of the cognitivist epistemology provides explanations as to how the observer processes information from the retinal image, how categories are represented, how new incoming information is compared to already stored category representations, and how the category representations are stored in memory.[28]

Second, the cognitivist epistemology views the human brain as a 'machine' of logic and deduction. The brain can be adequately reduced to 'embodied logic'; it employs logic in its processes of reasoning and it embodies logical principles in its physical structure.[29] Logic is thought of as a human competence that allows us to reveal the *truth* about phenomena observed, that is, logic is a vehicle for human beings to attain knowledge.[30] The competence consists in making propositions of various types connecting statements or objects by so-called 'truth-functional connectives'[31] in the form 'not', 'and', 'or', and 'if...then'. We recognize the use of truth-functional connectives in everday language; *If* A is the mother of B, *and if* B is my father, *then* A is my grandmother. Representations of events, phenomena, or states can be made by truth-functional connectives and propositions. They form a system of knowledge that is thought of as referencing to an external pre-given world. Discovery of this world is achieved through the systematic and careful formulation of propositions.

It is often postulated in the cognitivist epistemology that competence at logic enables internally consistent propositions, or in other words, that no propositions are contradictory. In constructing propositions that reveal truth about a phenomenon, and hence enable knowledge, internal consistency is the major criterion. For example, an apple cannot be big and small at the same time. It seems that the criterion of internal consistency in propositions should be easy to achieve.

However, as Cherniak showed, internal consistency may for all practical purposes be difficult to satisfy, even when the propositions are few in number and take on very simple forms.[32] Thus, there is a limit to competence at logic.

Competence at logic forms only part of the process of human reasoning. In discovering truth, probability assessements and judgements are also part of the process. In the epistemology pursued by cognitivists, to claim certain knowledge based on observation will rarely be the case. For example, you may claim that what you see on the table is an apple, but there will always be uncertainty involved in this claim. There may be a risk of hallucination, substitution of the object, or errors in category representation. Moreover, in most everyday situations the nature of the object, event or state to be represented may be more complex, making the representation itself more uncertain. There may also be time constraints on observation and thinking.[33] In the experiments of Kahneman and Tversky, subjects are presented with statements to which they assign probabilities. Typically, subjects are asked, based on the description of an imaginary person, to assign probabilities to the kind of occupation held by that person. Through their experiments, Kahneman and Tversky show that when faced with complex problems involving uncertainty, the use of simple heuristics is part of the reasoning process.[34] To summarize any cognitive representation of the world is associated with some level of uncertainty. The cognitivist assumption about the brain is that, in addition to competence at logic, the human brain has some competence at probability judgements and heuristics. The competences combined allow increasingly accurate representation to be developed.

The cognitivist epistemology has also affected the development of cognitive psychology. Varela offers the following commentary:[35]

> *[In cognitive psychology] computationally characterizable representations have been the main explanatory tool. Mental representations are taken to be occurrences of a formal system, and the mind's activity is what gives these representations their attitudinal color: beliefs, desires, plans, and so on.*

For example, a prevalent idea in cognitive psychology is that representational categories (e.g., of persons, things, events) can be stored in and retrieved from schemata of the individual,[36] and if an event frequently reoccurs, the corresponding categories are stored in scripts.[37] Nisbett and Ross coined the term knowledge structures to cover both schemata and scripts.[38]

An important finding of their work is the competence of probability judgements and heuristics; individuals frequently develop rudimentary knowledge structures by resolving ambiguity, making guesses about unobservable events, and inferring causal relationships.[39] Thereby the knowledge structures of the individual may not correspond directly to the world as it is.

In many ways the brain, as portrayed in cognitive psychology, resumes the functions of a computer: the computer like the brain, seems to be 'embodied logic'.[40] The cognitivist epistemology tends to be prevalent also in the design of computer systems ranging from simple programs to expert systems and artificial intelligence. The computer is built around the idea of symbolic representations and manipulation of problems, objects, events, or states.[41] Like the human brain, the computer is competent at logic: if a problem is given in a logical form (using truth-functional connectives and the criteria of internal consistency), computations can be performed and the problem solved. Truth functional connectives are the building blocks of programs that infuse logic into the very architecture of a computer.

The cognitivist epistemology on knowledge as representations allows the computer to be understood with the same conceptual system as the brain. This has also resulted in the emergence of a discipline of Artificial Intelligence (AI). Varela calls artificial intelligence the 'literal construal' of the cognitivist epistemology.[42] Important advances in robotics, expert systems, and image processing borrow insights from the study of AI.

The cognitivist epistemology with its cardinal idea of representation, and its two accompanying assumptions of transparency to information, ability to process information and competence at logic and probability judgements, can also be traced in studies of organization and management. At a very general level, several contributions assume that managers and organizations create representations of their environment.[43] Such representations may be implicit or explicit, and they may take the form of more or less dynamic beliefs among decision makers.[44] Moreover, representations may take various symbolic

forms. A market may be represented graphically in a corporate office, by charts showing market growth, market share,
customer retention rates, market segments, product-market
combinations, and so on. A new technology may be represented graphically by performance data, three dimensional
models, etc.

In some studies representations are storable and retrievable
in organization-wide knowledge structures that give organizational members a shared understanding of the world.[45] The
evolution of these knowledge structures, in turn, is dependent
on the specific experiences gained. For example, an unsuc-
cessful investment in a new market may cause a company to
terminate its learning about this market.

Several organization and management studies do, in accordance with the cognitivist assumption, also describe the organization as having a kind of glassy essence. The organization is
an input–output device: it picks up information from and
about its environment and processes it.[46] Several studies have
focused on sources of information in the environment, the
internal dissemination of information, and the actual processing of information, that is, the way incoming information
relates to already established knowledge structures and category representations.[47] According to Martin Kilduff, who analyzed the work 'organizations' of James G. March and Herbert
Simon through a method of 'deconstruction', the organization has been proposed as a 'non-trivial machine' or a computer.[48] As indicated above the link between cognitive
psychology and computer science is very much found in the
language used. Likewise, the link between computer science
and organization studies is found in a remarkably similar
system of concepts. Words like 'information input–output',
'information processing', 'instructions', 'procedures', 'rules',
'memory', 'information storage', 'programming', and
'retrieval through memory', have been used to uncover the
functioning of organizations. In their commentary on the
work by Ghemawat and Ricart i Costa,[49] Cyert and Wiliams
suggest that much of the strength in these authors' work
resides in the '*analytic language for modelling the organization as a
static and dynamic information processing mechanism*'.[50]

Studies of organizations also tend to capture the cognitivist
assumptions of competence at logic and probability

judgements in at least three ways: by viewing managerial knowledge as representable in a cartography of logic; by construing the organization as a problem seeker and problem solver; by viewing the organization as an instrument of strategic planning and forecasting.

First, there seems to be some support that management's knowledge can be represented in so-called cognitive maps, that is, using a cartography of logic. By applying a scheme of truth-functional connectives to transcribed interviews or corporate documents, like letters to shareholders, annual reports, strategic plans, vision statements, policies or procedures, knowledge can be revealed and adequately represented.[51] For example, management knowledge, applying category representations of 'technology', 'firm', 'industry' and so on, can be represented in the form:

IF	we invest in new technology;
AND	if that technology is generally available in the industry;
AND	if the cost of purchase of that technology and the benefits of its application is equal to all firms in the industry;
THEN	our firm may not necessarily gain competitive advantage over other firms in the industry;
AND THEN	it may not earn supernormal profits.

This way of representing knowledge assumes that management is competent at logic, and that *the task of the researcher is to reveal the logic used by the manager*. It further assumes that knowledge is time invariant; once knowledge has been 'captured' and represented, we may make inferences about future reasoning. Other ways of representing knowledge cartographically involve semiotics, and argument mapping[52] (we will focus more closely on arguments in chapter 7).

Second, organization studies frequently assumes that organizations are problem-seekers and solvers, and that they develop some task specific knowledge.[53] C.K. Prahalad and Richard Bettis take this argument a step forward by claiming that problem-solving behaviour ingrained in knowledge structures may be a potential source of a '*dominant general management logic, that is the way in which managers conceptualize the business and make critical resource allocation decisions*'.[54] Such conceptualizations and resource allocation decisions may be sustained in organizations and eventually develop into 'cognitive rigidities'. Several organization studies here demonstrate that novel problems may be approached by old patterns of reasoning, that is, already established logic. Here truth-functional connectives are again at play. Logic that seemed successful in the past tends to prevail; new problems are still approached by conventional If...Then...structures: e.g., If we invest in market share, then we will gain an increase in the return on investment. Several authors hence suggest that until a major crisis occurs or new top management replaces the old team, competence at logic and judgements cannot be successfully restored.[55] In sum, learning, that is changing or substituting existing representations, is found to be important but difficult.[56]

Third, competence at logic and probability judgements is also prevalent in several works on planning, forecasting, and management. In their classical work 'organizations', March and Simon identified the need in organizations to distinguish events that have previously been encountered from those that are new to the organization, and approach them differently. Previously encountered events will be met with a well structured representation of the situation that will include a repertory of response programmes. New events must be approached differently; the situation has to be represented and one or more response programmes have to be constructed. Due to the uncertainty involved in representing and responding to new events, March and Simon propose 'procedural planning'; planning for the event-response activity itself.[57] This kind of planning ensures that the organization reduces uncertainty involved in responding to new events. As a result, the organizational decison maker increases his competence at logic and probability judgements.

The work of Peter Lorange on strategic planning focuses on the clear formulation of goals, uses analytical rational decision procedures that enhanced the management's competence at logic and probability judgement. Such procedures involve the search for and processing of information to enable representation of alternative courses of action. The choice between alternative courses of action is based on their expected future consequences and on their influence on goal attainment. The process that Lorange recommends sets out to increase reliability and validity of current representations of future states of the organiszation.[58]

In a recent commentary by Nobel Laureate Herbert A. Simon on the nature and role of strategic planning, the cognitivist ideas of competence and logic and probability judgements are quite distinct.[59] A central argument in Simon's work is that three distinct types of managerial skills are of importance for the organization to survive and prosper in an uncertain environment (where few events are repeated): (1) skills in anticipating the shape of an uncertain future, (2) skills in generating alternative courses of action under alternative developments of the environment, and (3) skills in efficient and rapid implementation of plans. Logic and reasoning are central to such a skill base. More importantly, however, behind this conceptual system is the assumption that probability judgements about future states, as they for example appear in the work of Lorange, are of little value in management practice when the future is uncertain. When managers anticipate the future, qualitative, rather than quantitative, judgements are of importance. However, consonant with the conclusions of Nisbett and Ross,[60] the process of making qualitative and quantitative judgements are not 'qualitatively' very different. Human inference tends to follow some simple rules and be subject to cognitive simplification and heuristics.

The generation of alternative courses of action is accomplished through information search and processing. A key feature of information processing is combining information about the environment in novel ways, that allows the organization to see possible paths of development. Information processing, however, is selective and dependent on individual decision maker's representation of a situation. Recognizing this, Simon further claims that the organization has to be 'programmed' very much like a computer to represent the future and alternative courses of action and thereby to allow for implementation of a selected course:

> *To be effective a mission statement or description of the organization's comparative advantage must become part of the mind-set of every member of the organization who is responsible for making or helping to make decisions of any consequence... A new member of the organization has not been assimilated successfully until he or*

she has acquired the concept of what the organization is seeking to accomplish and how it proposes to go about it…the shared picture of the organization must be reinforced continually.[61]

The cognitive competence of an organization hinges on the mobilization of individual cognitive resources, and on the wide distribution of selected representations. The cognitivist epistemology allows for a specific formula to be adopted: representations can be 'firmly emplanted' in 'the hundred of heads' that comprise the organization. This formula in turn must dwell on the assumption that a cognitive system is essentially open; that it can improve representations towards the ultimate goal of attaining truth; that given the right information available to an organizational member and the right processing of information, these true representations will also be uniform. In fact, the cognitivist epistemology seems to manifest the correspondence doctrine of *truth*, where truth is viewed as the agreement of knowledge with observable facts.[62] This doctrine is not easily reconciled with a processual *Weltanschauung*, like the one developed in this book. Plato claimed that there can never be a science of Nature, because the visible world is a changing likeness of an eternal model, and since that would involve a final statement of exact truth about an ever-changing object.[63] The correspondence doctrine also subscribes to the mechanical metaphor that sees each addition to scientific truth as an individual brick 'in the wall', which clearly is analogous to the cognitivist epistemology.[64]

So far the cognitivist epistemology has had a great influence on our conceptions of organizational epistemology, not least manifested by the 1993 Winter Special Issue of the *Strategic Management Journal*.

THE CONNECTIONIST EPISTEMOLOGY

In the following we will briefly discuss the elements of an alternative to the cognitivist epistemology, namely the connectionist epistemology. The discussion will start by outlining the critique formulated by the connectionists toward the cognitivists, the central elements of connectionist theorizing, and the application of connectionist epistemologies to organization and management studies.

In the 1970s the cognitivist fundamentals of an architecture of computers started to receive some critical comments, and an alternative perspective, that of the connectionist, began to emerge. The criticism was mainly centred around two 'deficiencies' of the cognitivist work. Firstly, information processing is seen as sequential rule-based manipulation of symbols: one rule is applied after the other. Secondly, information processing is localized. If a rule breaks down or if a symbol is lost, this has serious implications for the global effectiveness of the system.[65] Varela phrases these two deficiencies in the following way:

> *the architecture and mechanisms are far from biology. The most ordinary visual tasks, done even faster by tiny insects, are done faster than is physically possible when simulated in a sequential manner; the resiliency of the brain to damage without compromising all of its competence, has been known to neuro-biologists for a long time.*[66]

By investigating the brain more closely, and comparing it, in what Goldman refers to as 'psychological realism',[67] to the computer, remarkable differences were detected. Rather than working sequentially starting with symbols, the brain seems to have dynamic global properties in a network of simple components, referred to as neurons. The simple components are active in their local environment and they are connected to other simple components. The components operate by their own local rules and there are rules for the connection between components. When components are active or inactive, each in their local environment, global properties emerge spontaneously in the total system of components. This spontaneous behaviour is what frequently was referred to as self-organization[68] in the founding years, and which today takes labels such as 'emergent properties', 'global properties', 'network dynamics', or 'synergetics'.[69] The global states emerge without a central controlling or programming unit ordering the activation of the components. Allthough most of the contemporary research on this type of network is based on assumptions from statistical physics and thermodynamics, it is not surprising to find that the ideas of the connectionists are often reconciled with those quantum mechanics.[70]

According to Varela, Thompson, and Rosch, a critical issue in connectionist epistemology, understanding the brain as a network of components (neurons), and the emergent behaviour that results, is *learning rules*. These govern how components are connected. One of the most frequently discussed rules is 'Hebb's rule'.[71] Donald Hebb proposed that human learning results from correlated activity between neurons. If two neurons are simultaneously active, their connections are strengthened, and if they are inactive, the connections are weakened. A different type of rules is found in the work of Paul Thagard. Here connections between components are governed by excitatory and inhibitory rules. If two components are connected excitatorily, then the activation of one component raises the activation of the other. If two components are inhibitorily connected, the activation of one component lowers the activation of the other.[72]

Like the cognitivists, *the connectionists see information processing as the basic activity of the brain.*[73] Information is taken in from the environment through our senses, and it will activate various components in the network of components that comprise the brain. However, information processing does not only depend on stimuli from the environment but also stimuli from the brain itself. According to Varela, Thompson, and Rosch; '*the behaviour of the whole system resembles a cocktail party conversation (between outside and inside) much more than a chain of command (triggered from a central unit)*'.[74] As a result, human learning is differently understood in the cognitivist and the connectionist epistemology. While cognitivists view learning as the increasingly accurate definition of representations corresponding to the external world, the connectionists understand the brain as global states in a history-dependent system where the learning rules, and the history of connections between components' affect present connections made. When the brain recognizes patterns, events, objects, states, etc. learning rules provide similarities in the emergent state of the system of components.

Still, however, the idea of representationism seems to be embraced by the connectionist epistemology. In a commentary by Wechsler on the state of neural network research, he chooses to quote Herbert A. Simon as outlining a fundamental doctrine:

> *All mathematical derivation can be viewed simply as change of representation, making evident what was previously true but obscure. This view can be extended to all problem solving - solving a problem then means representing...it so as to make the solution transparent. In other words, knowledge has to be made explicit if and when needed.*[75]

At first glance it may appear as though connectionists and cognitivists operate according to the same fundamental ideas: the representability of the 'real' world and the cognisers competence at representing. A closer look, however, uncovers how the two perspectives differ in the view on *how* representations are achieved. For example, a problem that has intrigued both connectionists and cognitivists is human recognition of rotating objects, like a pair of glasses. A *cognitivist* assertion would be that recognition of a rotating object would assume an infinite number of object representations, e.g., glasses represented from above, below, north, south, east and west. A typical *connectionist* reply is that the human mind only needs familiarity and practice: a few canonical representations, a limited learning of novel views of the object, and some landmarks for recognition.[76] What eventually matters is the global state that emerges as components are activated and deactivated through the learning rules.

This concern with the interaction between the world and the cognizer seems to be critical to the connectionist epistemology.[77] Knowledge is a state in a system of interconnected components, that interacts with its environment. It does not reside in each of the components of the system. As new experiences are gained new global states emerge in the cognitive system. At every moment in time, human thoughts are the result of self-organizing properties, some similar to previous states and others quite novel.

Our discussions of the cognitivist epistemology in organization and management studies revealed that the cognitive system is frequently understood as directed towards effective task resolution. Here is another similarity between the two perspectives. Cognitive competence, be it at logic and probability judgements, is aimed at resolving a required or pre-formulated task. This view of problem and task hinges on a pre-given, pre-defined, or pre-formulated world to be discovered and represented. These representations are inner-creations of the cognitive system that allows it to function adequately in the outer-world. If the system fails to accurately create, it fails to adapt in this world.

Neural networks have been a source of inspiration to computer design. 'Connectionist networks' are often built with a high number of simple information processing units that are connected according to various rules. The units, frequently referred to as 'nodes', have different functions: some are inputting data others are outputting data. Nodes are further connected in various layers, where some layers take care of input and output of data, and the rest are activated and deactivated as data is being processed.[78] Also here the role of history of emergent behaviour is important. Previous states are related to current experiences. Emergent behaviour makes time a part of any learning algorithm of a computer system based on a connectionist design. The system has to decide when to quit the attempts to resolve a task, for example due to limited exposure to the task, the intent not lose current investment in a task, or the need to allocate relatively more of a given time to complicated tasks than to simple tasks.[79] Lastly, we should also mention that the connectionist epistemology has contributed substantially to the advancement of artificial intelligence.[80]

What then does the connectionist epistemology have to contribute to our understanding of organizational knowledge? The immediate answer to most organization theorists would be found in the fairly well developed literature on self-organization of social entities[81] or that on the network approach to interorganizational cooperation.[82] This literature has as its focal points, evolving systems, structures, and processes.

However, the more subtle, but rarely touched upon, implications of connectionist epistemologies for organizations are two fundamental assumptions: the emergent and the historical *nature* of knowledge. As seen, previous states in the network, together with new information from the environment, will affect the resulting present knowledge of the organization. Here the organization theoretician confronts an obvious problem of unit of analysis: what is the component and what is the system? Should insights from the connectionist epistemology only be used at the individual level? Are neurons the only plausible component (if nothing else, due to its apparent simplicity)? Or should the component be understood as the individual organizational member (obviously not so simple)? If yes, what are the rules for connecting individuals, and how does organizational knowledge emerge?

Moreover, the connectionist epistemology portrays knowledge as historically dependent leading to a number of critical questions. How much does the environment matter in the development of organizational knowledge? What is the role of individual memory in the emergent organizational knowledge? What is the role of organizational memory in the emergent organizational knowledge? Under what conditions do organizations recognize previous events, states, objects, trends etc.?

The current state of development of organization studies do not seem to pay much attention to these and related questions. The connectionist epistemologies have much insight to offer, but have so far had little impact on theory building[83]. However, two studies in particular have come to our attention that we believe show fruitful directions of development.

First, the work by Lee Sproull and Sara Kiesler seems to suggest that the individual organizational member is the component of the networked organization, and that connections among individuals are partly but effectively facilitated by information technology.[84] The networked organization, they contend, is one *'in which large numbers of people...have easy access to good networking technology and information resources'*.[85] The rules that connect different users in the networked organization are rules of access, rules connected to various types of network resources, and rules of incentives that encourage connections. Knowledge in the network is stored in databases. It also effectively enables special types of processing like modelling, forecasting, designing, and publishing. The network allows people to enhance their task related competence through interaction with others and through interaction with network resources.

Organizational members may also increase their local knowledge of the global state of the organization through the organization–wide communications of messages.[86] Hence, the network, with its physical and structural characteristics, provides boundaries for the emergent knowledge of the organization. Because it entails data storage possibilities, this simplified conceptualization also allows the detection of historical knowledge. Typically, when an organizational member makes use of a database to provide illustrations in his message to another organizational member, the interaction between historical knowledge and information from the user allows new knowledge to emerge.

Second, rather than understanding emergent knowledge as a form of computer network, Weick and Roberts construe interpersonal connections as a social psychological problem.[87] They set out to understand the cognitive requirements for reliable coordinated behaviour on the flight deck of an aircraft carrier (zero failure), where the tasks that are played out are vastly complex and need substantial coordination often in a speedy manner. To this end, they develop the concept of '*collective mind...as a pattern of heedful interrelations of actions in a social system*'.[88] Organizational members construct their actions on the flight deck as contributions to a network of other contributions, and their actions are interrelated within the organization. In focusing on reliability of the organization, as well as the time needed for the total organization to respond to crisis-like events, like an aircraft with landing problems, Weick and Roberts are keeping with the initial 'biological' idea of the connectionist epistemology.

The components of the network are each organizational member rather than neurons. The rules that connect people are given by the 'representations' of the nework of activities performed by other organizational members. Each member knows what needs to be done in relation to what the others at the flight deck are doing (or are not doing). In simple terms, this is what is referred to as 'heedful interrelating'. This makes organizational members more than simple components, as Weick and Roberts carefully point out.[89] Still they believe that:[90]

What connectionism contributes to organizational theory is the insight that complex patterns can be encoded by patterns of activation and inhibition by simple units, if those units are richly connected. This means that relatively simple actors may be able to apprehend complex inputs if they are organized in ways that resemble neural networks. Connectionists also raise the possibility that mind is 'located' in connections and the weights put on them rather than in entities.

Thus, from this perspective knowledge emerges and resides not only in the brains of each individual organizational member, but also in the connections among members through the rules of heedful interrelating. A strong point for the understanding of collective mind is therefore the individual brain as a mechanism of representation of the network of activitities. Unless the organizational member adequately represents the world in which he interacts, collective mind will not emerge. Again, the idea of representationism is maintained in the connectionist view on knowledge. There is an external reference point, be it object, language, connection, for representation and recreation.

This concludes our brief discussion of conventional epistemologies and the way they apply to management and organization studies. From now on, what is said should be recognized as contributions to a new epistemology of organizations, one that is distinct from the previous ones in terms of its view on representation and cognition. The next chapter discusses autopoiesis theory; our starting point for rethinking organizational epistemology.

Notes

1. The other two branches are metaphysics and theory of value.
2. Montague (1962: 82).
3. For recent discussions of business ethics, see Hosmer (1994) and Donaldson and Dunfee (1994).
4. Goldman (1986: 13).
5. The term 'experience-distant', as opposed to 'experience-near' concepts was used by Geertz (1973). In anthropology, experience-near concepts are capturing the everyday language of the social system under observation. Experience-distant concepts, on the other hand, belong to the grand theorizing of the scholar.
6. Goldman (1986: 13).
7. Goldman (1986) is very specific on the need for extending epistemology from the individual to the social realm. This extension is of great importance to the development of the ideas in this book. As will be seen later, we are here concerned with knowledge both on the individual and the social level.
8. We will discuss this further at a later point in this book.
9. For a recent example, see Cyert, Kumar, and Wiliams (1993) explicitly suggest that the authors use information and knowledge interchangeably.

10. Several studies have dealt with the type of knowledge necessary to run a business and/or manage an organization. For example managers need knowledge of control principles, selection procedures, and appraisal systems (Boyatzis, 1982), and long-range planning activities (Hempill, 1959). For more examples of this type of literature see Silver (1991).

11. For more on the concept of knowledge workers see, for example, Handy (1989), Hage and Power (1992), and Sakaiya (1991).

12. Sackman (1991).

13. See Hærem (1993), and Hærem, von Krogh and Roos (1993).

14. Leonard-Barton (1992).

15. For a related discussion, see Ginsberg (1988).

16. Examples are bound to refer to contents.

17. Cognitive science the way it is used here includes many different disciplines ranging from neuroscience, linguistics, cognitive psychology, to computer science (artificial intelligence).

18. Varela (1992).

19. See Gardner (1985) and Varela (1992). For examples of some of the fundamental work of these scholars, see Newell and Simon (1972), Minsky (1975) and Simon (1989).

20. Goldman (1993).

21. von Krogh, Roos, and Slocum (1994).

22. Bruner and Anglin (1973: 397).

23. Rorty (1980).

24. Rorty (1980: 24–26).

25. Rorty (1980: 37). See also Dewey (1960) on the relationship between the spectator and the unchangeable object.

26. See discussions in Varela (1992) and Goldman (1993).

27. Goldman (1993: 6).

28. For an example of such a theory, see Biederman (1987).

29. This proposition was first stated by McCulloch and Pitts (1965). See also Varela (1992). By physical structure here we mean the way neurons are thought to connect to each other over time, through being active or inactive.

30. See our previous discussion of the grand divisions of philosophy, referring to Montague (1925).

31. Goldman (1993).

32. Cherniak (1986).

33. See Goldman (1986) on the imperfectness of human cognition and the possible constraints on human cognition.

34. See Kahneman and Tversky (1973), Tversky and Kahneman (1983).

35. Varela (1992: 240).

36. Anderson (1983), Bartlett (1932), Schank and Ableson (1977).

37. Schank and Abelson (1977).

38. Nisbett and Ross (1980).

39. Bruner (1964), Nisbett and Ross (1980), Kahneman and Tversky (1973).

40. According to Goldman (1993) some cognitive psychologists (functionalists) suggest that the brain should be studied in terms of input-

output relations and information processing algorithms, that is, using the computer as a starting point for understanding the human brain.

41. See Winograd and Flores (1987). They provide a critique of the prevalent view in computer science today, that computers are instruments of representation. They propose an alternative view in which the interaction between the computer and the user is given an increasing focus.

42. Varela (1992: 240). For more on recent advances in artificial intelligence, see Varela's accounts of the japanese ICOT, fifth generation program, able to understand human language and write its own programs.

43. See such diverse works as March and Simon (1958), Argyris and Schon (1978), Ginsberg (1990), Gioia and Manz (1985), Daft and Weick (1984), Weick (1979), Huff (1983), Hedberg (1981). Again it should be noted that in these works knowledge has often been substituted with less troublesome notions, like information, data, resources, reputation, etc.

44. Ghemawat and Ricart i Costa (1993).

45. Prahalad and Bettis (1986), Lyles and Schwenk (1992), Walsh and Ungson (1991).

46. See, for example, March and Olsen's (1975) idea of a complete cycle of choice in which the organization gathers information about its environments, attempts to learn from this information, and subsequently gives a response to the environment. It is further interesting to note how the Winter Special Issue of the *Strategic Management Journal 1993*, on Organizations, Decisions-Making and Strategy sets out to explore the nature of the organization as an information processing mechanism (Cyert and Wiliams, 1993). Another example which deals with organizational design is Galbraith (1977) where information gathering and processing are seen as determinants of organizational structures; as well as Stinchcombe (1990).

47. See Huber (1993).

48. Kilduff (1993). Kilduff's article is a milestone in understanding some of the often tacit assumptions behind organization and management studies.

49. Ghemawat and Ricart i Costa (1993).

50. Cyert and William (1983).

51. See the edited volume by Huff (1990). Her book is of great value to strategy scholars because in addition to research-based articles, it provides an exhaustive account of methodologies applied in each article. This structure allows the reader to more fully understand some of the fundamental assumptions that underlie cognitivist research into organizational knowledge.

52. See the examples in Huff (1990).

53. Cyert and March (1963), Lant and Meszas (1990), Lant et al. (1992).

54. Prahalad and Bettis (1986: 490).

55. See, for example, Hedberg, Nystrom, and Starbuck (1976), Grinyer, Mayes, and McKiernan (1988).

56. For more on organizational learning from a cognitivist perspective, see March and Olsen (1976), Huber (1991), Herriot, Levinthal and

March (1985). It should be noted that learning in the cognitivist conception of the organization is of a relatively recent date. Levinthal and March (1993) argue that models of the organization as a learning mechanism, that is, a special case of the organization as an information processing mechanism (Cyert and Williams, 1993), has come to replace the traditional models of organizations as rational actors that were prevalent in the 1970s.

57. March and Simon (1958).
58. Lorange (1980).
59. Simon (1993).
60. Nisbett and Ross (1980).
61. Simon (1993: 139).
62. This worldview of truth has its roots in Spinoza's (1677) scheme of things: *Truth is an affirmation (or a denial) made about certain thing, which agrees with that same thing; and Falsity is an affirmation (or a denial) about a thing, which does not agree with the thing itself* (quoted in Wolf, 1910: 102). This is similar to Kant's perspective of truth: *Ubereinstimmung der Erkenntniss mit dem Object Wahrheit ist* (quoted in Smith, 1947: 220).
63. See Cornford (1937: 23–29).
64. The correspondence doctrine is distinct from the coherence doctrine of truth, in which correspondence with an object is seen, at most, as a sympom of truth. Rather, ... *truth in its essential nature is that systematic coherence which is the character of a significant whole* (Joachim, 1939: 76). Where the former doctrine seem to be connected to Hegel's Richtigheit, the latter is connected to Hegel's Wahrheit.
65. Varela (1992).
66. Varela (1992: 243).
67. Goldman (1986: 328).
68. von Foerster (1962).
69. Varela (1992).
70. See, for example, Wechsler (1992).
71. Varela, Thompson, and Rosch (1992).
72. Thagard (1989). For other approaches to rules, see for example Feldman and Ballard (1982).
73. Wechsler (1992).
74. Varela, Thompson, and Rosch (1992: 96). Parantheses added.
75. Wechsler (1992: xix).
76. Eidman (1992)
77. An interesting stream of research that clearly shows what is meant here is the study of human perception of texture. We see different patterns in texture dependent on our efforts to look at individual detail or global appearance. For more on this, see Williams and Julesz (1992).
78. Uhr (1992). For more on this, see Varela, Tompson and Rosch (1992). See also Wechsler (1992).
79. Ballard and Whitehead (1992).
80. See Minsky (1986), and Minsky and Pappert (1987).
81. For examples of this wide variety of literature, see Ulrich and Probst (1984), Stacey (1993), Morgan (1986).

82. For example, Jarillo (1988)
83. See also commentary by Weick and Roberts (1993).
84. Note that there are apparent limitations in computer communications. See, for example, Meherabian (1971), Sproul and Kiesler (1991), and Kiesler, Siegel and McGuire (1984).
85. Sproul and Kiesler (1991: x).
86. Feldman (1987).
87. Weick and Roberts (1993).
88. Weick and Roberts (1993: 357).
89. See Weick and Robert (1993: 359). It seems, however, that the authors take a limited view on connectionism, suggesting that it is solely limited to the functioning of computers. This is only partly the case, as demonstrated in Varela, Thompson, and Rosch (1992) as well as the discussion above.
90. Weick and Roberts (1993: 359). See also the work by Sandelands and Stablein (1987).

3 Autopoietic Systems

We will begin this speculative enterprise by making a journey to another discipline, that of neurobiology. The objective of this chapter is to provide the reader with some 'food for thought' by visiting perspectives of cognition that are relatively unknown in the field of management and organizational studies, i.e. autopoiesis. Autopoiesis is, *per se*, distinct from the mainstream *Weltanschauung* of cognition discussed in Chapter 1. The beheaded, representation-based perspectives of management and organizations imply that business activities are contingent on external influences and respond to demands from the environment through internally representing a pregiven environment. The autopoietic perspective reflects the belief that cognitive activities in organizations are simultaneously open and closed. As will be seen throughout this book the autopoietic perspective not only sheds light on existing issues, it also opens up the management and organizational study realms for new probes into the unknown.

The concept of autopoiesis was originally developed in the field of neuro-biology by the Chilean scientists Humberto Maturana and Francisco Varela, and further developed together with Ricardo Uribe.[1] They wanted to understand better the nature of living systems, illustrated by cells and cell reproduction. The basic question addressed was: *What is common to all living systems that allows us to qualify them as living?* Thus, they recognized that all living systems share a common organization, by calling them living. The answer, they found, lies in self-production, which they labelled autopoiesis.[2]

Autopoiesis is a term of Greek derivation and means self *(auto)* production *(poiesis; poein)*. The main argument of autopoiesis theory is that living systems are created and recreated in an autonomous, simultaneously open and closed, self-referencing, and observing manner. Autopoiesis theory conceives living systems as being continually self-reproducing in terms of the processes that made them; not in terms of their relationship with an environment, nor in terms of their components *per se*. Therefore, the system's (internal) production of components does not depend on an input–output relation with the system environment. Everything the system needs for self-production (its autopoiesis) is already in the system. These properties make autopoiesis theory distinct from the cognitivist and connectionist epistemologies discussed in Chapter 2.

Not surprisingly, problems related to self-production, and self-reproduction[3] have triggered many efforts in several scientific disciplines. In the 1960s, for instance, von Neumann used cellular automata[4] to investigate the logical nature of self-reproducing systems,[5] and Moore discussed various 'finite-states machines' to theoretically analyse self-reproduction.[6] 'Artificial self-reproduction', incorporating features of living things, e.g., the capacity to pass on information to the next generation, has also been modelled. For instance, in the late 1950s, Penrose developed a self-reproducing machine with linked double hooks, tilted can-levers and various blocking devices. Even these attempts to 'materialize' the ideas of autopoiesis have not altered its speculative status. The realm of self-production is still seen as somewhat superstitious, the idea of an object reproducing itself '... *is so closely associated with the fundamental processes of biology that it carries with it a suggestion of magic*'.[7] In addition to addressing one of the most fundamental issues raised by man, i.e., understanding life, autopoiesis can also be seen as a reaction against reductionistic tendencies in natural sciences in general and in molecular biology in particular: the approach of breaking up complex systems into even smaller components, and so on, until the components are so small that at least one piece can be understood,[8] e.g., understanding DNA and its elements rather than cooperative relations of cellular systems.[9] By its very nature, autopoiesis also clarifies some of the confusion caused by intertwining history-dependent processes, e.g., evolution,[10] and history-independent processes, such as individual organization of systems.

In addition to helping us overcome the potential queasiness that may arise from trying to understand living systems, cognition, and, therefore, knowledge development,[11] autopoiesis has evolved into a theory also used to characterize the operations of non-biological systems[12] and their relationships with each other. Autopoiesis is instrumental in developing a new organizational epistemology: why and how knowledge, individualized or socialized, develops in organizations.

CHARACTERISTICS OF AUTOPOIETIC SYSTEMS

The theory of autopoiesis refers not only to self-production as such, but also to the characteristic of living systems continuously renewing themselves in a way that allows them to maintain the integrity of their structure (where 'structure' means the components and the relations of a system). Although a system can be formed in many ways,[13] if it is to constitute a distinct system in a given space-time continuum, then the system must allow for the *interrelations* between its components that define it as a *unity*. Unity means being distinguishable from the background and, therefore, from other units. Unity is the only necessary condition for existence in a given space-time continuum. In fact, the conditions that specify a unity determine its phenomenology, and whenever a unity is defined, a phenomenological domain is specified: '*A unity is brought forth by an act of distinction. Conversely, each time we refer to a unity in our descriptions, we are implying the operation of distinction that defines it and makes it possible.*'[14] Because self-production processes specify their *own* boundaries, rather than boundaries defined by an observer, autopoietic systems are units (as seen from the system).

The interrelations between the components of a system (unity) define the possible transformation the system may undergo, e.g., destruction. These interrelations are the answer to the question of how we recognize something as a unity, as well as signifying what must be present in order for the unity to exist. Thus, what specifies a system is the set of relations between its components, independent of the components themselves.[15] The term 'organization' is used by Maturana and Varela as a more generic term than 'structure':

> *its organization which are the necessary relations which define the system and its structure, which are the actual relations between the components which integrate the system as such. Thus ex-definitione, the organization is invariant while a system maintains its identity without disintegration; structures can vary provided they satisfy the organizational constraints.*[16]

The theory suggests that autopoietic systems are systems of a certain organization, independent of its components but dependent on their interrelations. Thus, over time an autopoietic system changes its components but maintains its organization. If the organization of a system as a whole changes the system in itself will change and form a new system with a new identity. However, when the structure changes and the organization is maintained, the system sustains its identity: '*A new structure may well be necessary to cope with a changing environment but the system maintains all these mechanisms that make it what it is; that is what is meant by not losing its identity.*'[17]

To better understand this relation between organization and structure, let us give a brief example. The organization of a bicycle requires two wheels connected by a frame. But the structure of a bicycle may be modified by replacing wooden tyres with rubber tyres, and a stainless steel frame with an aluminium frame. In order to understand autopoietic systems, however, we need to understand both the interrelations that define them and how the interrelations that constitute them are brought forth in the system. In cell reproduction, an example much closer to showing the true dynamics of autopoietic systems, not only are the cells reproducing themselves, but they are also reproducing their own capacity to reproduce.

After these general concerns, the reader should be prepared for the original definition of autopoietic systems given by Maturana, Varela and Uribe (1974: 188):

> *The autopoietic organization is defined as a unity by a network of productions of components which (i) participate recursively in the same network of productions of components, and (ii) realize the network of productions as a unity in the space in which the components exist.*[18]

From this definition we can see that the cell is an embodiment of autopoiesis – on the molecular scale. Although a cell rejuvenates its components many times during its lifetime, it maintains the integrity of its structure as a cell. It continuously regenerates its own interrelations through its operation as a system of production of its own components. Thus, the cell's own organization is invariant.[19]

All living systems are continuously self-producing (autopoietic) systems. But, what about evolution and reproduction? Because they are secondary to the establishment of a unity, reproduction and evolution cannot define the living organization.[20] Also, the feasibility of an autopoietic system depends on the presence of the required components and interaction between these. Therefore, the spontaneous occurrence of autopoietic systems is dependent on natural conditions under which the components arise spontaneously, like the well-known nucleic-acid-protein system.[21]

What then characterizes autopoietic systems, apart from their ability to form and reshape their unity? Four basic properties of autopoietic systems emerge: autonomy, simultaneously open and closed, self-referential, observing.

Autonomy

Autonomy means self-control/self-law, i.e., maintaining identity. Thus, a system is autonomous if it can specify its own laws for its own functioning.[22] Autopoietic systems are autonomous units; they subordinate all changes to the maintenance of their own organization: '*Autonomy is the distinctive phenomenology resulting from an autopoietic organization: the realization of the autopoietic organization is the product of its operation.*'[23] Because an autopoietic system reproduces its own components and recreates its own organization and identity, it acquires its autonomy. The rules for its functioning are found in the system's organization and the way it reproduces itself.

Autonomy is a property of living systems in general: '*... autonomy appears so obviously an essential feature of living systems that whenever something is observed that seems to have it, the naive approach is to deem it alive.*'[24] For this and perhaps other reasons, according to Maturana and Varela,[25] many biologists whose primary concern is to understand the living system, feel uncomfortable about the question of autonomy of the living organization.

Autonomous systems are distinct from systems whose couplings with the environment are specified or designed through input/output relations, like a computer:

mechanistic systems whose organization is such that they do not produce the components and processes which realize them as unities and, hence, mechanistic systems in which the product of their operation is different from themselves, we call allopoietic.[26]

In autopoiesis theory the notion of *control* exercised by the external environment on an allonomous system,[27] contingent on the input–output of information, is supplemented with the notion of *autonomy* of the autopoietic system. This view runs contrary to the modern conception of open systems adapting to, and at the same time shaping their environment.[28]

It should be noted that the property of autonomy makes autopoietic systems distinct from self-organizing systems:[29] they differ with respect to the criteria of autonomy they imply. *Systems first have to be self-organized before they can become autopoietic.* It follows that autopoiesis is *not* synonomous with self-organization, as suggested by some authors.[30] A process of self-organization may happen in two ways. Either the development of a self-organizing system's autonomy is a process of integrating various components that can be controlled by the need of the system to maintain its organization; or it is a process of rejecting various components at the system's boundary.[31]

Simultaneously Open and Closed

Changes in autopoietic systems are induced by independent events (sending signals). The system undergoes internal structural changes to compensate for these signals. Because such are subordinate to the maintenance of the system's organization, autopoietic systems do not have inputs or outputs in connectionistic or cognitivistic terms (Chapter 2). Otherwise, such inputs and outputs would have to be part of the definition of the autopoietic system, as a unity, which they are not.

This lack of input and output does, however, not imply that the system is isolated from its environment. The autopoietic system may be stimulated or disturbed by events in the environment, but under no circumstances are these 'perturbations' internalized as components in the ongoing autopoietic process – the system is not directing energy to the pertubation (like in allopoietic systems). Pertubations can only stimulate processes in the system itself, which always follows the self-defined rules of the system. Because the environment can never determine, direct or control these changes, the autopoietic system knows its environment in knowing itself.[32] Similarly, although the system, *per se,* may be the cause of structural changes in the environment, the final result can never be determined by the autopoietic system. Thus, the pertubations are reciprocal. The resulting continuous, mutually congruent structural changes are called 'structural coupling'. It follows that autopoietic systems are *simultaneously* open and closed; in the case of cells, they are open to energy but closed to information and control.[33]

This means that neither information nor knowledge is picked up or transferred from the environment, but are formed within the autopoietic system. Thus, information appears in the relative interlock between the describer, the systems, and their interactions.[34] Therefore, an autopoietic perspective forces us to reinterpret the concept of information as being constructive, '...*we are talking literally about in-formare: that which is formed within*'.[35] The notion of 'information' is derived from latin *informare* which literally means to-put-in-form. This is distinct from the way information is used in, for example, cognitivistic and connectionistic epistemologies. Here information means representation, independent of the system's structure and organization.[36]

An interesting conclusion emerges from the above discussion, that takes us further in understanding how human beings actually know, and how our conventional view on knowledge has been informed by the stringent use of notions like 'information' and 'control'. Any attempt to view a living system, e.g., the brain, as an input–output processing machine reduces it to a designed, allonomous entity.

Self-Referential

The concept of 'self-reference' is an abstraction that allows us to distinguish a particular class of systems by its functioning. Self-reference means that the knowledge accumulated by the system about itself affects the structure and operation of that system. Self-referentiality is prepared by self-organization, and self-reference is a feature of all living systems where the relating operation[37] is *life*. Autopoietic systems are self-referential.[38] In contrast, non-living systems, non-autopoietic systems e.g., a computer, refer to something given from the outside, like software, and consequently have a different relating operation.[39]

An autopoietic system may be self-referential with respect to a specific space-time combination, but also self-referential with

respect to its own evolution.[40] Once this circularity arises, the
processes attain coherence through their own operation, not
through interventions from the environment. Like logic, self-
reference cannot be conceived outside time and time is a part
of self-referencing. It has even been argued that circular, self-
referential processes are: '... *the nerve of the kind of dynamics we
have been considering in living systems and autopoiesis – in organizational closure in general* '.[41]

More implications emerge for how human beings know: we
know through (self-)reference to our previous knowledge.
Thus, self-referentiality is a way to abstract that what we know
was influence by what we knew, and what we will know
depends on what we know. This is another property that
makes a human being distinct from a machine.

Observing

Because the autopoietic process is not accessible directly to
anything or anybody except the system, but is only open to
observation, any characterization of an autopoietic system can
only be given from the standpoint of an observer.[42] An
observer, or observer-community, is '... *one or more persons who
embody the cognitive point of view that created the system in question,
and from whose perspective it is subsequently described* '.[43]

The observer can chose to either focus his attention on the
internal structure of the system, or on its environment. In the
former case, the observer sees the environment as background
and the properties of the system emerge from the interaction
between its components. In the latter case he treats the system
as a simple entity with certain interaction with the environment, e.g., imposed constraints, resulting in the problem of
controlling the behaviour of the system (cybernetics).

Observation is in itself, an operation of an autopoietic
system:

> it is we *who observe the event. The leaf, the wind, the frog, and the
> shadows are all part of* our *experience, and the events we describe,
> as well as the differences between them, are the results of the rela-
> tions we have established between parts of our experience ... we
> cannot step outside [our cognitive domain] and see ourselves as a
> unit in an environment ... what the observer now takes to be his*

*own environment is still part of his experience and by no means lies
beyond the interface that is supposed to separate the knower from the
world he gets to know.*[44]

A NOTE ON ITS APPLICATIONS

Not all processes can carry the label 'autopoiesis'. The main
requirement is that one must be able to give a precise conno-
tation to component production processes (what is the component and how do you guarantee its reproduction?) and the
system.[45] Still, given its four properties it is obvious that
autopoiesis is distinct from the cognitivist *and* the connectionist perspectives on knowledge and cognitions (see chapter 2).
The key to this distinction lies in that once symbols are viewed
as the system's own creation, any reference to representations
become superfluous:

> *Occam's razor can unburden us of the Trojan horse that was smug-
> gled from the land of Artificial Intelligence into Neuroscience.
> Perhaps the protestations that representations exist only in the mind
> of the observer who jointly beholds an environment and an observed
> organism (brain) will at last be heard.*[46]

Since its introduction, autopoiesis theory has gradually
evolved into a general systems theory.[47] In our opinion, this
theory has had an impressive impact in many fields. It has
even been claimed that autopoiesis is a theoretical paradigm
rather than a unified theory that '*like Marxist or psychoanalytic
theory, it comes in several forms*'.[48] The development of autopoiesis in understanding social systems is intertwined with the
main thrust of systems theory thinking during the last two
decades, i.e., towards seeing systems as adapting to their environment and, thus, being ever more open.[49]

In legal theory and the sociology of law, the basic concept of
autopoiesis has created awareness as to the legal system's lack
of renewal and resistance to adapt to problems in society.[50]
Autopoiesis has been combined with configuration theory to
better understand societal steering.[51] In the debate on ecological consciousness and corporate responsiveness to environmental issues, autopoiesis theory has helped increase the awareness
of communications problems (i.e. between environmentalists

and corporate decision makers) and advanced possible ways to overcome these problems.[52] Autopoiesis theory has also increased our understanding of how computers and their functioning are related to the evolution of human language, thought, and action.[53] In the philosophy of science, autopoiesis theory has been used to point out the constitution of 'everyday knowledge' as opposed to 'scientific knowledge'.[54] In the field of management, the concept of autopoiesis has been used to understand the firm as a living system[55] and address the development of organization knowledge.[56] It has also formed a reference point for understanding (more in a metaphorical sense), evolutionary organization change.[57]

In summary, through its biological roots autopoiesis theory focuses on processes and relations between processes realised through components, not on properties of the components of the systems *per se*. All metacellulars, like human beings, reproduce themselves through the coupled cells that they are composed of. Because all metacellulars are autopoietic systems, *whether we like it or not, you and I are autopoietic systems.*

Notes

1. Although the word 'autopoiesis' was coined by Maturana and Varela, many of its properties have, as we will see, their roots in studies published early this century .

2. It should be noted that self-production was discussed by several authors prior to Maturana and Varela. For instance, Weiss (1967; 1973) and Bertalanffy (1952; 1968) discussed living systems as self-producing and self-organizing flows of matter and energy. Smuts (1926) discussed living systems in terms of irreducible wholes in a continuous autogenesis. Bogdanow (1912) viewed living systems not only as self-maintaining but also self-producing. See Swenson (1992) and Zeleny (1980) for excellent reviews of historical sources of inspiration of self-production.

3. Self-reproduction takes place when a unity produces another unity with a similar organization to its own, through a process that is coupled to the process of its own production. For instance, cell division is a special case of reproduction that can be called self-reproduction.

4. Cellular automata was developed in the 1940s to understand seemingly simple systems. A cellular automation can be seen as an array of cells whose states depend on the states of neighbouring cells (Ulam, 1952). This technique has subsequently been used to explore a wide range of theoretical issues in dynamics and evolution.

5.   von Neumann (1966).
6.   Moore (1964).
7.   Penrose (1959: 105).
8.   See von Foerster (1972) for a somewhat ironical argument against reductionism in science.
9.   For a fuller discussion of this, see Monod (1970) and Berthelemy (1971).
10. Here, evolution denotes a development involving the interplay of both internal and external factors, as suggested by Spenser (e.g., 1851). This is distinct from its more familiar, and literal meaning of simply unfolding *pre-existing* structures through imminent forces, as suggested by the Swiss naturalist Charles Bonnet already in 1762 (see Miall, 1912), and later by Charles Darwin in his writings on the origin of species during the latter half of the ninteenth century. For a different view on evolution and co-evolution, see Kauffman (1991, 1995).
11. It should be noted that the frame of reference of Maturana and Varela in understanding autopoietic systems was 'specific objects called living systems, ... living cells' (Varela, 1979: 14).
12. The notion of non-biological is used in an alluding sense to illustrate that autopoiesis theory has been applied outside the field of biology. This, however, does not necessarily mean that authors have regarded such non-biological systems as non-living systems. For example, Vicari (1993), based on theories of autopoietic systems, outlining an alternative to a theory of the firm posed by Italian scholars (i.e. Onida, 1968; Zappa, 1950), suggests that the firm is indeed a living system (*L'impresa vivente*). In claiming this, he suggests that the concept and definition of life extends beyond the discipline of biology.
13. It is beyond the scope of this book to give a full review of systems theory. Readers interested in the foundations of systems theory and systems thinking have a wide array of paradigmatic writings to turn to, for example the early writings of Wiener (1961), Ackoff and Emery (1972), Emery (1969), Ashby (1960), Bertalanffy (1968), and Churchman (1968). Readers interested in the early application of systems theory to the theory and practice of management, should turn to Stafford Beer's work, e.g., Beer (1959) and the writings of C. West Churchman, e.g., Churchman and Schainblatt (1965).
14. Maturana and Varela (1987: 40).
15. The systems interrelations are typically characterized by processes that (1) recursively depend on each other in development and realization of the processes themselves, and (2) constitute the system, recognizable in the space-time continuum in which the processes exist.
16. Varela (1984: 25).
17. Gomez and Probst (1983: 3),
18. Varela (1979: 13) further developed this definition: 'Autopoietic systems are organized (defined as a unity) as a network of processes of production (transformation and destruction) of components that produces the components that: (1) through their interactions and transformation continuously regenerate and realize the network of processes (relations) that produce them; and (2) constitute it (the

system) as a concrete unity in the space in which they exist by specifying the topological domain of its realization as such a network.'

19.   Two basic distinctions emerge from this discussion: the cell (1) *reproduces* itself vs. not reproducing at all, and (2) it reproduces *itself* vs. reproducing something else.

20.   Reproduction requires the existence of a unity to be reproduced and evolution requires the possibility to change what is reproduced, i.e., the unity. The latter follows, by definition, the former.

21.   Varela (1979).

22.   Autonomy has been discussed in literature since Aristotle and several authors have previously used the term autonomy. See also Edgar Morin's (1982) essay on the intricate set of philosophical and scientific questions raised by the fundamental principles of autonomy.

23.   Varela, Maturana and Uribe (1974: 188).

24.   Varela (1979: 3).

25.   Maturana and Varela (1987:46–48).

26.   Varela, Maturana and Uribe (1974: 188–189).

27.   Control means external-law or external-control (allonomy).

28.   Taking his analysis of autonomous systems one step further, Varela claimed that: '... there is an autonomy beyond what we are used to seeing as individual biological entities, in the collective interaction in a social tradition.' (Varela, 1979: 271).

29.   See Jantsch (1980) and Andrew (1989) for a fuller discussion of self-organization.

30.   For example, Jantsch (1980), Andrew (1989), and Zimmerman and Hurst (1993). This assumption excludes several characteristics of autopoietic systems that allow more consistent and comprehensive system descriptions.

31.   These represent two distinct types of self-organizing systems: self-organizing systems that accept new components and concentrate their internal energies to integrate (order) these elements; and self-organizing systems that reject any new, external component at their boundaries. See Stichweh (1990) for an illustration of these types of self-organization in the development from pre-modern to modern science.

32.   This dialectic is further discussed in terms of the distancing of oneself in relation to oneself. This is called 'bootstrap' by Maturana and Varela (1987) and 'self-transcendence' by Dupuy (1988).

33.   Maturana and Varela's original discussion of strict organizational closure has subsequently been loosened, for instance, by Jantsch (1980). Furthermore, in Luhmann's (1986) view autopoietic systems must be understood as the recursively closed organization of an open system, that is, beyond the traditional dichotomy of open vs. closed towards a linkage of the two. This is the reason why we state 'simultaneously open and closed' (see also von Krogh and Vicari, 1993; von Krogh, Roos and Slocum, 1994).

34.   In the same way it has been argued that, for instance, legal systems are normatively closed and at the same time a cognitively open

system, and that (autopoietic) economic systems are open with respect to needs, products, services and closed with respect to payments.

35. Varela (1979: xv). This has been further discussed by von Krogh and Vicari (1993).
36. This is where information becomes what is represented, and what is represented is a correspondence between symbolic units in one structure and symbolic units in another structure. See the discussion in Chapter 2.
37. We use the term 'relating operation' to indicate what the system relates to in its functioning.
38. Varela (1979) and Goguen and Varela (1978) developed a calculus of self-referential expressions, showing that it is the rehentry of any expression into its own indicative space that permits recovering of all the basic forms of circularity. Also, their calculus illustrated that all self-referential situations can be treated on an equal footing as belonging essentially to one class.
39. In subsequent applications of autopoiesis to understanding other than living systems, the relating operation of self-reference is (of course) not life. In non-living systems in general the relating operation is *meaning*; in psychic systems it is *consciousness* and in social systems it is *communication*. See Luhmann (1984) for a fuller discussion of this.
40. Space does not allow for a full treatment of the differences and the similarities between evolutionary theory after Charles Darwin and the way 'evolution' is captured in the works of Maturana and Varela. For more on this, see Jantsch (1981), Maturana and Varela (1987).
41. Varela (1979: 107).
42. von Forester (1972).
43. Varela (1979: 85). The reader interested in studying in depth the biological roots of the theory of autopoietic systems, will discover how Maturana and Varela struggeled with the question of a definition of life, as mentioned initially in this chapter. In Maturana and Varela (1987) they strongly attack the approach of conventional biology, to define a list of characteristics of living systems that allows the observer to recognize one when (s)he sees it. Their chief claim is that such an approach would always meet the problem of making a complete list, covering all possible variations of life. Here we discover the amazing 'self-referential' capacities of the theory of autopoietic systems. Conventional biologists, themselves being living systems (observers) and embodying particular cognitive viewpoints, have created living systems of various kinds through developing lists of characteristics of these systems.
44. Varela (1979: 273–4).
45. Because an autopoietic system is defined as a system, and since either a system is autopoietic or not, the establishment of an autopoietic system cannot be a gradual process. To assess whether or not a system (unity) is autopoietically organized the following six-point key can be used (Valera, Maturana and Uribe (1974: 192–3):

1. Determine, through interactions, if the system has identifiable boundaries. If the boundaries can be determined, proceed to #2. If not, the entity is indescribable and we can say nothing.

2. Determine if there are constitutive elements of the system, that is, components of the system. If these components can be described, proceed to #3. If not, the system is an unanalyzable whole and therefore not an autopoietic system.

3. Determine if the system is a mechanistic system, that is, the component properties are capable of satisfying certain relations that determine in the system the interactions and transformations of these components. If this is the case proceed to #4. If not, the system is not an autopoietic system.

4. Determine if the components that constitute the boundaries of the system constitute these boundaries through preferential neighborhood relations and interactions between themselves, as determined by their properties in the space of their interactions. If this is not the case, you do not have an autopoietic system because you are determining its boundaries, not the system itself. If #4 is the case, however, proceed to #5.

5. Determine if the components of the boundaries of the system are produced by the interactions of the components of the system, either by transformation of previously produced components, or by transformations and/or coupling of non-component elements that enter the system through its boundaries. If not, you do not have an autopoietic system; if yes, proceed to #6.

6. If all the components of the system are also produced by the interactions of its components as in #5, and if those which are not produced by the interactions of other components participate as necessary permanent constitutive components in the production of other components, you have an autopoietic system in the space in which its components exist. If this is not the case and there are components in the system not produced by the components of the system which do not participate in the production of other components, you do not have an autopoietic system.

Please note that Varela Maturana, and Uribe use 'unit' where we use 'system'. See Zelany and Hudford (1992) for an application and evaluation of these criteria on various types of systems. It should be noted that these authors' direct application of these criteria has been criticized by, for instance, Geyer (1992).

46. Werner (1987: 183), referring to Maturana and Varela (1980).
47. Varela (1979), Luhmann (1987), van Twist and Schaap (1991).
48. See King (1993: xx)
49. For instance, Buckley (1968)
50. Luhmann (1988), Teubner (1988), Deggau (1988).
51. See the chapters in in't Veld, Schaap, Termeer, and Twist (1991).
52. Luhmann (1992).
53. Winograd and Flores (1987).

54. Maturana (1991), Becker (1991).
55. Vicari (1991).
56. von Krogh and Vicari (1993), von Krogh, Roos, and Slocum (1994), and in this book.
57. Morgan (1986), Smith (1982), Weathly (1992).

4 Organizational Knowledge, Individualized (and Socialized)

KNOWLEDGE OF ORGANIZATIONS

Organizational knowledge resides in both the individual organizational member and in the relations among organizational members, that is, at the social level. In keeping with the anti-representationistic stand, at our disposal we find strong theoretical foundations with respect to individual human cognition, and individualized knowledge. Little is written, however, about the knowledge of social systems *per se*. For this reason we have chosen to bracket socialized organizational knowledge until a mediating theory and accompanying language is found, that allows for a conceptualization of knowledge of the social system, compatible with the autopoiesis perspective.

At the individual level organizational knowledge is 'individualized'. In developing a concept of individualized organizational knowledge, we borrow concepts and their interrelationships from the autopoiesis theory of human cognition, applying the central terminology developed in Chapter 3. In particular we draw on the books *Principles of Biological Autonomy* by Fransisco Varela (1979), *The Tree of Knowledge* by Humberto Maturana and Fransisco Varela (1987), and *The Embodied Mind: Cognitive Science and Human Experience* by Fransisco Varela, Evan Thompson and Eleanor Rosch (1992).

We recall that the cognitivist and connectionist epistemologies assumed that the world is pre-given, and that the task of the cognitive system is to represent this world as correctly as possible. The cognitive system construes the world around it. The metaphor is that of a human mind mirroring nature.[1] The cognizing system subsequently acts on these representations. '*The ultimate court of appeal for judging the validity of (these) representation(s)*'[2] is the world, in which we act, unsuccessfully or successfully.

Autopoiesis theory at a very general level, suggests an alternative conception of the relationship between human knowledge and the world (see the discussion in Chapter 2). The discussion that follows points to various properties of knowledge of the human being: knowledge is embodied, it is self-referential and allows for distinction-making in observations, and it is brought forth in an organizational setting.

EMBODIMENT OF KNOWLEDGE

Cognitivist epistemologies suggest that knowledge is abstract in the sense of not being dependent on functions performed by the human body in an open-ended situation. A concept of knowledge as being abstract functions well for cognitive systems that perform tasks in a pre-defined, highly structured and bounded environment. When the degrees of freedom of movement, the items to observe and categorize, and the possible effects of actions are limited, there is a limited number of representations. An industrial robot, for example, has in its programs a limited set of movements based on the physical layouts in which it is placed, and the physical objects that it manipulates.

Human beings, however, very seldom encounter such pre-structured, bounded situations, and therefore, have to rely on their experiences and creativity in defining both the situation, the problem and the possible solutions to the problem. Unlike the cognitivist epistemology, a theory of knowledge rooted in autopoiesis theory suggests that knowledge is not abstract but embodied: '*everything known is known by somebody*'.[3] As the human being confronts new situations, experiences are gained through thinking, sensing, moving, etc. Knowledge is formed through the actions, perception and sensory and motor processes.[4] Autopoiesis theory also recognizes that the human being uses past experiences to orient itself in new situations: Thus previous experience will affect new experiences gained.

This view of embodied knowledge leads to a startling view of the relationship between the world and the knowledge of the human being. A key claim is that 'situation', or world, and 'knowledge' are structurally coupled, and hence co-evolve. Knowledge enables us to perceive, act, and move in a world, and as we act, perceive, and move the world comes forth as a result of our actions and observations. In the words of Maturana and Varela: *'knowledge is what brings forth a world'.*[5]

Knowledge and world are so intimately connected that it may be virtually impossible to say which started first. Thus, it is not surprising that most of us have difficulties defining what is knowledge. If looking at a bird in flight, who could say whether the bird or the eye was first in creating this event of observing an animal.[6]

So what then is world? Is it a pre-given world to be represented? We suggest that it is not. Rather the 'world' that is brought forth is a subjective world determined by previous experience. In the words of Alfred Schutz, *'The world...refers to subjective experience and comprehension. It is...a world of somebody, namely the concretely experiencing individual.'*[7]

The view of embodied knowledge also maintains the concern with autonomy that is so critical for autopoiesis theory. Knowledge develops in an autonomous manner for the human being, and thus cannot be transferred directly to other humans.[8] The ground for this claim is that the human being's history of structural coupling with the world is unique. Each human has its own history of movement and observation, *its own* pattern of structurally coupled interaction with the world. As a result, the evolving knowledge, because it is formed in structural coupling, also is unique.

This concern with autonomy and a unique history of structural coupling is not trivial and may bring new light to some previous commentaries on human knowledge. For example, the ideas of autonomous knowledge provide a strong warrant for Michael Polanyi's claim that individuals are in the possession of 'tacit knowledge'.[9] Polanyi argues that individuals have tacit knowledge, pertaining for example to the skills of making a violin, that cannot be articulated and hence of which little can be conveyed linguistically to others. The concept of embodied knowledge suggests that this is so, because training a certain skill is a highly private experience in which the body and mind together coordinate and perfect patterns of movements.[10]

In a training situation, the history of structural coupling between the human being and world, will also be a history of trial and error. This trial and error process, however, can only partly be captured by individual retrospection and representation.[11] As argued by Pierre Bordieu, human beings tend to forget all the details of a messy, non-linear training process, interpolating and generalizing about their own skill development. Personal accounts of skill development processes, then, are often rudimentary and partial. Nevertheless, having experienced the full trial and error process still makes a difference. Human beings who have 'lived through' the process make 'better judgements' and appear to be more 'flexible'.[12] In summary, a person's knowledge is a result of directly experiencing tasks through a history of structural coupling.

Let us give an example that we believe illustrates the power of the notion of knowledge as embodied.[13] We situate this example in a fairly complex setting that should be familiar to most readers: the office. Here machines, individuals, and documents interact, and patterns of interaction, light, time, space and locations can vary considerably across various offices.

Imagine that you are about to enter an office that is new to you. Your experience (knowledge) tells you both to take an initial sweeping look in order to locate the reception desk, your assumed point of entry into the inner circles of the office. Having located what you believe is the reception desk (world) you take the first steps towards the desk. In doing this you get a glimpse of a corridor on your right-hand side, in which you see a door, and on which you locate a name plate (world). You recognize the name on the door to be the person you are supposed to visit (knowledge).

Clearly, your bodily movement is a condition for new knowledge to develop. It also, however, constrained your view of the cloakrooms on your left-hand side (knowledge that could be of use). Now being in a position to talk to the person behind the desk, the person presents himself as being the director of administration with the additional message that the receptionist is away (world). Your reaction can only be determined by yourself: Am I allowed to ask this director to call the person I am to visit? Is the director not substituting for the receptionist but just fetching papers from the reception desk? How would the director react to my request?

From the example one is tempted to ask how the cognitivist can claim supremacy of one set of knowledge structures over the other, if at all? *It is not until you have moved, defined problems and attempted a solution that you can know about the world.* And your solution was indeed the trigger of creating a world. Following autopoiesis theory, one could suggest that knowledge affects what you eventually will know.

Autopoiesis theory allows us to take an additional step in our examination of individualized organizational knowledge. Observation and knowledge are closely connected in the concept of embodied knowledge, as seen above. A further step is to more closely examine how observation and knowledge co-evolve in the process of bringing forth a world.

KNOWLEDGE, DISTINCTIONS, VALUES AND BASIC SELF-REFERENCE

A central claim of autopoiesis theory is that knowledge of the individual human being arises from an operationally closed system.[14] Recalling the discussion in Chapter 3 of autopoietic systems as simultaneously open and closed systems, 'operational closure' means that the result of processes are the processes themselves. In effect, the human mind does *not* represent a world. Rather, it brings forth, or forms a world as a domain of distinctions that are inseparable from the structure of the cognitive system.[15] Moreover, the cognitive system is normatively closed in determining what it observes.[16] In the language of autopoiesis, in closing itself the brain enables the creation and re-creation of its own organization.

What does it mean that the world is a domain of distinctions and that human beings are normative in observations? In keeping with the notion of embodied knowledge, observation and knowledge are closely connected. Maturana and Varela's extended claim is that knowledge enables human beings to make distinctions in observations. Distinction-making is a process of isolating, or what resembles 'categorizing', elements of the world.[17] It is a process that mainly distinguishes a unity from its background, e.g., a tree from the forest. Every time human beings refer to something, implicitly or explicitly, a 'criterion of distinction' is specified.[18]

Specifying a criterion of distinction may also imply that some form of 'value judgement' is employed. By value judgement we mean assigning value to observations.[19] Little, however, is said in Maturana and Varela's version of autopoiesis theory about normative closure arising from such individual value judgements. Of course, value judgements are in themselves distinctions, and hence have their own criteria, e.g., a tree can be seen as beautiful, as distinct from ugly.

We believe it necessary to separate distinctions pertaining to value judgement from more conceptual and categorizing distinctions. The reason is that value judgements *per se* open new avenues of philosophical investigations, ranging from metaphysics to methodology and theory of value. A new language for describing knowledge, especially because of its embodiment, must be richly equipped to describe historical patterns of structural coupling between human beings and the world, not only in terms of observations of distinct elements, but also in terms of autonomous value judgements.[20]

Our use of these two basic distinctions will become clearer to the reader as we proceed to discuss organizational knowledge socialized. Here, however, it suffices to note that *knowledge enables both conceptual distinction making and value judgements*.

As previously elaborated on, autopoietic systems are self-referential. In making use of autopoiesis theory to understand human cognition, the requirement to basic self-reference, like the requirement of autonomy, must be satisfied. In all human knowing basic self-reference is accomplished in the dynamic relationship between knowledge, observation, and distinction-making. *Knowledge enables distinction making and distinctions, in turn, enable (the development of) knowledge.* This knowledge refers to previous distinctions and previous knowledge, and it simultaneously refers to a *potential* for new knowledge and distinctions. How should we understand this 'reference to a potential'?

First, previously (referred) knowledge/distinctions make up human cognitive resources. As the psychological theory of Jean Piaget shows, these cognitive resources, grounded in conceptual and observational experiences, allow for the accommodation[21] of new experiences.

Second, the cognitive resources also allow for imaginization. New experiences can be derived from thought without observation. Also here, self-reference plays an important role. Referring to cognitive resources, situations, events, and concepts can be envisioned. These envisioned 'states' presuppose emodied action.[22] but they do not have to be limited to such. In a way they are 'cognitive actions' in a pure sense.[23] Imaginization is about creating new distinctions, and hence, new knowledge. This should not be confused with a cognitivist perspective in which individuals with high imaginative (or creative) capacity would have a strong ability to score high on creativity tests like connecting nine dots arranged in a three-by-three matrix.[24] Nor should it be limited to artists only, who can imagine whole worlds composed of life-like characters. Rather, it is an integrated feature of human knowledge development.

Let us finally illustrate knowledge, distinction making and self-reference through an example. In supervising the construction of a building, the engineer distinguishes the ground from the building, the ceiling from the floor, the doors from the wall, etc. In order to act in the world, that is, to see deviations from the designs or problems with the use of poor quality materials, this distinction-making is essential. It is also based on his knowledge/distinctions developed through encounters with other construction sites and through his education (observing). However, also his imaginization allows him to act. At home he might for example envisage a particular technical solution to a practical problem. His previous knowledge of the construction site, and his imaginization, allows him to make new distinctions around which he can develop knowledge. These distinctions in turn can allow him to test out the technical solution on the construction site. Next, when observing the construction site, he can make new distinctions based on his implemented technical solution.

The concept of self-reference has strong implications for the way we view human knowledge. Knowledge is intimately connected to creativity, action, observation, hearing, smelling, etc. The broad reportoire of human activity contributes to knowledge. Cognition is not, as many cognitivists would claim, processing of information in a central processing unit based on input from an external pre-given world. Rather cognitive processes refer to themselves. In effect all knowledge will always be 'self-knowledge'; as you know (bring forth a world) this will reveal something about yourself.[25] Even when humans are acting spontaneously[26] in hindsight their actions reveal something about themselves to themselves. Whenever I experience a sense of joy, for example, I can refer back to this experience as joyful, telling me something about a particular mood as well as a particular setting for experiencing that mood (a joke, passion, etc.).

ORGANIZATIONAL KNOWLEDGE WHEN INDIVIDUALIZED

Having clarified how indiviuals know, we are now in a position to more clearly specify what is meant by individualized organizational knowledge. Our starting point is that the organization functions as a specific domain of structural coupling that allows the individual organizational member to realize its autopoiesis (reproduce cognitive processes). Every day organizational members experience a history of structural coupling with other organizational members. Thus, as a domain of structural coupling the organization presents itself to the organizational member as a set of variable experiences and events, some of which have a kind of recurrent character. Other events give the organizational member a sense of having experienced them for the very first time. Sometimes these events, same or different, are experienced at the same or at different times.[27] Organizations provide this kind of regularity to organizational members and allow them, in the context of what they experience as the organization, to distinguish events and the time at which they occur. We call these *event – time* distinctions and we shall return to these later.

Knowledge of the organizational member of the organization hinges on the making of at least two more fundamental distinctions. First, there is a distinction between 'self' and the organization. This, to most of us, seems like a natural distinction. It is not, however, a trivial one because, as seen above, the difference between the environment and the knowing human is constantly being reproduced autopoietically. A cognitive system reproduces its own processes, and these processes distinguish it from its environment. Autopoiesis is necessary for the awareness of 'identity'.[28] We name this distinction *identity – organization* distinction.

The second type of distinction refers to the isolation of the domain of organization from the environment of the organization. Subsequently, many distinctions are made pertaining to this first distinction, such as, this is a part of activities that belong to the organization, these norms are the norms of the organization, etc. We label these *organization – environment* distinctions. This type of distinction is so often taken for granted in the organization theory literature. Chester Barnard, for example, had already chosen to look at activities when identifying organizational boundaries.[29] Moreover, Max Weber used the legal system as distinguishing the organization from its environment.[30] Yet another criteria is membership of an organization.[31] From the perspective of our organizational epistemology, the boundary of an organization is an issue of knowledge. The boundary is created by individual's knowledge pertaining to the organization – environment criterion.[32] Each individual will form his or her own boundaries of the organization, and recreate these dynamically as a part of their individual knowledge base. For example, a director of finance may be day-dreaming in his office until the CEO calls him up to ask about the quarterly results. When is the organizational boundary maintained? In a strategic alliance, a production engineer working with a production planner from the partner company may forget about his (so called) mother company, and focus on their common task. He may even become exuberant about the excellence of the production process, and reveal production secrets to the fellow from the partner company. As these two examples illustrate, the fundamental organization-environment distinction varies with time and location.

The organizational members' knowledge of the organization then comes forth as a particular set of norms and distinctions dependent on the individual's interaction with various parts of what he distinguishes as the organization at various locations and time. *Therefore, it is meaningful to talk about individualized organizational knowledge.* This should not be confused, however, with a concept like 'individual knowledge of the organization' The latter would be misleading since it implies that there is an organization (out there) to be

represented and the individual experiences the organization
in a private manner. The notion of individualized organizational knowledge rather suggests that through making event –
time, identity – organization, and organization – environment
distinctions in observations, and subsequently many organizational specific distinctions, the organization is brought forth
for the individual organizational member. (S)he can *never*
know what others know is the organization.

Does this understanding accentuate the need for rethinking
established understanding of the knowledge of individual
organizational members? A very common understanding of
individual knowledge of an organizational member is that type
of knowledge that arises as the member resolves certain tasks
of an organization. The task presents itself to the organizational member as a collection of events, like problem formulation, generation of problem solutions, implementation, and
control of task performance. Like a notion of 'learning curve'
suggests, the individual organizational member becomes
better at resolving a task as time goes by. A common managerial response to this increasing proficiency is to implement a set
of work descriptions or other *organizational routines* that ensure
the capturing and repetition of successful task resolution
behaviour (normally triggered by individual behaviour).[33]
Task perfection along these lines requires that the task presents itself to the organizational member as a set of recurrent
events. However, the question we are led to ask by viewing
knowledge as embodied is, of course, how new are these 'old'
events, and further, if these new events are not old, does it
matter?

The first question is critical because it may raise important
issues related to the suitability of a classical concept of organizational and other types of routines given our understanding
of human knowledge.[34] To answer the question a precaution
must be taken, however. Since any observer of an organizational member necessarily must follow the dynamics of
autopoietic cognition, there is a need for making explicit the
reference point for the observation made.

An external observer watching behaviour by an organizational member can gradually describe the organizational
member as becoming increasingly competent with respect to a
certain task. For example, the observer may describe the

pattern of competence evolution in a higly complex task[35] domain in accordance with the scheme suggested by Dreyfus and Dreyfus.[36] First, the person is a novice, just working hard to recognize objects, and events, and the rules of behaviour that may lead to succesful task performance.

The observer may describe the next stage as the stage of an advanced beginner at which the task solver can take on small deviations in the tasks based on previous experience. Competence, the third stage, is achieved as the task performer recognizes certain situations where certain conclusions are drawn, decisions made, and expectations investigated. Fourth, proficiency is not achieved before the task solver is able to relate previous situations to present situations in an automatic manner, without decomposing and analyzing each element of the situation. The fifth, ultimate level of task resolution proficiency is when the task solver becomes an expert. At this stage, *'when things are proceeding normally, experts don't solve problems and don't make decisions; they do what normally works'.*[37]

For an external observer, the behaviour of the task performer reaches some kind of stability as he achieves the level of an expert. The observer has seen a process of trial and error as the organizational member increased his competence. At this time, stable behaviour can be captured systematically in work rules, refined in work procedures, and further, perhaps, developed into computerized models.

From the viewpoint of the expert, on the other hand, through recurrent interactions with the complex task, his knowledge and distinction-making have gradually evolved. When he has reached the expert stage, his knowledge enables him to detect small variations in the task situations that he himself brings forth. He also knows that his actions influence how the task appears over time. If we assume that structural coupling with a task environment makes the task solver's knowledge different from the observer's knowledge, then we can also claim that these very fine distinctions necessary for bringing forth tasks, detecting and correcting variations in the task, may be beyond the 'horizon' of observation of an external observer. By horizon we mean that it cannot be described by the external observer. Events are never the same, but are recreated from time to time, not in the environment alone, but by the human mind in interaction with the environment. And since human cognition is never invariant, but consists of processes that reproduce their own processes, these events, by definition, can never be exactly the same. Does this conclusion matter?

We believe it does. The argument raises important implications for descriptive and prescriptive views on the functioning of organizations. Behaviour of organizations has long been captured in the form and formats of organizational routines. In reading for example the work by Cyert and March.[38] we are led to believe that organizations function as their routines prescribe. These routines have been based on successful behaviour of organizational members or what is imagined to be necessary behaviour for successful task performance. Alternatively, organizations function not in accordance with their written routines, but rather by their unwritten or tacit routines.[39] Over time, organizational members repeat their behaviour and knowledge as they become socialized into the values and norms of the organization, giving rise to more informal routines.[40] A necessary implication of this view of human cognition and task performance, is that the organization at various moments may appear as highly fragmented where each individual holds his own view of what the organization is.[41] Thus for management of organizations, a critical task becomes the coordination and integration of these highly fragmented views.[42] By coordination one achieves the necessary stability for routinized behaviour.

This is first and foremost possible because one assumes a pre-given world, a fixed reference point in how the organization 'really is'. Finally, as argued by March and Olsen,[43] organizations function as 'garbage cans' where problems, decisions, and people are intertwined. Nevertheless, the elements of the garbage can by themselves exhibit some kind of invariance over time. Where, however, does organization theory capture the non-stability required for human cognition, and hence, life? And how does it cope with the knowledge that humans beings create their own worlds, and that there is never a fixed reference point against which to measure whether or not the individual organizational member has created a 'correct representation' of the organization.[44]

(ORGANIZATIONAL KNOWLEDGE WHEN SOCIALIZED)

So far an approach to human knowledge founded on autopoiesis theory has had little to say about knowledge that extends beyond one individual to others. Varela, Thompson, and Rosch nevertheless offered some indications where they see further development:[45]

> *One provocative possible extension of the (autopoiesis) view of cognition is to the domain of cultural knowledge...Where is the locus of cultural knowledge such as folktales, names for fishes, jokes...is it in the mind of the individual? In the rules of society? In cultural artifacts? How can we account for the variations found across time and across informants? Great leverage...might be obtained by considering the knowledge to be found in the interface between mind, society, and culture rather than in one or even in all of them.*

In keeping with the autopoiesis theory of human cognition, our discussion has centered so far on the knowledge of the individual, that is, knowledge within the individual organizational member. As we begin to consider the possibility of some organizational knowledge that extends beyond the individual (for this reason we call it socialized knowledge) two critical questions arise. The first question is a methodological question that we as observers of organizations must ask: What is our observational scheme by which we can observe knowledge extending beyond individuals and, at the same time, keep with the environment – organization distinction? Second, where does knowledge reside? Does it reside in the individual or, as suggested by Varela, Thompson, and Rosch, in the interface between the individual mind and culture?

As mentioned in Chapter 3, the German sociologist Niklas Luhmann has attempted to apply autopoiesis theory to a broader class of systems. Luhmann has suggested a scheme for the observation of autopoietic systems. He attempts to distinguish between a general theory of autopoietic systems and applied theories of autopoietic systems. At the applied level, autopoietic systems are of three categories: living systems, psychic systems, and social systems.[46]

Most of the traditional work on describing the structure and functioning of cells and metacellulars belongs to the category of living systems. The systems use life as their mode of reproduction. Both psychic systems and social systems use meaning as their basic form of reproduction; meaning is created and recreated over time. However, psychic systems use consciousness and social systems use communication as the basic mode of meaning-based reproduction.[47]

In this scheme, knowledge can both be of the individual as a psychic system, or it can be of a social system. For example, in his sociological systems' theory, Luhmann differentiates a specific sub-system of society, namely science, whose function is to produce knowledge according to the basic distinction 'true' and 'false'.[48] Individuals are not seen as members of the system of science, but they contribute to its autopoiesis by engaging in communication about science. This communication is the component of the social system's autopoiesis and consists not only of a specific statement, but also of a particular meaning again pertaining to certain established criteria (like true or false). Thus, for a communication to be meaningful, it is very often discipline specific (meaningful to the discipline) and follows certain rules that can be accepted by the discipline. In the words of Krohn and Kuppers:

> *Science, like every social system is conservative. Although the knowledge produced by the system is always new, the rules generated by the recursive interaction of researching, and which control the production of knowledge, do not generally change.*[49]

However, the startling conclusion of Luhmann's scheme for observing autopoietic systems, is that the communication does not have to be accepted by one specific other 'scientist' for it to be part of the social system of science. If, for example, an opponent on a doctoral dissertation 'feels uncomfortable' with a proposition made by the candidate, this does not necessarily pass for knowledge in the system of science. At the level of basic distinctions, a feeling of discomfort is not easily categorized as true or false. Thus, even if coming from a so called 'scientific authority', his communication does not necessarily contribute to the system of science.

The reader by this time has begun to see the very controversial conclusion of Luhmann's use of autopoiesis theory: that the individual human being is not the 'stuff' of a social system, like the social system of science, but belongs only to its environment. The system has its own knowledge and its own communication. It follows its own rules of interpretation as distinct from individual interpretation. Through communication, it brings forth its own world: the system of science brings forth its own world of scientific exploration and proof. A consequence of this scheme then is that the idea of the collective as the interface between individual and social system is abandoned.[50]

In spite of these radical consequences, treating the social system of science as a system, or unity to use the language from Chapter 3, opens up a range of possibilities with respect to specifying the functioning of the system. For example, Luhmann is able to suggest that science as a system observes (like an individual), that it communicates, and that it understands itself.

Luhmann's theories suggest the primacy of the social system over the individual, and thereby open up a new domain of investigation. For example, the organization would be one system that carries its own knowledge and must be studied at its own premises. Nevertheless, one might ask if his observation scheme is overly restrictive with respect to the relationship between individual and organization. Luhmann does *not* follow up on Varela, Thompson and Rosch's suggestion to study social knowledge at the boundary between individual and the social system. In doing this he would ultimately have to rely on the theories of social stratification, the relationship between the collective and the individual in the form of roles and values,[51] the very theories to which he claims to have an alternative. His approach raises a number of questions, however.

First, Luhmann assumes a general theory of autopoiesis, but since he does not discuss the relationship between individual and social (other than saying that the individual exists in the environment of the social), it is difficult to understand the *nature* of the dynamics between the individual and social autopoietic systems, and, hence, between individualized and socialized organizational knowledge.

Second, Luhmann further suggests that individuals belong to the environment of the social system. Does the same hold for the individual? Does the social system form the environment of the individual? Could one conceive of a social system *without* individuals (e.g., all scientists become lawyers), and likewise, could one conceive of an individual (psycic) system *without* the social?[52] For example, Matruana and Varela suggest that one of the functions of language for human beings is to allow for consciousness.[53]

To summarize this far, when the *individual* is the primary unit of analysis, knowledge of the individual brings forth a world. When the *social* system is the primary unit of analysis, the knowledge of the social system brings forth a(nother) world. *Organizational knowledge, when socialized, has to be knowledge of the organization,* that is, based on the latter claim.

Using our already established scheme of basic distinctions, organizational knowledge at least allows for the basic distinctions organization – environment[54] and organization – individual.[55] Still, as seen above the individual organizational member brings forth an organizational world. This world contains both the basic distinctions individual – organization and organization – environment. In many ways, dependent on these sets of distinctions, worlds emerge within worlds, and knowledge emerges within knowledge. Since distinctions are never static and are constantly being reproduced, the individual's organ-izational world and the organization's individual world are constantly pulsating, changing and flowing.

A metaphor that may be used is that of running tap water. The water stream emerges as hundreds of thousands of small water drops flowing along. Yet it is not composed of a finite number of these water drops. It is impossible to say which water drop is actually within and which is outside the water flow. The water stream is just a distinction we are able to make when observing the flowing water drops at a higher scale. Likewise, individual worlds reproduce themselves autopoietically. Like taking off in an airplane, the shape and contours of a new world can be recognized: the organizational world.

From this, several important questions surface: What is the relationship between individual knowledge and organizational knowledge? What language is appropriate to describe this relationship? Based on our discussion it appears that at each level the system contains itself: the organization is autopoietic and supposes yet other level of autopoiesis. What does this mean?

It seems that an alternative observational scheme can be suggested; one that captures similarities and differences in autopoietic processes, one that describes the boundaries of the phenomenon explained, and provides a language that can help us, in observing and describing socialized organizational knowledge. We will make use of a distinct, and more natural *Weltanschauung* in our attempt to understand these phenomena, that of scaling and self-similarity.

Notes

1. The metaphor is borrowed from Rorty (1980).
2. Varela, Thompson and Rosch (1992: 136).
3. A paraphrase of Maturana and Varela's (1987) famous statement that 'everything said is said by an observer'.
4. See Varela, Thompson, and Rosch (1992: 173), and Merleau-Ponty (1963). This is clearly linked to previous conceptions of human knowledge in phenomenology. See Schutz (1970).
5. Maturana and Varela (1987).
6. Merleau-Ponty (1963).
7. Schutz (1970: 323).
8. This would mean that these others would give up their autonomy. Knowledge, like information, is never taken in from the environment. The relationship between the environment and the autopoietic system, or the world and the human being, is not specified in terms of input output of information, nor of knowledge. For more on this, see Chapter 3.
9. Polanyi (1958), Spender (1993). See also Nelson and Winter (1982) and Winter (1987) for a discussion of the role of tacit knowledge in economics and organization theory. Note that Polanyi uses a different definition of knowedge than we have used here. We suggest that all knowledge is autonomous for the cognizing system. Polanyi, on the other hand, suggests that knowledge is not only tacit, but also articulable. Articulable knowledge can be conveyed linguistically to other human beings. In terms of autopoiesis theory, this presupposes another scale of observation, and it is not meaningful to talk about how the individual shares his knowledge. See Chapter 3.
10. We use 'skill' here very much in the sense of Schutz and Luckman (1985) to give particular attention to knowledge enabling bodily movements. In particular, we use skill as it may be used by an external observer looking at a person in a training situation.
11. Bordieu (1977).
12. See Dreyfus and Dreyfus (1986). It follows from the discussion this far that the autonomy of embodied knowledge makes it difficult to label and analyze patterns of observation, movement, etc. This lack of complete representation in turn makes it difficult to convey something about tacit skills to others. Representations can never fully recover intuition, judgement, and flexibility exhibited by human beings in an open-ended situation. This incompleteness has severe implications for

the possibility of building expert systems based on the knowledge of human beings. See Dreyfus and Dreyfus (1986) for a full discussion of this problem.

13. Varela, Thompson, and Rosch (1992) provides excellent examples of embodied knowledge.

14. See Chapter 3.

15. Varela, Thompson, and Rosch (1992: 140). On the relationship between distinction making and observation, see Maturana (1978) and Winograd and Flores (1987).

16. This is referred to as normative closure by Luhmann (1988). See also von Krogh, Roos and Slocum (1994).

17. Categorization theory is covered in an extensive amount of literature. See Lai (1992) for a review.

18. Maturana and Varela (1987: 40).

19. Value judgements will be further discussed in Chapeter 6.

20. Note that we also see these value judgements as enabled by knowledge. Seldom do such value judgements arise as a result of long 'judgemental' processes in which various pros and cons of the observation are weighted. Rather, knowledge enables immediate judgements, like the one expressed in 'this is a house, not a barrack, – and I like it'. Knowledge even enables simultaneous value judgements and conceptual distinctions, like the one expressed in 'what a sharp cookie...'

21. Change in cognitive schemata. Piaget also uses 'assimilation' of experiences where experiences do not change cognitive schematas.

22. For example, in order to be able to envisage yourself bicycling, you must have observed and distinguised a bicycle. However, envisionaging yourself riding a bicycle, does not guarantee that you will be able to ride a bicycle using your body.

23. For example, the eighteenth-century Swedish scientist and philosopher Emanuel Swedenborg imagined a conversation with inhabitants of the planet Mercury, posing the question how they would react to what they found on Earth (Swedenborg, 1758). Other philosophers have done the same. Rorty, for example, in order to shed light on the nature of personal experiences and language, imagined the meeting between two peoples, of which one is equipped with a different type of language. The science fiction genre attempts to make use of such 'mind games'. In *Star Trek* the recurrent theme is that of man going 'where no man has ever gone before'.

24. See Howard Gardner's (1990) critique of such a limited view of creativity. Please observe that many studies seem to associate creativity and imagination with slightly pathological states of the human mind. Creative painters or writers are said to look at art as a form of therapy in which they may confront traumatic experiences (Albert and Runco, 1990).

25. Garreth Morgan (1986) suggests that autopoiesis theory reveals the 'narcissistic' tendencies of the knowing subject, in his example, the organization. Rather than revealing a obssession of the human in himself, autopoiesis theory suggests that knowledge will always be self-referential and revealing something about the knower. The catego-

rization of some organizations as 'narcissistics' thus, reveals more about the world brought forth by an observer than the observed system (see Chapter 3).

26. Here 'spontaneity' has a strict meaning as being 'the basic mode of immediate, essentially active experience. It means being immersed in ongoing experience and excludes self-awareness' (Schutz, 1970: 322)

27. Weick and Bougnon (1986).

28. On the problems of identity and autopoiesis theory, see Varela, Rosch and Thompson (1992)

29. Barnard (1938).

30. Weber (1947).

31. For a full discussion of organizational boundaries, see Scott (1987).

32. This idea has a strong resemblance to the discussion of 'virtual corporations'.

33. The literature on organization theory and behaviour has substantially discussed these aspects of the increasing proficiency of organizational members. See as diverse works as March and Simon (1958), Cyert and March (1963), Thompson (1967).

34. We are of course not the first to address the question of the need for organizational routines. Management practitioners have long recognized the limitations of organizational routines in capturing learning, providing stability and control. This is also fully in line with much of the upsurge in literature on the post-industrial society. Today, authors argue, very few tasks are actually routinized (Hage and Powers, 1992). However, authors have tended to conceptualize organizational knowledge in terms of the level of sophistication of the routines they develop (Nelson and Winter, 1982). With the perspective of knowledge presented herein, the role of organizational routines must be rethought.

35. On the notion of task complexity, see Campell (1988).

36. Dreyfus and Dreyfus (1986).

37. Dreyfus and Dreyfus (1986: 31).

38. Cyert and March (1963). See also some of the followers like Lant and Mezias (1990).

39. Argyris and Schon (1978).

40. See Nelson and Winter (1982).

41. In organizational culture literature this problem is frequently referred to as the 'differentiation problem' (Frost *et al.* 1990.). The problem is not foreign to sociologists. For example, Talcott Parsons suggests that consensus on values and shared symbolic systems are necessary for social systems to emerge (see Østerbeg, 1988).

42. See, for example, Peters and Waterman (1982), Schein (1985), Deal and Kennedy (1982). The writings of these authors belong to what is frequently referred to as the 'integration perspective' on organizational culture. In some instances managers have also resorted to this very strong view on the knowledge of the individual. The former CEO of Scandinavian Airline System, Jan Carlzon, for example actively used television, radio, and newspapers to communicate the 'SAS vision' to the employees of SAS. In doing this, he believed, the organizational

members would come to share a common view on the company and its future.

43. March and Olsen (1975).
44. The assumptions that no human beings have equal knowledge, and that knowledge of human beings, by definition, is constantly drifting provide a foundation for the development of a new *organizational theory*. It is not the task of this book, however, to fully discuss the implications of the new organizational epistemology for organization theory.
45. Varela, Thompson, and Rosch (1992: 179).
46. Luhmann (1986).
47. Thus, Luhmann has taken autopoiesis into complex, non-life situations, beyond the individual-as-unit-of-analysis stage, while not directly translating autopoiesis from its biological roots. Cells are not replaced by individuals, nor are metacellulars replaced with organizations.
48. Luhmann (1990a; 1992). Maturana (1991) has seen some of the same tendencies in science, but goes even further than Luhmann in suggesting that only explanations that fulfill criteria of valid scientific explanations, which in turn depend on the structural coupling between scientific discipline and individual scientist, will be scientific explanations. Note here the apparent tautology of science. Luhmann has also pointed strongly to this characteristic of science.
49. Krohn and Kuppers (1989: 165).
50. Østerberg (1988)
51. See Luhmann (1986).
52. See Maturana and Varela's (1987) discussion of the social malfunctioning of two girls that at the age of eight and five were discovered and rescued from a wolf pack. Having lived among the wolves for many years, deprived of human contact, they had no language that made them able to communicate with other humans.
53. Maturana and Varela (1987).
54. This corresponds to the I – organization distinction of the individual.
55. This follows Luhmann's premise that the social system is able to distinguish itself from its environment, given that this environment is composed of individuals.

5 Unbracketing (Socialized Organizational Knowledge) by a Theory of Scaling

UNDERSTANDING SCALE

Knowledge is what brings forth a world, and the world is what brings forth knowledge; knowledge is a process brought forth by individuals, groups, departments, organizations, etc. We cannot say what is the chicken and what is the egg. They seem to be two sides of the same coin.[1] Dependent on our observational scheme, knowledge development is really knowledge development at various *scales*; autopoiesis at various scales. A theory of scaling may help us to understand the relations between individual and social knowledge development, the dynamics of individual and social autopoietic systems; in fact, it may help us unbracket (socialized organizational knowledge). The objective is not to uncover mathematical principles of scaling *per se*, i.e., taking a microscopic approach to scaling.[2] Rather, our intention is to uncover a phenomenological understanding of scaling without calculating it directly like in a scaling function.

What is scale? The great determinist and French mathematician Pierre Simon de Laplace speculated about scale:

> *One of [the] remarkable properties [of Newtonian attraction] is, that if the dimensions of all bodies in the universe, their mutual distances and their velocities were to increase or diminish proportionately, they would describe curves entirely similar to those which they at present describe; so that the universe reduced to the smallest imaginable space would always present the same appearance to observers. The laws of nature therefore only permit us to observe relative dimensions...if we diminish [a circle's] radius, we are forced to diminish also in the same proportions its circumference, and the sides of all inscribed figures. This proportionality seems to be much more natural an axiom than that of Euclid.*[3]

Scale concerns arrangement of classes of phenomena into some kind of sequence, an issue that many mathematicians and philosophers have struggled with over the years. In addition to its meaning in music, scale is a commonly used concept in many fields. Scale implies similarity, which is one of the basic notions of geometry. Two objects are similar if they have the same shape regardless of their size. Scaling means moving across the scale. Mathematically, the meaning of scaling is 'similarity transformation' (of dimensions). Although scientific discourse on associated phenomena are emerging,[4] there is no 'unified theory of scaling' that we can apply in our understanding of scaled autopoiesis. One reason for this might be that scaling various dimensions is often accompanied by a change from simplicity to complexity. Still, the quest for a unified description and mathematical origin of a scaling theory has just begun.[5]

In its most intuitive meaning, scaling concerns the design of nature, or more precisely, its multi-level, even hierarchical structure.[6] In its Euclidian version scaling represents the search for the physical organization within cosmos: '*a global design that may transcend spatial and temporal limits*'.[7] Scaling in phase transitions has been discussed and there is even a scaling theory where quantities are measured directly from mathematical principles, e.g., thermal phase transitions and percolation clusters.[8]

Scaling *is* a fundamental aspect of nature and, therefore, possibly of autopoiesis. The wave that pulsates towards the shore, the growing tree, and the weather are dynamic (and nonlinear) phenomena and processes, whose states change only over time and space, i.e., across scale. Because size alone has vast consequences for human beings and the behaviour of things, *spatial* scaling is perhaps the most discussed type of scaling. Take, for instance, the enlargement of a photograph. The enlarged photograph is a scaled version of the original in proportion to it. Its corresponding angles are the same and the corresponding line segments, oblique or not, have the same scaling-factor.[9] Likewise, think about the scaling involved in making a science-fiction movie.

Spatial scaling has also been used to bring forth underlying messages in literature, like in *Gulliver's Travels* . In this political satire, that later appeared as a story for children, Captain

Lemuel Gulliver experiences the challenges of being on a relatively larger scale in his travel to the country Lilliput.[10] If one takes a panoramic view of the universe it is natural to talk about the relative size of things. The search for the *largest* scale has been a long and rewarding one. With the enormous advances in telescope technology, electronics, instrumentation and space flights during this century, astrophysics and cosmology have increased our present understanding of the largest scale, what we call the universe. In fact, we can now observe objects and radiation up to distance of several hundred million light years away.[11] Scientists have so far developed a rough, four-level scale of the universe, the atomic, stellar, galactic, and mega-galactic scale.[12]

The quest to reach the *smallest* scale has also been a long one. From Democrito's notion of 'atom' as the smallest thing, our present understanding of the smallest scale goes well beyond what we call the atom. Today, classes of elementary particles include leptons and quarks.[13] *If* the quarks and leptons are the ultimate building blocks of all things, the two-and-a-half-millennium quest for the smallest scale would be at an end![14]

The famous 1978 film *Power of Ten* by Ray and Charles Eames is an excellent illustration of spatial scaling.[15] In eight minutes we are taken from the scene of a relaxed picnic on a lawn in Chicago towards the limit of our knowledge about the universe, i.e., the largest scale, every 10 seconds increasing the distance with a power of ten. Furthermore, the spatial scaling is reversed and continued towards a molecule in a blood vessel of the hand of the man picnicing on the lawn, i.e., towards the limit of our understanding of the smallest scale. Thus, the world at arm's length is scaled somewhere in the middle of the extreme large and the extreme small, from our own experience, and illustrated so well in *The Power of Ten*. But, what about scaling of dimensions other than size?

Time can also be scaled. Another Eames film, *The Downturn and Fall of the Roman Empire*, is a great illustration of *temporal* scaling. In this short film the geographical changes of the various empires during 500 BC to AD 450 (e.g., the Roman Empire, Alexander's Empire, Carthage, The Huns) are captured and illustrated in just four minutes. From this temporarily scaled-up version of history, the geographical changes stemming from wars and conflicts appear in a very dynamic way, almost like increase and decline in bacteria growth.[16]

In architecture, scale alludes to the relationship between the two-termed relationship of the parts to the whole and the dimensions of the observer.[17] In garden design, scale refers to the apparent size of a landscape space or the element within it.[18] Other examples of frequently studied scaled phenomena include: temperature, including negative absolute temperatures;[19] evolutionary scales, including the subtle behaviour of animals;[20] scaling of quantum effects;[21] mental activity, such as, speech and memory;[22] scaling of aspirations, including hopes and fears, of people.[23]

To summarise this far, scaling is a profound property of nature, and everything in nature and all dimensions can be scaled. Even this book is scaled, the headlines being a scaled version of the text. As brought forth by Eoyang, it might be that '...*size is an abstraction of the mind, time is a figment of human imagination; chronology an accident of history*'.[24] What has this to do with organizational knowledge?

Scaling is important because it is an everyday activity. Let us assume that when you walk into your office one morning one of your collegues approaches you with a curious look on her face, asking: *Have you been a reliable person lately?* How would you respond? Surely, your answer depends...but on what? What does she really mean? Although you feel you are, and have been a faithful, loyal, dependable, staunch, devoted, and trustworthy person, for (almost) all your life, does this self-perceived 'reliability' (over time) correspond to not only being reliable, but being reliable lately in the world brought forth by your collegue? Not necessarily. Why?

The adjective 'reliable', and the temporal expression 'lately' have different meanings on different scales, so perhaps the most natural answer in the above example would have been: *Reliable on what scale...?* and *Lately, on what (temporal) scale..?* Surely, such an answer would force the collegue to specify if she means, for instance, at work, in connection with a specific task, or privately, as well as whether she means last week, the two years you have been colleagues, or all your life.

All adjectives, verbs and temporal expressions are scaleable. What is right and beautiful for me, given my own theory of value, i.e., ethics and aestethics, might not be right or beautiful for someone else. What is the beginning for me probably means something different for you. Even truth has different scales of meaning. As argued by Joachim, no truth is truth for any man until he has rethought it for himself; truth is not truth at all, except in so far as it is the living experience of a mind.[25] Truth has two Hegelerian connotations: *Richtigheit* ('correctness') and *Wahrheit* (beyond provisional: *...the truth in which the thought content is in agreement with its own essential character*).[26] Or, as stated by Lord Cherbury: '*...all instance of truth will be relations...all truth, except for the thing itself, is conditional*'.[27] If such scaling discrepancy is ignored, an observer-independent assumption regarding scale is made, thereby assuming that all parties are on the same scale.

What scales are found in organizations? On the organizational level there are scales like 'degree of' internationalisation, unionization, performance, and scope of activities. Scales on the divisional or departmental level might include, for instance, degree of project organization vs. operations management, perspectives on time, socialization between employees. On the individual level, we find scales like level of education and experience, work morale, degree of political or religious beliefs, environmental awareness, sense of urgency, and so on. Given that there are virtually infinite numbers of scales in organizations we now start to see the importance of *not* assuming that all parties are on the same scale. Thus, the scale of observation *is* important. At arm's length, direct, real-time observation of, for instance, a social phenomenon may appear as processual, whereas on another, arbitrarily chosen scale, the same social phenomenon may appear sufficiently stable to be called structural, and in addition this may vary over time.[28]

Additional questions surface: How can we be so sure we are on the right scale? And, by the way, what is the right scale – yours, mine or someone else's? Because knowledge is a process that is simultaneously and continuously brought forth autopoietically on many scales, scaling provides a language for better understanding knowledge development and the linkage between individualized and socialized organizational knowledge. The scaling issue discussed here goes beyond the discussion of the 'level of theory', that is, specifying homogeneity of sub-units within higher level units (e.g., among group members, independence of sub-units from higher-level units (e.g., independence of individuals with respect to a group), and heterogeneity of sub-units within higher-level units (e.g., the individual within a group).[29]

Now when we have recognized that the autopoietic process/knowledge development is scaled, like most other phenomena, the next question is not far away: What is the *nature* of the scaling involved in making organizational knowledge individualized and/or socialized? Is it like a photograph and its enlargement proportionally scaled? *We suggest that, like living systems, the autopoietic knowledge development process is not only scaled in general, but similar across scale.* But, what does similar across scale mean?

SCALING THAT IS SIMILAR ACROSS SCALE

> *The OLD NEW INN at Burton-on-the-Water in the heart of the lovely Cotswold country has an unusual name, but its name is not the most unusual thing about it. Its fame has spread over the world because of the remarkable Model Village which has been built in its garden and which has delighted many thousands of tourists since its opening on Coronation Day in 1937.*

This is the first paragraph in a brochure describing a model of an English village, built by the late Mr C. A. Morris, landlord of the inn.[30] In Mr Morris's vegetable garden six men spent four years carefully building a scaled-down version (1:9) of every building and every feature of the landscape in Bourton-on-the-Water: trees (resembling bonsai trees), the river, bridges, and so on. Furthermore, in the garden of the Old New Inn in the model village, a scaled down version of the model village was constructed, similar, but not identical to its arm's-length model of the original village. In turn, a third model village was built in the garden of the inn in the second model village, in the garden of the inn in the first model village, in the garden of Mr Morris, in Bourton-on-the-Water, each of the models being similar but not identical to one another.

Why is this model village of interest in our attempt to better understand organizational knowledge, individualized and socialized? Because we think that it is a great illustration of scaling – more precisely, scaling that is similar, but not identical across scale: just as we shall claim that the autopoietic, knowledge development process is scaled. The grounds for this claim are rooted in the knowledge stream called chaos theory. Briefly reviewing chaos theory will allow us to draw on one of its properties: self-similarity. Our intention is only better to understand the *phenomenology* of self-similarity, not its specific or exact mathematical properties.

A Note on Chaos Theory

Having its roots in dynamic systems theory in mathematics, chaos theory challenges the Euclidean and Newtonian legacy. As pointed out by Hayles, it all started with the 'three-body problem', i.e., the moon making the earth-sun relation too complex to be handled with Newton's equations of motion.[31] The moon attracted earth, causing perturbations in the earth's orbit, changing the earth's distance to the sun, which in turn disturbed the moon's orbit around the earth, and so on. This problem was not understood until Henri Poincaré's paper in 1890, which proved, that in general, a solution was *not* possible by means of Newtonian equations.[32] By proving that it was not sufficient to introduce small perturbations in linear equations in order to solve nonlinear problems, Poincaré laid the groundwork for general dynamic systems theory and, subsequently, chaos theory. However, it was not until Edward Lorenz's article on deterministic nonperiodic flows (applied to unpredictability of weather systems) in 1963 that chaos theory came into full swing.[33] His findings made many researchers across various diciplines more aware that small fluctuations on the micro-scale often propagated through the system, resulting in macro-scale instabilities.[34] Thus, sensitivity on initial conditions is a fundamental property of chaos theory/nature: just think about the instabilities our childhood has caused in our grown-up life.[35]

Chaos theory holds that some systems are nonlinear in their dynamics, and in such nonlinear dynamic systems, islands of order arise from the sea of chaos. Although a system can be said to be chaotic, this in itself does not show much new insight. An example is molecules bouncing off one another in a gas. Because there are so many particles involved, a statistical description is all that can be given, and this decription can be done without chaos theory. Analogously, a social system with many people involved might be seen as chaotic, but that fact alone does not reveal much. There might simply be so many degrees of freedom that the system effectively is random.[36] Different initial conditions may evolve to different attractors: equilibrium points, periodic orbits, quasiperiodic orbits, or chaotic/strange attractors.[37] A chaotic attractor arises when the overall contraction of volumes takes place by shrinking in some of the directions while stretching in others. This will result in an unstable motion even within the attractor. Pairs of orbits which originate from points near one another on the attractor become exponentially separated over time. Thus, small errors of measurement of initial conditions are magnified to cover the entire attractor so that accurate prediction of the future course of the orbits becomes impossible, except in the short run. It follows that there is no causal connection between the past and the present. This condition is referred to as sensitive dependence on initial conditions.[38]

Thus, simple deterministic systems with only a few elements can generate random behaviour, and interaction of components on one scale can lead to complex behaviour, on a larger scale, which cannot be deduced from knowledge about the individual components. Gathering more data does not make this randomness go away. Exactly this type of randomness is called chaos. But, is chaos chaotic? Paradoxically, chaos is generated by fixed, simple rules that do not incorporate elements of chance. The determinism inherent in chaos also implies that many random-looking phenomena (in nature) that were thought never to be predicted can be explained, at least to some extent, in terms of simple laws. In fact, chaos theory '...*decenter all claims of perfection, finality, normality or historical necessity and thus provides an elegant theoretical envelope in which to locate postmodern science and politics*'.[39] It allows for free will within a world governed by deterministic laws.[40]

Cultural history explains why chaos theory is seen as revolutionary within the Western tradition. The word 'chaos' derives from a Greek verb-stem, *kha,* meaning 'to yawn, to gape'. This is the root of the definition in the *Oxford English Dictionary,* a gaping void, yawning gulf, chasm, or abyss.' Many myths in the West depict chaos as a negative state; it is a disorder that must be conquered for creation to occur, e.g., in *Enuma Elish*.[41] Thus, if order is good, chaos (anti-order) is bad because it is the opposite of order. This can be contrasted with Taoist myths, e.g., in *Zhuangzi*, where chaos is the necessary other, the turbulence that challenges and complements the transparency of order. Here, the Western binary logic order vs. anti-order is complemented by 'not-order'. This becomes clearer if one considers that chaos may either lead to order as in self-organized systems or it may have complex structures of order encoded in it. Thus, chaos's relationship with order is much more complex than the traditional (Western) binary perspective.[42]

In natural sciences, fields as diverse as meteorology, thermodynamics, epidemiology and nonlinear dynamics, have used the theoretical lens of chaos theory. What about the social sciences? Here, the change is more evolutionary than revolutionary. The traditional linear perspective that underlies most management and organizational studies, such as economics and marketing, seems to give way to new, nonlinear perspectives,[43] in particular the property of sensitivity of initial conditions[44] Also, chaos theory has been used, in a metaphorical sense, to better understand the boundaries of firms.[45] In some instances, chaos theory has emerged as a serious challenge to conventional world views, e.g., finance and investment theories (the efficient market hypothesis, portfolio theory, capital asset pricing models, and internal rate of return models). Seeing financial markets as complex, dymanic systems has, *de facto*, undermined the above mentioned models; financial markets are neither 'efficient' nor move in 'random walk': Might investors beat the market?[46]

Chaos theory has also attracted increasing attention within the humanities, in particular the relationship between order and 'disorder'. In Katerine Hayle's 1991 book, authors within the humanities have discussed, for instance, fictions as dissipative structures,[47] the chaos of metafiction,[48] chaos theory in relation to deconstruction,[49] and reciprocity between literature and physics,[50] Some of these authors, reflecting on the application, relevance, and importance of chaos theory, are quite critical of the claims by natural scientists, as well as science writers, that chaos theory implies a new metaphysics; for instance:

> *To imagine that profound philosophical questions can or should be answered by advances in irreversible thermodynamics [the author is referring to Prigogine and Stengers (1984)] is apt to evoke uneasiness among most scientists and outright skepticism among humanities scholars...Even more problematic, in my view, is whether the new paradigms are causes of social change or are themselves reflections of larger cultural currents. In light of these uncertainties, it is especially important to be clear about what different research programs within the sciences of chaos have accomplished, and what they have so far merely promised or suggested .[51]*

To sum up, conventional social science presumes that there is only one equilibrium state in normal social systems, and that all unstable systems mean social disintegration and complete lack of order. Small changes will produce small consequences and large changes will produce large consequences. Chaos theory has helped us to rethink this conception. The system's dynamics will push the system into instability and subsequent chaos; the ability to control the system fades. In chaotic systems, small changes may result in enormous changes, and large changes may result in no change – the system becomes unpredictable.[52]

The Property of Self-Similarity

Already in the mid sixteenth-century, Galileo observed that rules based on proportional scaling put a limit on the size of many natural things: for instance, trees. Similarly, a baby is not a scaled-down version of its parents: for instance, its head is much larger and its facial features are different.[53] Chaos theory shows that the wilderness of nature, trees, mountains and lakes cannot fully be understood in terms of Euclidean geometry. In plane geometry, curves have a dimension of exactly 1 and no width, whereas in nature all curvilinear features have width and most have dimensions greater than 1 but less than 2. Coastlines, for instance, look the same when viewed at different scales.[54]

Think about a cloud. Regardless from what angle you observe the cloud, you will find that it is almost impossible to judge the distance to it. It is equally difficult to assess all Euclidean dimensions of the cloud. Why? Because the cloud has virtually every scale: You can focus on parts of it and see that these are more or less similar. Likewise, the cloud you observe looks similar now compared to a few minutes ago. This is because clouds are similar across scale. What does this mean?

For any given system, change from one equilibrium state to another yields a set of predictable and unpredictable outcomes, and the boundaries between these states is not binary, it is 'fractal'.[55] This term describes systems with fractional dimensionality, e.g., the coastline of Britain.[56] Formally, a fractal has infinite detail, infinite length, and no slope or derivative. In Euclidean geometry the homogeneous distribution on a line, plane, or space is invariant under change of scale. In 'fractal geometry' this invariance is restricted or modified, or as stated by Feder: '*Once one leaves the secure ground of conventional geometry a whole zoo of fractal dimensions appear.*'[57]

A property of fractals is 'self-similarity', which means invariance with respect to scaling. For instance, a line is a special set of points in space. If we change the length of the line we recover the same set of points. The same goes for planes, spaces, and, we believe, other dimensions and/or social phenomena and processes. Thus, self-similarity is about patterns, not at one scale or another, but across scales – it is a way to collapse complexity.[58]

Self-similarity is frequently illustrated by the well-known Mandelbrot set, a colourful, almost magical exhibit of islands of order in oceans of chaos.[59] At first, no part of this set resembles any other part at *any* scale. But if the scaling continues, any segment, no matter where it is and how small it is, will, when the scale of observation is changed, reveal new structures each resembling the main set. Although Mandelbrot coined the word 'fractal', self-similarity had been discussed by many other scientists before him, e.g., Georg Cantor in the 1880s, Helge von Koch in the early 1900s (on non-differentiable curves), and Felix Hausdorff in the 1920s (on fractional dimensions).[60] Lorenz explained self-similarity of fractals:

in many fractal systems, several suitably chosen pieces, when suitably magnified, will each become identical to the whole system. This

*implies, of course, that several sub-pieces of each piece, when
magnified, become equivalent to that piece, and hence to the whole
system...Other fractals are only statistically self-similar; small
pieces, when magnified, will not superpose on the entire system, but
thy will have the same general type of appearance.*[61]

The property of self-similarity has been very useful in advanc-
ing understanding of many other fields of inquiry within the
realms of natural and social sciences. There are many self-
similar structures in the human body, e.g., neurons, network
of blood vessels, nerves, ducts, and cardiac mucles; airways of
the lung, mechanical and electrical dynamics of the heart.[62]
Auditory and visual perception also exhibit self-similarity.[63] It
has even been suggested that the universe, its galactic and
atomic structure and dynamics, is self-similar, which has been
called the 'self-similar hierarchical cosmology'.[64] At one of the
most recent academic conferences on fractals, the 1994
Gordon Research Conference on Fractals,[65] the vast spectrum
of topics discussed illustrates how natural sciences are
advanced through the lens of fractals. Papers presented
covered: fractal aspects of sub-monolayers in thin film growth;
dynamic scaling in surfaces during etching and thin film
growth; morphological instabilities during solid state reaction;
design principles for biological organisms, pattern formation
and cellular dendritic growth; different modes of self-organization in the growth of plants; cross-over in self-similar and
self-affine fractals; properties and functions of non-coded
regions of DNA; fractal correlation in DNA; impedance of
capacitive fractal electrodes; wave interactions with fractal
objects; structure of branched rivers and their associated
topographies; fractal hazard assessment-floods, earthquakes
and volcanic eruptions; fractals in general relativity; fractality
in particle physics; multi-fractal tools for image processing;
frustrated percolation; and fractal cracks.

Many social phenomena *appear* to be self-similar in nature.
Democracy, for instance, is self-similar: We find it on the
supra-national level, like the European Parliament, the
national level in the form of national parliaments, and at
the organizational level, in the form of various interest organizations. The form of democracy may vary but its principles
are similar across the scale.

Social processes also exhibit self-similarity,[66] for instance, HIV transmission,[67] density waves in traffic flows,[68] classical and contemporary music.[69] Language may be self-similar, for instance, Chinese tends to mimic phenomena rather than define it and is rich in repeated compounds, and these can be seen as a form of verbal self-similarity.[70] Thus, many social phenomena and their dynamics are self-similar in nature. This was underscored by Young:

> *the behavior of a mother or a priest or a marriage or a capitalist system, does not take the form of a euclidian structure; the distribution of units acts which correspond to each person in social harness takes on fractal features. One is not a mother, clark or a criminal over one hundred percent of the unit acts which one embodies. Mothers embody other roles in the same time-space dimensions in which she mothers...The worst criminal one can imagine engages in criminal behavior but a tiny fraction of the unit acts s/he embodies over time.*[71]

In fact, we could probably generate 'Mandelbrot sets' in different social settings and for processes, like industries, organizations, education, health care, and individual behaviour. Economic systems, for instance, have fractal basins with changing regions of (in)stability when they undergo bifurcation. Think about political decisions regarding new corporate taxes, for instance. The new policy can be seen as an (chaotic) attractor of corporate and individual behaviour, which in one country might boost its infrastructure and in another result in large scale tax evasion, reduced corporate morale, and national economic problems.

SPECULATIONS ON SELF-SIMILARITY IN ORGANIZATIONS AND MANAGEMENT RESEARCH

From our perspective self-similarity means invariance over operations, any operation. Whatever is done with the self-similar phenomenon or process, its fundamental principles remain similar across scale.

Imagine you are a newly hired member of the corporate staff in a large firm that, without you being aware of it, has developed a self-similar organizational learning process. At first, when you try to uncover the organizational learning practices of your new company, no part of the process implemented in the Strategic Business Units (SBUs) resembles any other part at *any* level. Gradually you uncover more and more details of the process, such as the governing principles, how people are involved in different activities and what responsibilities people have at what time. No matter where it is or how small it is, when the scale of observation is changed, (for instance, when you study the learning process at individual, group or SBU level), new processes are revealed, each resembling the overall process. In fact, they are always similar but never identical.

To what extent have processes and phenomena within the realm of management and organization studies been recognized and, therefore, been addressed as self-similar (or even scaled)? Only to a very limited extent. By revisiting everyday knowledge, conventional models and theories by means of the theory of scaling and self-similarity, then new insights will emerge, and existing literature can be enriched. Let us illustrate this by revisiting well known conceptualizations in literature and viewing them from the perspective of self-similarity. It should be noted that this is just a brief revisit to a few areas, *not* an in-depth theoretical treatement of each issue.

Within the field of international business, for instance, rudimentary distinctions are often made between 'international', 'multinational', and 'global' operations of companies. In the process of globalization, many firms follow a developmental path from international to multinational to global. The international stage is characterized by an increasingly autonomous international division, separate from the domestic business. A firm at the international stage maintains a strong distinction between the domestic and international divisions, and also operates with a strong hierarchy within the international division. So the application of management processes, such as planning, budgeting, performance review and compensation will tend to be different.

In contrast, the global stage is noted by its increasing geographic integration of activities and strategies. As a firm moves into the global stage, a degree of differentiation will return as different subsidiaries take on different roles, and as the value chain is allocated out to a limited number of countries. So, for example, profit responsibility will have a different scope for the global headquarters of a business unit, for a country that has both manufacturing and selling, and a country that has selling only.

The 'intermediate' multinational stage, on the other hand, is characterized by an increasing duplication of activities across countries and local autonomy. A firm at the multinational stage often operates with a United Nations mentality, whereby each subsidiary is given equal treatment.[72] Thus, this is where self-similarity occurs. Not surprisingly, this stage has been given many labels – for instance, multidomestic[73] and 'multilocal'.[74] Thus, the strategy and structure of multinational firms exhibit self-similarity.[75]

Organizational ecology is another example of a self-similar theory within the realm of management studies. Organizational ecology is a macro-sociological theory of organizations that builds on general ecological and evolutionary theories of change in populations:[76]

> *an ecology of organizations seeks to understand how social conditions affect the rates at which new organizations and new organizational forms arise, the rates at which organizations change forms, and the rates at which organizations and forms die out.*[77]

The underlying, self-similar principle of this line of thinking is that '*organizations develop lives of their own, with action at least partly disconnected from ostensible goals, from demands of relevant environment, and often from the intentions of organizational leaders*'.[78] Concepts frequently used in the organizational ecology (or population ecology, as it is often referred to) discourse include demography, populations, boundaries of forms, niche, selection, and mortality. All these concepts have been imported from biological theories, i.e., from theories pertaining to life cycles on a different scale, that of biological life.[79]

Another set of theories that appear to be self-similar pertains to power in organizations.[80] First, in the light of our previous discussion, 'power' is a scaled phenomenon. Why? Because an individual has power only with respect to a specific context. For instance, people might agree[81] that Mr Silversaw is, on the one hand, very powerful in his role as CEO of the automotive company but, on the other, appears powerless at home. It falls into our category of value judgments, previously alluded to.

It has been argued that to understand power in organizations, and organizational sub-units, one needs to understand politics on the international and national level. Authors in this realm frequently refer to cosmopolitical behaviour of (former) politicians when they are trying to understand organizational politics and power.[82] Similarly, the seminal study by Allison of the Cuban missile crisis has given rise to a fuller understanding of power and politics on the organizational level.[83] Thus, management, like governmental activity, is, in itself a political activity, which takes the concept of power across scales, from international and national politics, to organizational politics, and further to the organizational and individual levels.[84]

Another example is 'classical' organizational theory: how tasks are performed. Frederick Taylor, who investigated the 'effective use of human beings' in industrial organizations, gave rise to the area of 'scientific management'.[85] These theories were mainly concerned with the task performed by people on the production floor or in clerical departments, that is with largely repetitive tasks requiring limited problem-solving by the worker handling them.

The language used by scientific management literature reveals its self-similar nature. Workers were described in terms of capacity, speed, durability and costs. These were concepts imported directly from the understanding of how to 'deal with' machines, subsequently applied on another scale, people.

Although distinguished from Taylor's machine perspective, *Organizations* by March and Simon also illustrates self-similarity.[86] They focused on tasks that involved decision-making, like determining a price, designing a product, as distinct from the repetitive nature of the tasks studied by Taylor. March and Simon make use of a computer Gestalt when they develop their theories of how decisions are made, illustrating the self-similar nature of their thoughts.[87] Still, where Taylor's self-similar models of task performance ranged between manufacturing machinery and workers, March and Simon's self-similar models of 'decision making processes' range between computers and brains: the brain functions like a computer.

An additional contribution to organization theory as mentioned in chapter 2 is the concept of organizational and/or collective mind[88] as well as organizational memory.[89] Collective mind is conceptualized as '*a pattern of heedful interrelations of actions in a social system*'.[90] Organizational memory is seen as the ability to both store and retrieve information in organizations, analogous to the brain. Thus, the self-similar theories discussed within the realm of organization studies have been applied across machinery, computers, organizations, people, and brains.

Decision making in organizations, including rational choice models, bureaucratic models and political models of decision making, can also be said to be self-similar.[91] Because it has been prominent in the social choice literature, we chose to limit our illustration with the model of 'rational choice'.

This model is often prescribed as the 'best' way to make choices in organizations. In this line of thinking events are purposive choices of consistent actors and, consequently, behaviour reflects purpose and intention.[92] According to this model, how are decisions made? First, the rational choice model presumes that there is a consistent set of goals that characterize the organization.[93] Second, in order to make decisions a number of differentiable alternatives is considered. Such alternatives are produced by a search process that is conducted only until a *satisfactory* alternative is uncovered, in turn,[94] dependent on the social actor's level of aspiration.[95] Third, the likely consequences of the various possible courses of action are assessed, including calculation of probabilities. It is assumed that consequences can be fully anticipated, with some uncertainties. Finally, a rational choice involves selecting the alternative that maximizes the social actor's likelihood of getting the highest value in terms of the objective.

Why is this model self-similar? Because the authors bringing forth this model of decision making in organizations claim that it is also descriptive of actual choice processes in *individuals*:[96] it has been applied both in the cognitive sciences and on social systems.

CAN AUTOPOIESIS BE SELF-SIMILAR?

It has been argued that autopoiesis is a phenomenon of both biological and social systems (see Chapters 3 and 4). Still, there is an ongoing discourse within, in particular, the realm of general systems theory regarding the application of autopoiesis on understanding systems in general.

A basic question raised by Maturana and Varela is whether metacellulars are autopoietic unities, and they conclude that '...*whatever the organization of metacellulars may be, they are made up of first-order autopoietic systems and form lineages by reproducing through cells*'.[97] They further discussed the similarities of autopoiesis in cellular and metacellular systems in terms of the degree of autonomy an observer sees possible in their components. Based on this the observer should put them in a series according to the degree of dependency of their components (in their embodiment as autonomous unities)'.[98] From this they infer that organisms have minimum autonomy of components, whereas human societies have maximum autonomy of components; social insects, for instance, are somewhere in between: '*Organisms and human social systems, therefore, are opposite cases in the series of metasystems formed by the aggregation of cellular systems of any order.*'[99]

Still, Varela stresses that the term 'production' (poiesis) only refers to single natural phenomena as living cells. This view has been supported by some social scientists.[100] However, neither Luhmann nor Teubner, two chief writers on social autopoiesis, directly translate it from biology to sociology.[101] In fact, cells are *not* replaced by individuals, neither are metacellulars replaced with organizations. Rather, social systems are defined as systems of meaning, autopoietically reproduced.[102] It should be noted that Luhmann and Teubner seem to differ in their views of autopoiesis of social systems. The latter accepts partial autopoiesis whereas the former does not.

Given the discussion of scaling and self-similarity in this chapter, our perspective on this discourse regards whether autopoiesis is *identical or not across scale*. In the observational scheme presented in this book it might be useful to view autopoiesis as a scaled phenomenon, perhaps a self-similar phenomenon. Our task as observers is to recognise patterns across scales that allow us to use this terminology. Although firmly rooted in the cellular language, the fact that Maturana and Varela discuss first-order and second-order autopoiesis, imply to us the possibility of self-similarity: '...*everything we are going to say will apply both to first- and second-order autopoietic systems; we shall make no distinction between them unless it is strictly necessary*'.[103]

For our purposes this paves the way for conceptualising that how an individual (autopoietically) produces new knowledge (new distinctions) is similar to the way a group (autopoietically) produces new knowledge, which is similar to the way an SBU (autopoietically) produces new knowledge, which, in turn, is similar to the way an organization (autopoietically) produces knowledge, and so on – or the other way around. At various levels of scales of observations,[104] the individual, group, or organization are autonomous, simultaneously open and closed, self-referential, and observing systems.

Scaling, and in particular, self-similarity, provides a language for, and a lens through which we may advance our understanding of the dynamics of organizational knowledge, individualised and socialised.[105] It will be an important part of our observational scheme, the organizational epistemology brought forth in this book. The language of scaling and self-similarity also sheds light on the debate between protagonists of biological and sociological applications of autopoiesis. It should be noted that our conceptualization of a self-similar autopoiesis goes beyond its extension to social systems through communication, as suggested by Luhmann.[106]

From now on we will discuss how organizational knowledge occurs on the social scale; scaling and self-similarity will be the means to investigate the social knowledge development. From now on everything we are going to say can be seen as scaled, or more precisely self-similar phenomena and processes.[107] We will start with languaging.

Notes

1. Or is the hen just a means for the egg to bring forth new eggs?
2. For this we recommend Berka and Riska (1983).
3. Laplace in his *Systems of the World*, 1879, Vol. VI, as quoted in Mandelbrot (1983: 419–20).
4. For example, the Santa Fe Institute (SFI) workshop on Self-Organized Criticality in 1991.

5. SFI Bulletin (1993).
6. See Bonner (1969) for an illustration of this.
7. Oldershaw (1982b: 37). See Anderson (1977) for a discussion of the *broken* symmetry of the hierarchical structure of science.
8. See Stauffer (1979) for an extensive review, discussion, and simulation of scaling theories of percolation clusters.
9. Here, some simple mathematical rules capture the transformation: If a two-dimensional object is scaled-up, its area increases with the square of the scaling factor. If a three-dimensional object is scaled-up, its volume increase with the cube of the scaling factor, and so forth.
10. For instance; '...when bending my Eyes downwards as much as I could, I perceived it to be a human Creature not six Inches high, with a Bow and Arrow in his Hands, and a Quiver at his back...when in an Instant I felt above an Hounded Arrows discharged on my left Hand, which pricked me like so many Needles' (Swift, 1726/1940: 6).
11. The complexity involved in this scaling-up is appalling. An earth-bound observer must take into account the 30 km/sec at which the earth orbits the sun; the 230 km/sec of the solar system's rotation within the Milky Way; the 40 km/sec at which the Milky Way is drawn toward our closest neighbouring galaxy, Andromeda; the Local Group's (a few neighbouring galaxes) movement of 600 km/sec with respect to the fabric of space, the gravitational attraction of the Virgo cluster of galaxies and the much larger attraction from the Hydra Centaurus supercluster of galaxies, which is itself moving towards what is known as the Great Attractor, a vast collection of galaxies. See Fabbri *et al.* (1980), Dressler (1987), and Hawking and Ellis (1973) for further insights into the largest scale.
12. Oldershaw (1981a).
13. The former class consists of the electron, the neutrino and other particles that do not feel the 'strong nuclear force', whereas the latter consists of the neutron, the proton and other particles that feel the strong force. According to quark theory, leptons are elementary, but hadrons are not. Hadrons are made of quarks, which are treated as elementary.
14. In May 1994, physisists at the Fermilab outside Chicago announced that they have discovered the 'top quark', the last of the 12 quarks. The evidence, to be published as a 200-page paper by a team of 440 physicists, shows, however, that there is still some doubt (Cookson, 1994).
15. See Morrison and Morrison (1982).
16. Another example of temporal scaling was provided by Voltaire's philosophical tale *Micromégas* from 1752. In this tale the inhabitant Micromégas (from Greek meaning *small* and *big*) from one of the planets of the star Sirius travels to other planets. During a stop-over on Saturn he learns that this people 'only' live some fifteen thousand earth-years, Micromégas responded that his kind lived 700 times longer than that, but were still frustrated over the lack of time (Voltaire, 1988: 12).
17. The observer not only see the proportions of, for example, a door and its relationship to those of a house, as he would in a two dimensional

drawing. It is a matter of balancing the scale of the individual features with the whole, often based on metaphysical principles.

18. Here, scaling is closely linked to the determined relations among the sizes of all the parts within an element and of all the elements within a space. Similarly, the scale of sculpture must often be considered in relation to the scale of its surroundings. The sculptor often tries to make the sculpture in scale with the rest. This is particularly important for outdoor sculptures, silhouetting against a sky.

19. Proctor (1978).

20. Best (1963).

21. Reif (1964).

22. Geschwind (1972).

23. Cantril (1963).

24. Eoyang (1989:280).

25. Joachim (1969).

26. Arber (1954: 71), that is, more of a philosophical thought of truth, rather than the 'hard' scientific approach of *Richtigheit*. This distinction also illustrates the difference between the correspondence and the coherence doctrine of truth previously discussed.

27. Herbert (1937: 88). Arber's discussion of biology and truth also points to the scaled nature of truth: 'Since what is true for a man is thus inseparable from his whole personality, the 'truth', even of a relatively simple object, may seem entirely different to two different observers, even if they are endowed with equally acute senses and intelligence; what is truth for either of them depends upon his individual field of interest, and the channels in which his mental life naturally flows' (Arber, 1954: 68). Similarly, Kant's *Phenomenon* and *Nomenon* can be seen as an extreme point on a 'truth scale'.

28. Please note that to reduce complexity we are *not* including 'emergent behaviour' into our discussion of scale.

29. See Rousseau (1985) and Klein, Dansereau and Hall (1994).

30. We are grateful to Mr. Ken Slocum for pointing out this example to us.

31. Hayles (1991).

32. Poincaré wrote his paper in response to a reward offered by King Oscar II of Sweden to the person who first proved that a solution was *possible*. Although Poincaré did the opposite, he got the prize.

33. Based on a small difference in his specification of initial conditions he discovered aperiodic solutions of numerical integrations of a set of three ordinary nonlinear differential equations. The interesting finding was that a very small change in initial conditions could result in complicated aperiodic behavior. This was, on the other hand, not a new insight *per se*. Already in 1776 Laplace discussed prediction of everyday phenomena. According to him, randomness in the vast majority of phenomena was due to imperfections in observations.

34. Lorenz's finding, and further developments in chaos theory, implies fundamental limits to the possibility to make predictions. Small uncertainties are amplified so that although the behaviour of, for instance, the stock market is predictable in the short term, it is unpredictable in the long term. See Crutchfield *et al.* (1986) for a fuller discussion of this.

35. Although the term 'chaos' was coined by Li and Yorke (1975) to describe the ability of nonlinear systems to generate temporal solutions that look like a random process, Lorenz's name has become synonymous with the discovery of chaos.

36. The early works on the theory of multiplicity of solutions formed a branch of mathematics called bifurcation theory, including the areas on 'critical solutions', 'stability', and 'structural stability'. The development of bifurcation theory has enhanced the understanding of how multiple solutions can exist in nonlinear systems and how the number and stability of solutions change as parameters are changed. See Weissert (1991) for an analysis of literature through the lens of bifurcation.

37. An attractor is what the behaviour of a dynamic system settles down to, or is attracted to. Any system that comes to rest over time can be characterized by a certain region of state space (state space is an abstract space whose coordinates are the degree of freedom of the system's motion). The motion of a pendulum is, for instance, determined by its initial position and velocity. Thus, its state space is a point in a plane whose coordinates are position and velocity. Its swing represents a path through this state space. Such regions are called attractors. The simplest form of an attractor is a fixed point to which nearby orbits are attracted. An example of this is the point at which a pendulum spirals and stops. A system may have several attractors. It should be noted that chaotic systems generate a randomness of their own without any external random input. This random behaviour comes from more than amplification of initial errors, it is due to the complex stretching and folding of the trajectories generated in the attractor. This is different from the function of, for instance, noise amplifiers where the deflection in pattern can be adjusted by, for instance, lowering the temperature.

38. For instance, see Medio (1993) for a mathematical definition.

39. Young (1991: 289).

40. Crutchfield *et al.* (1986).

41. The Babylonian history of genesis, probably written during Nebuchadnezzar I around 1100 *BC.*

42. See Eoyang (1989) for a fuller discussion of this.

43. See the discussion in Stacy (1992; 1993).

44. E.g., Zimmerman (1993).

45. E.g., Zimmerman and Hurst (1993).

46. For a fuller discussion see, for instance, Nichols (1993), Osborne (1980), and Weiss (1992).

47. Porush (1991).

48. Stoicheff (1991).

49. Knoespel (1991).

50. Weissert (1991).

51. Hayles (1990: 92).

52. It should be noted that the assumptions of chaos theory have been somewhat loosened with the development of theories of self-organized criticality and anti-chaos, theories used to further understand and

explain the behaviour of complex, dynamic systems. See Waldrop (1992), Stein (1989), Kauffman (1991), Bak and Chen (1991).
53. Stern (1988).
54. See Dutton (1981) for a comparison between original, fractalized, smoothed, and different combinations of these, when scaling coastlines.
55. Mandelbrot coined the word by combining the Latin adjective 'fractus' and fractional; it connotates both fractional dimensions and complexity of form.
56. Mandelbrot (1967).
57. Feder (1988: 4).
58. Still, it should be noted that we acknowledge the argument by the condensed-matter theorist Philip Anderson that, despite striking similarity across scales, we expect to encounter new things on each scale (Anderson 1977; Horgan 1994).
59. It should be noted that Mandelbrot used the phrase 'scaling fractal' for fractals that are invariant under certain transformations of scale. A fractal invariant under 'ordinary geometric similarity' is called self-similar: 'In the compound term *scaling fractals*, the adjective serves to mitigate the noun. While the primart term *fractal* points to disorder and covers cases of intractable irregularity, the modifier *scaling* points to a kind of order. Alternatively, taking *scaling* as the primary term pointing to strict order, *fractal* is a modifier meant to exclude lines and planes' (ibid. p. 18).
60. See the classical papers in Edgar (1993) for a fuller discussion of the scientific roots to the principle of self-similarity. Also, Manderbrot (1983) acknowledged that self-similarity is an old idea, referring both to Laplace and Liebiz.
61. Lorenz (1993: 170–171).
62. Goldberger, and West (1987); Goldberger, Rigney and West (1990). See Sander (1987) for a simulation of self-similar growth in nature.
63. See Schmuckler and Gliden (1993) and Keller, Crownover and Chen (1987).
64. See Oldershaw (1981; 1982a; 1982b).
65. May 1–6, 1994, San Miniato, Tuscany, Italy.
66. Cellular automata have been used to study many dynamic processes that appear to be self-similar in nature, e.g., spread of forest fires and epidemics, propagation of chemical reaction, turbulence, urban growth processes, tumor growth, layout of rooms in houses, snowflake growth, growth of dendritic crystals, diffusion-limited aggregation. See White and Engelen (1993), Witten (1993) for a more extensive discussion and illustration of this.
67. Wallace (1993).
68. Herrmann (1994).
69. See Bolognesi (1983) for a discussion on self-similar music.
70. Eoyang (1989). See Shannon (1993) for a fuller discussion of fractal patterns in language.
71. Young (1991: 291).
72. See Bartlett and Goshal (1989).

73. Hout, Porter and Rudden (1982).
74. Yip (1992).
75. See Roos, von Krogh and Yip (1994) for a fuller discussion of this.
76. See Hannan and Freeman (1989) and their previous works on organizational change (and life cycles) in various industrial settings, e.g., Hannan and Freeman (1977). See also the collection of papers in Singh (1990) and Aldrich (1986).
77. Hannan and Freeman (1989:7)
78. Hannan and Freeman (1989:5)
79. Likewise, in this book we scaled a theory of cellular self-production, autopoiesis, to enhance our understanding of organizational knowledge, it is similar but not identical across the cellular and social scale.
80. See Pfeffer (1981) and his previous works with Salancik on power and organizational processes and structures, e.g., Pfeffer and Salancik (1978).
81. But not necessarily understand!
82. For instance Pfeffer (1992) refers to Richard Nixon and his behaviour as president of the US.
83. Allison (1971).
84. It should be noted that we do not subscribe to the concept of power as discussed by Pfeffer (1981) and others professing the same worldview. Our view of power is more in line with Foucault (1980): Power does not come with position, it flows around in organizations and shows in events.
85. For instance, Taylor (1911; 1947).
86. March and Simon (1958).
87. The reader will recognize that these ideas are the basis for the cognitivist perspective discussed in Chapter 2.
88. See Weick and Roberts (1993).
89. Walsh and Ungson (1991).
90. Weick and Roberts (1993: 357).
91. See Allison (1971) for a discussion and application of these three models in the same situation, the Cuban missile crisis.
92. Ibid.
93. March (1976).
94. Simon (1957) introduced the concept of 'satisficing' to illustrate that the search for alternatives was not costless and that a large number of alternatives was not necessarily considered.
95. March and Simon (1958).
96. Here, it should be noted that many of the properties of the rational choice model are based on the cognitivist perspective alluded to in this book.
97. Maturana and Varela (1987: 89).
98. *Ibid.* p. 198.
99. *Ibid.* p. 199.
100. For instance, Zolo (1992), and Blankenberg (1984). The primary criticism is that social autopoiesis is unscientific because, contrary to its

biological origin, it has not been validated by empirical evidence.
101. King (1993) refer to this as 'social biologism'.
102. Luhmann (1984; 1986).
103. Maturana and Varela (1987: 89).
104. Please note that our concern with 'observation' comes from an attempt to be sensitive to our previous treatment of knowledge of an individual. A kind of textual self-reference requires us to be consistent in our development of the organizational epistemology presented herein.
105. Is self-similarity holography? Because each scale does not necessarily contain a condensed version of the highest scale, self similarity and the 'holographic paradigm' are two distinct *Weltanschauung*. See Wilber (1985) for a fuller discussion of the roots of the holographic perspective and Shanon (1991) for a discussuion of analogies with cognitive psychology. By the holographic view all reality is ultimately the manifestation of an omnipresent consciousness; under the explicate realm of things and events is an implicate realm of undivided wholeness, which is simultaneously available to all explicate parts, i.e., the universe is a gigantic hologram. See Hedlund (1986) for an example of a holographic perspective within strategic management.
106. This is an important distinction because it opens up autopoiesis theory to new applications and, therefore, to the advancement of knowledge. Our attempt to develop a new organizational epistemology is but one manifestation of this.
107. Still, we want to, again, acknowledge Anderson's (1977) argument on broken symmetry.

6 Organizational Knowledge and Languaging

'THE WORLD IS BROUGHT FORTH IN LANGUAGE'

Individualized organizational knowledge depends on a structural coupling between the individual and the world. This happens in observation, but, above all, in language. The coordination and cooperation between different organizational members, as seen by an observer, exists because of the language they use. This is not a new insight; for two single cells to form a single multicellular creature a 'cellular language' is required.[1]

According to Maturana and Varela, since the observer can identify this structural coupling between individual organizational members, a new domain of possible study arises, the domain of language.[2] This domain achieves a status of its own for the observer, in the sense of being independent of *particular* organizational members. According to Varela: '*I am saying then, that whenever we engage in social interactions that we label as a dialogue or conversation, these constitute autonomous aggregates, which exhibit all the properties of other autonomous units.*'[3] Following what was said in Chapter 5, this domain of language and conversation is where we should scale when searching for socialized organizational knowledge.

The scale between socialized and individualized organizational knowledge is achieved by means of language. As we speak or utter, a new domain, at a different scale, is achieved. *The world is brought forth in language.* Still, we do not first have a language and then name things with it. Rather, the world and language shape one another. Eskimos have some thirty words for different kinds of snow because their world is, to a large extent, made up of snow. And perhaps Eskimos can distinguish between some thirty kinds of snow because they have so many words for it: '*The language we use influences how we experience our world and thus how we know our world.*'[4]

As will be seen in this chapter this claim is distinct from the notion of an ideal language perfectly mirroring the world, rooted in Aristotelian, analytical, philosophical pedigree, that is: to know an object is to know its essence and differentiate. Thus, we are moving towards an 'anti-representationistic' worldview of language: '*The world does not speak. Only we do. The world can, once we have programmed ourselves with a language, cause us to hold beliefs. But it cannot propose a language for us to speak. Only other human beings can do that.*'[5]

We do not attempt to investigate the philosophy of language. Rather, we will build on certain philosophies of language, like that of Wittgenstein, and treat language as the means through which organizational knowledge gets socialized.[6]

Although we recognize that there are several systems of language used by human beings over time, e.g., olfaction, touch, gesture, facial expression, posture, pheromones, vocal intonation and text, the term 'language' used in this book refers primarily to *spoken language*. In Chapter 7, however, we also address text.

The relatively older language systems, like gestures, continue to function effectively and simultaneously with more recently developed ones, such as the spoken language. This simultaneity in language systems '... *enables our loved ones and our pets to recognize our moods and intentions, and to sometimes guess what we are going to say before we say it.*'[7] It should be noted that although members of the Animal Kingdom have several language systems, almost all creatures are lacking the most recently acquired brain tissue, the neocortex. Even those with considerable neocortex, like our fellow primates, do not possess a brain area unique to humans, the angular gyrus, which is the centre for production of spoken language.[8] Thus, human speech is grounded in embodiment of human cognition. To utter recognizable statements is not sufficient for communication. What computers lack is the human body's other language systems, like gestures, and activity to form speech which is as meaningful as human speech: like cartoon animals imitating human behaviour, only by behaving as humans can computers communicate with humans.[9]

What then, following our discussions of autopoiesis, is the meaning of language? As individuals distinguish objects, name them and convey their experiences about the objects to other individuals, a world is brought forth that lends itself to observation by those who have conversed and by those who have only observed conversations. Thus, there are two types of distinctions that are required in order to speak of language.[10] First, the spoken language[11] has to be isolated from its background of noise or pause.[12] When somebody talks he breaks the silence, and thereby makes way for a description of the spoken language.

Second, a distinction must be made with respect to *elements* of language; like concepts, prepositions, nouns, verbs, etc.[13] In listening to somebody talking the observer must be able to distinguish words and their usage. For example, 'sense' can refer to two different usages: 'my body senses' and 'this makes sense'. In a social system with its own history of interaction among its members, these double distinctions can be made by members who have participated for some time. The newcomer, however, does not necessarily possess the knowledge necessary for adequate descriptions of what is going on, that is for making these distinctions in observations, and thus has problems in for example, distinguishing between 'babble' or 'sense'.[14]

A domain of language is dynamic, because it changes based on the experiences of the individual organizational members that help generate it.[15] The act of making new double distinctions is in itself an experience which allows for new distinctions to be generated. For example, A, uttering the very first words in a new language can allow for a response by another, B, who is proficient in that language. The response introduces new distinctions for A: for example, enabling him to articulate better (clearer distinctions) a word already uttered, or exposing him to a new vocabulary by pointing to an object and pronouncing a word.[16] Thus, *language is a process, not a 'fixed stock' or an 'asset'*. According to Maturana and Varela the term 'languaging' describes the processual characteristics of what humans do when they coordinate their behaviour through speaking.[17]

Over time, organizations develop their own distinct domains of language. There are two explanations for this. First, the obvious explanation is that languaging may be understood as 'the stuff', that the organization is made of. By introducing the concept 'organization,' we linguistically distinguish it from something else (i.e., the organization–environment distinction).[18] Hence, the emergence of an entity/organization presupposes languaging.[19] The organization, or other distinctions substituting for this, like, 'Exxon', 'the jungle', 'the firm', 'the factory', etc., is conserved as a concept over time as organizational members continue to bring it up in their conversations (or writings).

Second, the broad linguistic distinction of organization – environment allows organizational members to make finer linguistical distinctions. In other words, this basic distinction allows them to coordinate their other linguistic distinctions given the concept of the organization. For example, the term 'customer' requires the environment–organization distinction.

We may understand a domain of language as tradition. In the process of languaging an organizational tradition is formed. This tradition will affect languaging, or in the words of Varela: *'Everything said is said from a tradition.'*[20] A lawyer speaks from the tradition of his law firm and the legal society; a production engineer speaks from the tradition of his manufacturing organization; a doctor speaks from the tradition of his professional organization; an Eskimo speaks from his 'Arctic' tradition.

Given this specificity, as well as the variability of language,[21] it is meaningful to speak of *organizational languaging*. Organizational languaging presupposes socialized organizational knowledge and gives rise to distinctions that form an integral part of the concept of organization. The organization has no substance except for being a self-similar, autopoietic system of knowledge and distinctions. Rather it has its tradition from which new conversations can take place. *It demands of its members to continue to language about it on all scales in order for it to survive, or in other words, continue its autopoiesis.*

If a tradition of languaging gives rise to the autopoietic reproduction of socialized organizational knowledge and distinctions across scales, an interesting question to ask is what properties languaging has in organizations. Organizational languaging covers at least two domains; *writing* and *conversations*. Because we deal primarily with language as spoken language, we will concentrate on conversations. Still, in Chapter 7, we will also give some comments on the role of writing in organizations.

USAGE

As pointed out by Wittgenstein, the usage of words plays an important role in how we communicate with each other. Particular usages of words tend to be specific to national cultures, to regional sub-groups within a nation, as well as to organizations. For example, the usage of the word 'cop' may differ not only in criminal circles in Chicago and Beverly Hills, but also between a street gang and a police station around Hill Street.

It is in the organizational tradition of languaging to make particular use of words. Wittgenstein suggests that words are embedded in so called 'language games' (*Sprachspiele*); they derive their meaning from the content of their use rather than the objects, events, or actions they denote.[22] The use of words follows certain history-dependent rules that are specific to an institutional setting.[23] Such rules are created and recreated in languaging and form the basis for the social system's knowledge of the world. The very uses of the double distinction-making of languaging carry, in themselves, their own distinguishing capacity. *Thus, the very use of a word in a particular way is distinct from a different way of using the word.*

Let us illustrate the power of the notion of language games by three examples. First, in his exemplary ethnography of Disneyland, John Van Maanen has uncovered how the service staff of the theme park use a wide array of words for 'customer'. These words do not come randomly, but rather as a conscious choice of the staff to convey meaning; particular experiences, moods, feelings, attitudes, etc. The customer is referred to as 'guest' in order to create an 'inviting' and 'friendly' atmosphere in which the customer may feel well. In private with their colleagues, however, the staff may refer to troublesome or annoying guests as 'ducks'. There are, however, distinct socially embedded rules that guide the usage of words in the description of a customer; where, when, and how to say what.[24]

Second, Percy Barnevik, the CEO of Asea Brown Boveri has decided on a linguistic policy in which the word 'foreign' is banned in all the subsidiaries throughout the world. Experiences related to the encounter with foreigners, foreign technology, foreign culture, foreign systems, etc. cannot be conveyed legitimately within ABB, at least not by using the word 'foreign'. Mr. Barnevik has even stated that he will 'fine' managers who use the word 'foreign'.[25]

Third, in an organization the CEO wanted to instal a procedure for strategic planning. Therefore, the phrase, 'strategic planning' was introduced into the conversations among top managers and middle level managers. The possible contents of a procedure were subsequently discussed among managers on many scales. At first, the use of the word 'strategy' took many forms and there were few established rules for its usage. During meetings top managers typically discussed possible issues that were perceived to be covered in the strategic plan. At first, discussions touched upon a vast range of issues, from acquiring a new company to adjusting the salaries of switch-board operators. At that time, conversations about strategy had few rules regarding the usage of the term 'strategic planning.'[26] After reading strategy texts and discussing further, managers attempted to prioritize issues to include, for example, those pertaining to the possible impact on financial performance. Over time, the usage of the word 'strategic plan' and 'strategy' became increasingly narrowed. As the conversations were carried out, certain rules became attached to the usage of such words. For instance, one rule was that the word 'strategy' should be restricted to the conversations among members who defined themselves as being part of the 'top management team'. Middle-level managers should concentrate on 'policies' of various types. As time goes by, consequently, a linguistic tradition unfolds that coordinates the organizational members' use of words.

Do such rules of usage make any difference? Yes, we believe so. The relatively formalistic rule the word 'strategy' is only used in discussions among the top management may, for example, inhibit redirection of the strategy based on bottom-up initiatives and conversations from the rest of the organization.[27] The conversations encounter a block that inhibits new socialized organizational knowledge from emerging. This is of primary importance when trying to understand knowledge of the organization. As the flip-side of the coin, usage of words is intimately connected to socialized organizational knowledge, and it is, hence, a necessary property of organizational languaging.

The language game has many functions. First, it helps to conserve the organization as a knowledge system. Each organization carries its own unique set of rules, distinct from other organizations and other rules, that provide a distinct system of meaning. The organization provides some coherence for the usage of words for organizational members[28] and this coherence allows organizational members to distinguish the 'right' use of words from the 'wrong' ones. As such, language games of the organization provide a template from which to coordinate meanings, and subsequently interpret and coordinate action. For example, to give orders or to obey orders, organizational members must use words like 'action', 'policy', 'time', 'control', 'perform', etc. to allow for initiation of action and observation as well as description of action once it occurs.

A normal part of organizational languaging, unavoidable in a world where knowledge of the individual is embodied, is to contest, challenge, and question rules. Rules are subject to innovation as organizational members make new uses of words. As noted by several authors, frequently managers need to innovate in the way they state their policies. Difficult issues are settled in an ambiguous form that allows them to have multiple interpretations by various groups of organizational members.[29] Issues become defined, not by a reference to particular objects, events or actions, but by the way they are used in the organization. What must be understood with 'coherence', thus, is that *the organization always provides a context for playing new language games*; there are always starting points from which new words and rules for the uses of words can be developed.[30]

Second, the rules help to decrease the time needed for conversation to initiate competent action[31] or further conversations. For example, as the surgeon operates, he shouts 'scalpel'. The assisting nurse, being familiar with the rules of the usage of words, immediately gives him the scalpel. She does not have to hear, by contrast, Nurse, could you give me the knife-like instrument, frequently referred to as scalpel, that is situated at the table of instruments, please. *The function of socialized organizational knowledge is to allow for rules and languaging that give way for effective action.*

Third, the rules for the usage of words allow the organization to adapt to uncertainty related to a presently envisioned future. The organization may conserve itself as a system of meaning over time, through the continuous reproduction of rules. The language game allows for reflection on past and present events. However, it also structures conversations about the future taking place in the present. Conversations about future events take as a starting point the present rules of the usage of words and invent rules and words beyond these. This may be necessary, for example, in talking about the future of the industry, or the 'vision of a company'. Here managers may use ambiguous terminologies, metaphors, stories, invent new words, etc. In the words of Astley and Zammuto: *'Managerial language serves as a lens for structuring ... what is fundamentally unstructured, thereby providing the psychological confidence necessary for the exploration of new courses of action.'*[32]

There are numerous possible rules for the usage of words (language games), some of which are preserved, discarded, or evolving as the languaging of the organization continues.[33] There are also numerous words in the organization being introduced, discarded, or maintained in conversations. In principle, there are four possible combinations of words and rules creating meaning. First, previous rules are maintained in the use of previous words. For example, a company uses 'share-price' to report about its performance to its shareholders on a yearly basis.

Second, previous rules can be given new words. For example, in explaining about what an observer may label the 'strategic planning' activities of a company, the management may decide to 'do some thinking about the future of this company'. At a later point 'thinking' may be substituted by 'planning', 'contemplation', 'long-range planning', 'idea-generation', 'strategic planning', or even 'bifurcation analysis'. The meaning may still be to allocate some thought activity to figuring out aspects of the future of the company.[34]

Third, new rules can be given to previously used words. For example, in refining the 'process of thinking about the future', the management of the company may decide to apply a SWOT analysis, going through the steps of identifying strengths and weaknesses of the company, and the opportunities and threats in the environment of the company.[35]. Management may still prefer to use the words 'thinking about the future', rather than 'strategic planning', but may give some new rules to these words by suggesting that thinking implies the more formal SWOT analysis.

Fourth, new words and new rules may accompany each other. See, for example, the introduction of strategic planning in the company, as given above. We may illustrate the four options as shown in Figure 6.1.

Fig 6.1. can also be used to identify possible changes in words, and rules for their usage, indicating a dynamic process of organizational languaging. Some words, for example, may be introduced with new rules[36] accompanying them. For example, in introducing the word 'customer satisfaction' into the organizational language, there may be very few and open rules, like 'our sales personnel should discuss what drives customer satisfaction'. Both the words and the rules may, after some time of being used and guiding use in organizational languaging, emerge into a more stable pattern, referring to previous words and previous rules, e.g., customer satisfaction may subsequently be used whenever a sales person reports an event in which a sale did or did not occur. Otherwise the words will have a very limited use and history will render them 'obsolete' or 'out of fashion'.[37]

Innovations in both rules and words exhibit the richness of the process of organizational languaging. Roald Dahl's final short story, *The Vicar of Nibbleswicke*, illustrates an amusing version of this.[38] In this story we learn that Mr. Robert Cape, who had suffered from a peculiar form of dyslexia in his youth, sud-

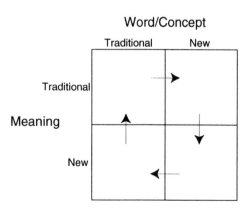

Figure 6.1   Change in languaging

denly developed a variety of this illness during his first day as the new vicar in Nibbleswicke. When he spoke, he unconsiously mixed-up the characters in the words, making new words for what he thought he said. Although many people thought the vicar was amusing, most thought he was mad. The cure, it was found, was for the vicar to go sideways and turn around while talking.

Finally, considering the dynamics of organizational languaging one should perhaps avoid being overly analytical. Just as it would be impossible to write up a list of every word used in an organization, it would be overly restrictive (and perhaps wrong) to attempt to write up a complete list of all possible language games ensuring meaning in the organization. However, Wittgenstein mentions some worth repeating here: giving orders, and obeying them (the nurse and doctor), describing the appearance of an object, reporting an event, speculating about an event, forming and testing hypotheses, presenting the results of an experiment, making up a story, guessing riddles, making jokes, asking, thanking, cursing, greeting and praying, and many, many more.[39] The point is that the process of languaging gives a range of opportunities for new words and new rules. As observers of organizations we are looking at a tremendous plasticity of rules: organizational members make jokes about the vision/value statement issued by the top management; 'strategy' is used not only at board meetings, but also by a sales-representative planning his meetings with the clients of the firm, or by the staff of the personnel canteen discussing next week's menu; over a lunch with her friends, the nurse imitates the low-pitched voice of the surgeon shouting 'scalpel', while trying to imitate the characteristic posture of his head.[40]

It is also interesting to note that the most apparent and trivial rules, like a joke in the corridor about the company's vision statement, carry rich implications for the way we understand the socialized organizational knowledge. Joking about a vision statement may forward a new type of enquiry: Why do people make jokes about it? Has it provoked some hidden tension in the organization? The current organizational epistemology may provide a tentative answer in that the joke provided the mean to new organizational knowledge. As a new distinction, it opened the way for subsequent, new distinction-making. The examples of similar questions and processes of languaging are manifold: are there some organizations, or parts of an organization (different processes of languaging) where questions related to performing the task of management are 'banned'?[41] Are there situations where speculation is used not only to puzzle, but to encourage new ideas?[42] Are there situations where making up stories and telling them is seen as an integral part of management?[43]

For an external observer of the organization, an important task is to analyze the meaning of what is said.[44] To this end, the following observational scheme may be applicable: (1) to identify the rules and words as they appear in the process of organizational languaging.[45] (2) to identify the changes in words and rules in the organization (see Figure 6.1), and (3) to compare rules and words to other words and rules, especially to those found in other organizations. It should, however, be noted that rules seldom are explicitly defined in conversations, and have to be brought forth through interpretation by the external observer.[46] Only in a very few cases can an observer hear a statement like: 'We use the term 'strategy' only in discussions between top managers of this company'; or even more explicitly: 'When I use the word 'strategy' in this situation, I am referring to the rule we have about 'strategy' being restricted to conversations among top managers'.

ORGANIZATIONAL ARGUMENTATION

In organizations language games, as we have seen, come in many forms and serve many functions. However, specific rules, more tangible in their character, apply to argumentation. Observers of organizations frequently hear organizational members refer to a specific 'line of argument',[47] a 'scientific argument', a 'legal argument', an 'economic argument', a 'sales argument', a 'unionized argument', a 'political argument', a 'medical argument', an 'ethical argument', 'aesthetical argument', or 'emotional argument'. Whenever a reference is made to an argument, rules must be at play, which distinguish particular words and their sequencing as something that passes for an argument. Because such rules are dynamic and perhaps organization-specific, the process of isolating an argument is not trivial. A manager may claim something at one time without really having to justify his claim. Listeners may 'just know' why he made that statement. At other times, it seems that statements and explanations are completely entangled, inseparable by analyses. Nevertheless, the area of argumentation processes in organizations is exciting because they appear to be involved in various stages of decision-making, planning, implementation, control and follow-up, and other managerial activities.

As in the realm of managerial cognition, research on the argumentation processes in organizations has mainly followed a cognitivist tradition. Here, the claims of the authors are that the argument somehow 'mirrors' or represents the reality faced by the one who argues.[48] The words and the structure in which they are embedded in a statement are taken to denote objects, events and actions.

Staying with the idea of organizations as autopoietic in their knowledge development, these ideas seem difficult to pursue consistently. Still, 'argument' is a form of communication that we frequently recognize in organizations in which we participate. Either we observe how people structure their statements in a particular way, or we observe them describing their statements as being argumentative. Rather than abandoning the realm of argumentation from our analysis, we believe that it is beneficial to look at these rules of structuring the use of words as pertaining to particular language games. Thus, by understanding the nature of arguments we might better understand organizational knowledge when socialized.

To present something as an argument (Wittgenstein frequently does this himself), means that one employs a specific set of rules. It does not, however, mean that one (re)presents the world as it is (like claiming that there is an industry). Rather we should begin with the question posed by Stephen Toulmin: '*What sorts of arguments could be produced for the things we claim to know?*'[49] This question could, of course, refer to the wide array of arguments that could be performed by the individual organizational member. However, because the focus here is on socialized organizational knowledge, and since languaging establishes an autonomous unit of analysis, *arguments refer to the arguments as they surface in organizational conversations*.[50] The question posed by Toulmin is highly relevant for our understanding of organizational knowledge.

If we accept that the study of arguments in organizations may reveal something about the socialized knowledge of that organization we run the risk of looking for (like many others have done) generic arguments that extend beyond the world of a specific organization. We should, however, assume that *because the socialized knowledge of the organization is organization-specific, the arguments of an organization (claiming knowledge) should also be organization-specific.* Here Toulmin seems to lend us some support:

> *What has to be recognized..is that validity (of an argument) is an intra-field, not an inter-field notion. Arguments within any field can be judged by standards appropriate within that field, and some will fall short; but it must be expected that the standards will be field dependent., and that the merits to be demanded of an argument in one field will be found to be absent (in the nature of things) from entirely meritorious arguments in another.*[51]

Although he investigates certain fields of argument Toulmin's point is that arguments must be sensitive to the context in which they occur. This, we may add, is consistent with the idea that arguments are a particular form of language games across different scales.

At the very general scale an argument consist of four parts; (1) a claim (*C*) distinguishing something from something else, (2) the grounds (*G*) supporting the claim, as being distinct from the claim, (3) a warrant (*W*) that shows in which way the grounds support the claim, and finally, (4) qualifiers (*Q*) that amplify or dampen the claim by indicating limitations.[52] This is illustrated in Figure 6.2.

At any one time arguments in organizational conversations do not necessarily contain all these elements. For example, a manager may claim that *The environment is becoming increasingly complex* without giving further grounds for it. A more full-blown argument may be in the form:

> *The environment is becoming increasingly complex (claim)*
>
> *... because a new competitor of ours has recently been acquired by a foreign competitor ... (grounds)*
>
> *... and since, any acquisition we have seen by the foreign group has implied that the acquired company obtained new products, and easier access to capital ... (warrant)*

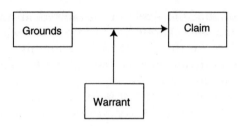

Figure 6.2   A generic argument

However, what is claimed here, only holds if the foreign group does not change its acquisition policy. (qualifier)

Organizations are likely to produce a variety of arguments on all possible scales. Some will be incomplete in the sense of not containing all the elements of a full-blown argument, and for good reasons, as will be seen later. In some instances a claim will function as grounds for other statements. Yet other claims will be warrants or qualifiers for further statements. In this sense, *conversations allowed for by the organization, are like a pool of knowledge for further knowledge development.*

Under certain circumstances particular types of arguments will be employed by the organization reflecting a particular socialized organizational knowledge: that is, certain rules for what passes for a good argument will evolve in association with particular contexts and scales. We believe that little can be said by way of classifying arguments; this is essentially the task of the individual observer of an organization. Nevertheless, we would like to propose a broad observational scheme for studying arguments in organizational conversations. This includes functional arguments, temporal arguments, value arguments, intertwined arguments, and self-similar arguments.

Functional Arguments

The first type is that of functional arguments. These are arguments that through their use: (1) distinguish various functions of the organization, (2) make claims related to various functions performed, and (3) maintain the organization – environment distinction. Functional arguments, then, involve claims, grounds, warrants and qualifiers related to either intra or inter-functional activities.

For example, in a business organization arguments can be made about a marketing function, to its organization, procedures, planning systems, customer orientation, etc. Functional arguments can also be made about the relationship between the marketing function, the production function or the finance functions. Functional arguments in themselves do not have to be made by people in the functional organization, i.e. 'marketing arguments' made by 'marketing people'. Nor do they have to be bounded by or limited to any specific functional area in a classical sense. Rather, the arguments distinguish a set of functions performed each time they are made, and claim some knowledge about these functions. For example, they may refer to 'the budgeting functions of marketing and production', or the '(internal) marketing of the budgeting functions'.

Functional arguments carry descriptions of the organization, the functions performed, and hence the purpose of these functions. Being arguments made possible by socialized organizational knowledge, functional arguments result from observations of the organization (of itself).[53] Because functions require functional arguments in order to exist as a function, and since arguments, like any conversation, are highly dynamic, an interesting conclusion is that a function and its purpose are also dynamic. Consider the following example bracketed from an everyday conversation among the administrative staff of a sales organization:

C (1): The purpose of the secretarial function is to buffer and prioritize the manager's contacts with internal personnel and customers.

G (1): The reason for this is that the manager has been overloaded with meetings lately.

W (1): And we all know that if our manager has not got available time, he cannot concentrate on doing his important work.

C (2): What..? The important work of our manager is to meet with people!

W (2): And nobody can know what is important, and who is important until they have met with them and heard what they have to say.

C (2): The secretarial function should be more effective in organizing a queueing system for the people who come to his office.

G (2): The reason is a good one. The office looks like a battle-ground when all these people come in at 8 a.m.

This chain of functional arguments shows how one claim might function as a ground for a new argument.[54] More importantly, however, it shows the inherent instability of, in this case, the secretarial and managerial functions and their purposes. In analyzing this passage as an *autonomous unit of conversation*, we see how the daily life of the organization gives an inherent dynamic quality to socialized organizational knowledge. And it follows that a cognitivist goal of 'fixating a best representation' of a function and its purpose, seems unreachable.

Temporal Arguments

The second class of arguments we label temporal arguments. These arguments, in their structure, indicate various temporal horizons for the organization. Temporal horizons may occur in both grounds and claims, as well as in warrants and qualifiers. Consider the following example:

C: The assumptions behind the strategic plan should hold for at least two years.

In this claim, the temporal horizon is given as a part of the claim. Now, consider the following example where the temporal horizon is explicitly given as a qualifier:

C: The strategic plan suggests that we should diversify into the consumer electronics industry.

Q: This is valid only if the acquisition is made within our two year planning horizon.

In general, temporal arguments are arguments made in the present[55] about the past or the future.[56] Temporal arguments speculate about what has been and what will be. They may indicate clearly a temporal horizon according to hours, days, months or years, but frequently, they just refer to 'past' or 'present'. For example:

C: We have to become more responsive to our environment.
G: Because the environment is changing rapidly.
W: In the future, no organization will survive if it is not sensitive to changes in its environment.

Temporal arguments often accompany conversations about the ideology, basic values, or norms of the organization. As suggested by Niklas Luhmann,[57] 'conservatives' in favour of maintaining a strong ideological platform in the face of change, claim that 'nothing is the same any more' while the 'progressive side', in favour of changing the ideological platform in the face of stability, argues 'we have not yet achieved our wanted state'. Both, however, structure their arguments with reference to different temporal horizons, the past and the future.[58]

Conversations about what could be are surely important conversations in organizations from the viewpoint of maintaining its socialized organizational knowledge. In discussing the present future, options for further conversations inevitably arise. Imagine a proposed future situation in the organization. This proposition can be verified only if in the future, conversations can *refer back* to the previous conversations about this state. Therefore, the statement 'time will show' has more than a trivial meaning. It is a lucid example of a statement that opens for the possibility of future conversations referencing today's conversation, and hence, an important element of conversation providing coherence to the socialized organizational knowledge. Thus, we recognize an important property of autopoiesis, namely self-reference.

Temporal arguments may also involve 'idealization',[59] which may be understood as generalizations refering to historical conditions and specific experiences. In this particular instance, temporal arguments are structured so as to ground the claim by concrete experiences. The argument also contains an explicit or implicit warrant that 'it can always be done again', bridging the past with the future. For example:

C: The management should not yield in negotations with the unions about next year's salaries.

   G: It usually works out fine.
   W: Since we have done it before, we can always do it again.

Conversations involving temporal arguments are inherently unstable, and the 'definition of the situation' might change accordingly. Thus, it might be expected that temporal arguments of idealization will not prevail, but will be changed during the process of argumentation and counter-argumentation.

Value Arguments

Even though temporal arguments play an important role in conversations about for example the ideology of an organization, we see the possibility of another class of arguments, namely value arguments. Value arguments are judgemental, and distinguish relative values, and positive and negative values.[60] Such arguments make statements about values in the form of claims, grounds, warrants, and qualifiers; thus, they are scaled in nature. A value argument may for example take the following form:

   C: It is unethical of a manager to talk negatively to other employees about the strategies of the organization.
   G: This is because (s)he has previously committed him/herself wholeheartedly to the strategy.
   W: All managers participate in an iterative, participative planning process where they are allowed to voice their concern before the plan is formalized.
   Q: This only holds if the manager has been given a fair-chance to participate.

This argument involves value judgements in all of its components, and it raises important questions of further value judgement: What does it mean to 'talk negatively'? What does it take to be 'wholeheartedly committed'? What is it that makes a planning process 'participative'? What is meant by 'a fair chance to participate'? The answers to these questions depend, like any value judgement (see Chapter 5), on what scale the discussant refers to, i.e., value arguments are observationally contingent.

Intertwined Arguments

Although our observational scheme has distinguished four different classes of arguments, in any one conversation the classes are intertwined. By 'intertwined' we mean that any argument may have the grounds, claims, warrants, and qualifiers from different classes of arguments. At least the following combinations are possible as 'middle-ground' classes of arguments:

- functional-temporal arguments,
- functional-value arguments,
- temporal-value arguments,
- functional-temporal-value arguments

Consider the following example of a functional-temporal-value argument:[61]

> *C:*   The main function of the personnel department is development of human resources as a part of strategy development of the corporation.
>
> *G:*   The reason is that our physical resources are easy to imitate by competitors compared to the knowledge and skills embedded in our personnel.
>
> *W:* Only the types of resources that can withstand imitation can give a sustainable competitive advantage.
>
> *W:* Human resources are difficult to imitate.
>
> *C:*   Today, the personnel department performs traditional functions like hiring and firing, and setting salaries.
>
> *C:*   They definitely have to improve if we are to survive in the long run.
>
> *G:*   Presently, they are not good enough.
>
> *Q:*   If they do change, however, we may have to change the people in the personnel department.

This class of intertwined argument is perhaps the most common in an ordinary organizational setting. The observational scheme developed here would aid the observer to distinguish classes of arguments, and, hence their roles in the organization. Thereby, the observer would better understand the various arguments that could be produced about what the organization claims to know. Its knowledge enables the organization to produce a wide variety of arguments distinguishing events, issues, opportunities, people, concepts, things, etc. from their environment. While doing that, the organization produces new socialized organizational knowledge, that in turn enables new meaningful conversation.

Self-Similar Arguments

Based on our previous discussion on self-similarity we suggest that some arguments may be (made) self-similar. The principles of a self-similar argument are depicted in Figure 6.3.[62]

It is not the content of the argument that necessarily is similar across scale, like claiming that 'everything is relative'. Rather, it is the process by which the argument is brought fourth; an example of a self-similar argument is:

C: We cannot get an exact understanding of this problem
G: because of the uncertainty principle
W: and since we assume that this principle is applicable to this problem

In this argument, the grounds encompass a reference to Heisenberg's 'uncertainty principle', which in turn is an argument in itself. This can be seen by investigating the grounds, warrants, and claim used by Heisenberg.

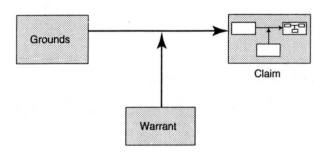

Figure 6.3   Principle of self-similar argument

One could also envision a class of argument that *encompasses* another argument, which, in turn, may encompasses yet another argument, and so on, in a self-similar manner. For example:

> C: Please develop some options, in line with our management principle, regarding new potential diversifications during 1995.
>
> G: Because I would like to have more knowledge before I decide.
>
> W: And since I have the authority to order you to do this.
>
> Encompassed, similar claim (on a lower scale):
>
> C: These options are only valid if they have been developed in accordance with the company's management principle: minimum 30 per cent of total turnover steming from the Far East.
>
> G: Because our owners have enforced this principle.
>
> W: And since this is the maximum risk level the owners are willing to take.

In turn, there might be yet another level of similarity (third-order, fourth-order, etc.) claim, grounds, and warrant.

Self-similar arguments may be functional, temporal or intertwined in nature. This form of argument may serve a particular purpose of reducing complexity in managerial practices of an organization. In most organizations, however, pulsating, reoccurring processes of sense-making and sense-giving often tend to induce differences in arguments at various levels of the organization at various times. For example, as shown in a study by Gioia and Chittipendi,[63] the CEO may suggest a strategic direction, a set of core-values, or guiding principles for the organization, to the next level of subordinates (sense-giving). These give their own perspectives and reactions back to the CEO, who in the next instance modifies or reinterprets his previous statements to accommodate the feed-back (sense-making). In this instance, the arguments change over time as the CEO learns about the reactions of his subordinates, and the arguments of the subordinates change as they learn about the reactions of the CEO. We suggest that unless some kind of directive action is taken to change these dynamics, this will be the normal situation.

Self-Referential Languaging

Before finishing our treatment of the specific language games of organizational argumentation, we would like to discuss a property of organizational argumentation that stems from what we have established as the self-referential nature of knowledge. We argued that individualized organizational knowledge has self-referential properties since it stems from observation and distinction-making by the individual. The, by now well known, statement that *everything said is said by an observer*, is an illustration of this kind of self-reference.

Languaging of organizations is also self-referential. Previous language games and previous arguments form a tradition necessary for the production of new language games and arguments. Remember the statement 'everything said is said from a tradition'. The organization, then, emerges as a *self-referential system of knowledge*, that, like any such system, has self-knowledge and is able to describe and act on itself.[64] It can for example produce arguments about its own argumentation processes; why they work or do not work, and how they should change. Next, recursively, the organization can even produce arguments about the argumentation about argumentation (converse about the conversations about conversations).[65] For instance, it can, decide on which types of argument it wants to use as grounds or warrants or qualifiers for next arguments.

The organization can never 'step out' of its own processes of argumentation. The only basis for further argumentation and knowledge development will be previous argumentation and knowledge development. Everything conversed about within the organization, will be kept in words and language games rooted in the tradition of the organization, on all scales. Every observation introduced in conversations, will be introduced in the languaging processes of the organization. According to Niklas Luhmann the processes of such self-referential systems will be fraught by paradox and tautology.[66] For this reason, we can, of course, as observers of organizations expect to find many arguments that may appear paradoxical or tautological. For example:

C: We have to invest in a new computerized printing press.
G: Because we simply have to do it.

The self-referential nature of organizational knowledge and languaging also surfaces in other instances. Organizations may observe and distinguish certain events and trends, and, like Toulmin suggests, claim knowledge about them. Many organizations produce arguments like *the environment increases in complexity* without any further justification for such a claim. Sometimes, however, awareness of self-referentiality gives rise to doubts, and may produce qualifiers like, *That is, if we have perceived it correctly ...* or, *That is, if we have got the right information ...*

If the organization claims to know about the environment, and given that it is aware of possible flaws in observations or descriptions of the environment, there are certain reservations regarding the validity of this claim. Because they would indicate a kind of 'pointless doubt', the organization rarely burdens itself with constantly making such qualifiers.[67] Doubt would be pointless if every statement made in the organization would have to be disqualifed (because everything said is said by an observer). It is only in those instances where the organization 'has reasons to doubt' that qualifiers and disqualifiers complement the arguments.

Reasons to doubt may come from several sources: the awareness of possible flaws in observations, or descriptions, the belief that a falsified claim (proposition) may have negative repercussions for the speaker;[68] the fact that the tradition of the organization is to seldom claim anything with certainty until certain procedures have been fulfilled (i.e., science);[69] a crisis that has occurred or is about to occur in the organization;[70] the exposure to misleading arguments. Doubts may in themselves help to fuel the autopoietic process of organizational knowledge in the sense of leading to further discussions trying to resolve the doubt. In this sense, the qualifiers of an argument, because they indicate doubt with respect to the knowledge claimed (not only doubt on the part of the counter-argument), serve an important function in sustaining the autopoietic process, for individuals, groups, department, etc.

ON STABILIZING LANGUAGING

So far we have established that organizations create socialized organizational knowledge through languaging, and that languaging is made possible, self-referentially, by socialized organizational knowledge. We have also discussed the role of language games, or the rules for making use of words, in organizations. In doing this, an anti-representationist epistemology has gradually evolved that recognises the inherent constructive function of any cognitive system, and the lack of any environmental reference point for making accurate representations.

As an important part of this epistemology, we have tried to develop an observational scheme distinguishing various classes of arguments as being particular rules for the usage of words in organizations. All these discussions have been based on the ideas of autonomy, autopoiesis, scaling and self-reference. Through these ideas, we have been able to specify the fuzzy boundaries of what may be called socialized organizational knowledge, and shown how this concept is dependent on languaging. We have also been able to allude to the coherence and change of socialized organizational knowledge and the dynamics of languaging.[71]

It follows from the concepts of languaging and organizational knowledge, that neither can be conceived as fixed entities: they continously change. Each time a new statement is made, knowledge changes, and allows for yet another, different, statement to be made. At the same time, change presupposes stability. A new statement, argument, or conversation will always be distinct from the previous statement, argument, or conversation, but at the same time, it presupposes the previous elements to be recognized as something new.[72] This inherent change–stability duality will always be present for self-referential systems. Moreover, the duality enables the discussion of forces or effects that keep languaging and socialized organizational knowledge coherent over time (this would simultaneously be another view on the issue of self-reference). To address this stability we will focus on the argument as a form of language game in organizations.

Socialized organizational knowledge and languaging have a mutual stabilizing effect on each other. *By stabilizing, we mean that coherence and consistency are maintained over time.* In the structure of an argument, socialized organizational knowledge plays a particular role in stabilizing languaging through enabling the making of warrants. Partial arguments are often made in organizations where warrants are tacit; 'private', 'hidden', 'concealed', 'unspeakable', 'taboo' or 'taken for granted'. Take for example the following functional-temporal argument:

C: It can be asserted that Mr Temple will be the next managing director of our company.

G: Because Mr Temple is favoured by two-thirds of our board of directors.

In looking at this partial argument, clearly the warrant is missing. For the observer of the organizational conversation, finding the warrant is like 'filling in the blanks'. For an organizational member making the statement, and another, listening to the statement, however, this 'silence',[73] the lack of a warrant, does not lead to further inquiries like, 'why is that?'; 'how can you be so sure?', etc.

Conversations and individual memory are both important. Both of the organizational members may, for example, have established through previous conversations, that:

W: In electing the company's managing director, the board of three people always votes, and the outcome of the vote determines who will be the managing director.

Hence, socialized organizational knowledge allows for less to be said than what is known. In this sense it stabilizes the arguments as they are made, by concealing warrants. Concealed warrants are not exposed for further criticism and questioning, unless the observer explicitly asks 'why' questions.

If arguments contain concealed warrants, the knowledge base of the organization allows for at least one stable element in the arguments made. In a way this is a 'lubricating mechanism' of organizational knowledge; we may say that socialized organizational knowledge allows for effective conversations. If this was not the case, if every warrant was exposed in every argument made in organizational conversations, then two things could happen: (1) the conversations would become increasingly complex and intertwined, maybe leaving organizational members in a state of inaction, fatigue, or dispair (see our previous example of the surgeon and the scalpel); (2) a troublesome search would begin where warrants had to be produced for warrants, or in other words, 'why questions' had to be answered by 'why questions'.[74]

Recognizing the function of concealed warrants, what kinds of warrants are they, and hence what socialized organizational knowledge do they conceal? We have found that few concrete answers can be given to this question. However, we still believe that it is meaningful to outline an observational scheme whereby various classes of warrants can be found.[75] Such an observational scheme could cover a wide variety of possible warrants.[76] For the purpose of the present text, however, we suggest three classes of warrants.[77]

Definitional Warrants

Definitional warrants establish definitions in organizations. Some words have a definition that does not surface in each conversation, statement or argument. Such definitions may have sedimented through years of using them. Definitions may be more or less formalized, unique or manifold. Some words may even have a mathematical definition. Consider for example the following argument:

C: We have to improve the quality costs in our production line.

G: Because our quality cost is 3,000 USD and the average of our competitors is 2,000 USD.

The concealed definitional warrant for this argument may be:

Definitional warrant: Quality cost is defined as the sum of the cost of inspecting each product plus the cost of rejection of products.

By using words in a legitimate way in conversations, that is, following the established rules, further inquiries or questions are not posed about the definitions of words. *Definitions, concealed in warrants, may evolve into rigidities that are not questioned.* Occasionally, however, definitions, may drift over time, by their very use, or by an occasional decision to redefine words.[78] For example, newcomers may use words in a new way or context; organizational members or consultants may question the use of words and how they fit with what is real to them, new words may be picked up, for example from literature,[79] and in an effort to incorporate them into the existing language games of the organization, the words themselves challenge existing definitions and use of words.

However, the celebration of new definitions in the organization will not always isolate and exclude old definitions automatically. Definitional warrants, because they often are concealed in arguments, will persist and stabilize the languaging in the organization. Until the form of conversation and the contents of the argument itself are questioned, for example by discussing the inclusion and exclusion of definitions, the organization will reproduce conversations with dual and perhaps even contradictory definitions. Interesting conversations can be imagined, in which organizational members hear the same words being used, but where the conclusions do not follow the way they would expect them to. 'Linguistic battles' would be fought in which the reason for the battle would be difficult to identify, resembling a kind of shadow boxing.

Propositional Warrants

Propositional warrants establish the relations between concepts in terms of change and causation (see chapter 2 regarding 'truth-functional connectives'). They also specify properties of concepts with respect to quantity, order, number, and time. As in the case of definitional warrants, propositional warrants may have sedimented through their recurrent use in the organization. The above example of the board of directors' vote for a new managing director is an example of a propositional warrant. It is, however, a *formal warrant* in the sense that the relationship between the succession and voting of the board of directors is specified by a rule and a number.

Not all warrants of an organization are formal. Some take a very *rudimentary*[80] form, encompassing unclear properties or relations between concepts. Such warrants may also be in the form of stories that are handed down through conversations in the organization. Consider the following example of a functional-value argument with a concealed rudimentary propositional warrant:

C: One should not make complaints about the behaviour of customers while they are on our premises buying our services.

G: Because it is not the way this company does things.

Propositional warrant: And since our managing director clearly showed that this is really not how things are done around here. Before firing one of the service staff members, she shouted to him; 'I will fire anyone who says anything negative about a customer. At any time'!

Here the story is what gives 'substance' and 'power' to the claim. The story may also be coupled with another warrant suggesting that this should never be brought up in conversations and discussed.[81] Concealed propositional warrants, whether formal or rudimentary, as well as concealed grounds, allow the organization to avoid, for each argument made, the 'burden of proof'. Few, if any, organizations can devote their conversations to exploring the proof of any argument put forth. At each partial argument, questions would have to be posed like; 'what are your grounds?', 'how do you link your grounds to your claims in this instance?', 'by what proof do you claim this?', 'what is the logic of your argument?'. Such questions, as suggested above, would render ordinary day-to-day conversations extremely complex. For members of an organization, it is enough to (individually) know about formal and rudimentary propositions, as well as to know (individually) that others (socially) know about these, to speak effectively. Nevertheless, concealed propositional warrants are a 'double edged sword' for the organization; they do also hinder individualized and socialized knowledge development.

Paradigmatic Warrants

Paradigmatic warrants establish the overall purpose of an organization, be it to make profit for its owners, to serve the public, a profession, or its members, or to maintain an ideology. Furthermore, a paradigmatic warrant may place the organization with its purpose into a larger social, political, or economic context in which the purpose gives meaning. A political organization would, for example, uphold a certain charter to maintain or reform the creation and distribution of wealth within a society, fight crime, and provide good living conditions for senior citizens.

Paradigmatic warrants are often concealed, seldom questioned or debated, and tend to persist over a longer time. Nevertheless, they frequently form a basis for organizational conversations. An example of an argument using a paradigmatic warrant is the following:

C: This school must improve its teaching
G: Because the average student evaluations of our courses shows a low score.
Paradigmatic warrant: and since the purpose of this school is to effectively educate high quality professionals for a demanding business community.

In this example, the paradigmatic warrant was precisely stated, almost as if it was taken out of a 'mission statement' for the school. This level of clarity and consistency will not always be the case, however. Paradigmatic warrants can surface in many different statements, in many different forms. However, the warrants express a part of socialized organizational knowledge necessary for the coordination of conversations, and thus, even if they find different forms, provide traces of the same answer to the question what is this organization all about – the *raison d'être*. Paradigmatic warrants are thus closely linked with what is often conceptualized as the 'identity' of the organization.[82]

It should be noted that organization theory literature has taken a great deal of interest in changes in identity and paradigms of an organization. Scholars have identified at least two conditions under which the organization is said to learn, or undertake a 'paradigm-shift': (1) when new management comes in and questions old paradigms; and (2) when the organization confronts a crisis.[83] Given the concept of concealed paradigmatic warrants, an additional condition for change of paradigm may have been identified: it is not until day-to-day conversations, arguments and statements are based upon a new set of paradigmatic warrants, that a paradigmatic change really has been accomplished in the organization. The very idea that paradigmatic warrants serve a stabilizing purpose, however, shows how slow organizational identity change is likely to move. It also shows the need for a new view on the nature of organizational change. Running the risk of being normative, good change management at the level of the paradigm of the organization is really about making good conversations on various scales: bringing up old warrants, questioning them, and replacing them with new warrants.

Counteractive Warrant

As seen, the three types of warrants may persist over time in organizations, having a stabilizing effect on languaging. Another warrant with a stabilizing effect is the counteractive warrant. This type of warrant may be definitional, propositional, or paradigmatic. A counteractive warrant establishes alternative and competing definitions, propositions and paradigms by inclusion, not by exclusion. In this sense, the counteractive warrant is different from a counterclaim. The counterclaim would simply provide a contradictory statement, while the counteractive warrant is a sophisticated strategic element being a part of a stabilizing argument. Let us give an examples of counteractive warrants. Consider the following partial, functional-temporal argument:

C: The garment manufacturing company has to acquire an investment banking company.

G: Our knowledge of finance is not sufficient.

Let us now consider two different propositions backing and opposing (refuting) the claim. First, one proposition could be that given the high risk of acquisition activities, the company should buy other companies in related rather than unrelated businesses. The garment manufacturer would lack the necessary management competence, physical assets, market and distribution channels to be able to implement any synergies with the investment banker, and so should refrain from an acquisition. Second, an opposing proposition could be that an acquisition essentially is a learning process, and that in due time, and with effective processes, skill transfer between two companies is to their mutual financial benefit.[84] Given the knowledge of these two propositions, an effective warrant can be made which disqualifies one of the two propositions. For example,

W: Remember that the company must strengthen its knowledge in order to prosper in the long run. Hence, the synergies to be obtained are those of gaining a fast and speady access to a new stock of knowledge rather than doing more of what it already knows. The criteria for judging whether the acquisition is appropriate will therefore be access to knowledge and its long term effect rather than relatedness of operations, and its possible short-term effects.

A warrant such as this may be concealed or revealed. Note that, in any case, a counterclaim or a counter argument would be answered trivially, by statements like *the company has thought of that* or *we have tried that, and it did not work,* two statements that are frequently heard in organised life. A *non*-counteractive argument, would have to follow up by providing counterclaims and new warrants, indicating a new line of argumentation and inquiry. Thus, counteractive warrants have a stabilizing function on languaging in organizations, as well as on the development of new socialized organizational knowledge.

A final note on stabilizing languaging: over time, warrants, whether definitional, propositional or paradigmatic, change as the organization uncovers them, challenges them, and substitutes them. However, changes in warrants do not necessarily mean that the rest of the argument, grounds and claims change. It may merely alter the meaning of the argument, linking the grounds to the claims in novel ways.[85] Therefore, in studying the creation of meaning in organizations, an observational scheme, like the one outlined above, will be helpful. The observer should also ask questions related to what is normally not made explicit, to look for traces or clues that may indicate the change of meaning.[86]

Notes

1. It has been argued that the initial means of cellular communication took place via electrical discharges, like the surface membrane of a living cell is maintained by electrical forces and the interaction between macromolecules. Via alterations in the electromagnetic and electrochemical forces, molecular cellular structures are able to interact. See Joseph (1993) for a fuller discussion of the languages of the body and brain.

2. Maturana and Varela (1987) give status to the domain of language as a new 'phenomenal domain'.

3. Varela (1979: 269). The term 'autonomous unit' here refers to a broader class of autonomous systems. The characteristics, functions, and limitations of autonomous systems have spurred a considerable debate. Some of the important issues raised concern the meaning of natural and artificial life, cognition, and artificial intelligence. See Varela and Bourgine (1992) and Morin (1982). This line of research

is interesting to follow for everyone involved in understanding the epistemology of complex systems.

4. Sorri and Gill (1989: 71).
5. Rorty (1989: 4).
6. See Martinich (1990) for a collection of articles on the philosophy of language.
7. Joseph (1993: 8).
8. Still, although non-humans do not have the ability to speak, they still utter in a primarily emotional way, e.g., barks, grunts, screams, moans, coos, whimpers, clicks of the tongue, in situations involving sexual arousal, terror, anger and helplessness. (Joseph, 1993).
9. Sorri and Gill (1989).
10. Maturana and Varela (1987)
11. Luhmann (1986) uses 'utterances' to denote sounds associated with speech.
12. Becker (1991).
13. We will neither discuss grammatical relations nor denotative features of language in this book.
14. The best examples of the 'stranger' trying to learn about a language are found in works of anthropology. See for example Geertz's (1973) studies of cock-fights arranged by males on Bali. What enable him to give an adequate description of the cock-fight and its more profound layers of meaning, was a set of distinctions that made him aware of what kind of action that was played out. For example, he was able to distinguish utterances. Again, it should be noted that we do not discuss in this book the importance of the loudness, intensity, cadence, melody, rhythm, and emotional qualities of the spoken language. It should also be noted that when we speak of language in the present text, we do not refer to the 'grand' languages *per se*, like French, German, Italian, or English, but rather to language as evolved in the organization.
15. So far, the idea of the individual conveying his experiences, is consistent with the idea of externalization (*Entauserung*) of Hegel, employed by for example, Alfred Schutz (Schutz, 1970; Schutz and Luckman 1985/1989; Berger and Luckman, 1966). Care must be shown, however; the phenomenology of Alfred Schutz not only restricts externalization to the use of language, but it also covers signs, tools, marks, etc. Please note that the issue of the individual expressing experiences raises another question of the ways or means of expression. Does the individual have a private language in which to express experiences? Our later teatment of language games in organizations in keeping with the writings of Wittgenstein (1958; 1953), presupposes that rules for language games are public, and not private. It is only by publically using a word, that a correct or incorrect use of a rule can be identified (you may just think that you use a rule correctly). The present text does not allow for further discussions of private languages, a theme that has received substantial attention. See Kripke (1982). It is also unclear to us what the stand of Maturana and Varela would be towards the issues of private language.

16. This is the simplest form of training, what Wittgenstein calls *'demonstrative teaching of words'* (Wittgenstein, 1958: 77). This can also be seen as combining two language systems, the spoken language with gestures.

17. Again this perspective is limited to spoken language. This perspective of 'languaging' is very different from many of the previous contributions to the understanding of language in organizations. For example, Fiol (1991), contributing to organizational economics (e.g. Barney, 1991; Barney and Ouchi 1986: Mahoney and Pandian, 1992), sees language as a *stable* system of signs and symbols. She encourages management of organizations to manipulate this system occasionally so as to ensure that their organization differs from other, competing, organizations.

18. The role of language in this respect has been discussed by Fiol (1989) who suggests that language defines boundaries of the organization.

19. This has interesting parallels with the work by Bittner (1974) who studied how the concept of 'organization' varied across the members of an organization.

20. Varela (1979: 268).

21. Of course, if we include paralinguistic nuances, e.g., melody, pitch, and grammar, the variability would have been much larger.

22. It should be noted that the term 'language game' underscores the fact that speaking is something people do, it is an activity within our broader social existence. Likewise, language emphasizes games underscores that languaging takes place in relation to other persons. Both these (obvious) properties are obscured by the representationistic perspectives previously discussed (see Sorri and Gill, 1989).

23. Wittgenstein (1958; 1953). A full treatment of Wittgenstein's philosophy of language is beyond the scope of this text. Nor are we in a position to give a sufficient analysis of the tremendous transformations in the thinking on language that have resulted from Wittgenstein's ideas. We urge interested readers to turn to the analyses in Martinich (1990, section vii), as well as in Kenny (1973).

24. See Van Maanen (1991).

25. Percy Barnevik speech at the Academy of International Business Conference (AIB), Hawaii, November 1993.

26. Note that, for example in the works of Westley (1990) there is no mentioning of the possibility that conversations about strategy vary to a considerable extent across organizations. What is strategic to one organization may be highly operational to another. See for example Haspeslagh (1982) on the differences across organizations in the use of portfolio planning instruments.

27. Compare the term 'emergent strategy' (Mintzberg and Waters, 1985; Mintzberg, 1989).

28. Eisenberg (1984), Eisenberg and Witten (1987), Astley and Zammuto (1992).

29. Astley and Zammuto (1992). See also Meyer (1984).

30. This conclusion must be seen as stemming from our view that conversations in organizations form autonomous units that reproduce them-

selves autopoietically on many scales, and perhaps, in a self-similar manner. Conversations form a starting point for the emergence of new conversations on the same and on different scales.

31.   Note that 'competent·action' is judged by the one who issues the orders, and alternatively, by the one who carries them out. It is not referred to a third party's observations.

32.   Astley and Zammuto (1992: 452).

33.   What does Wittgenstein say about changing rules of language games? *'We can easily imagine people amusing themseles in a field by playing with a ball so as to start various existing games, but playing many without finishing them, and in between throwing the ball aimlessly into the air, chasing one another with the ball and bombarding one another for a joke and so on. And now someone says: The whole time they are playing a ball-game and following definite rules at every throw. And is there not also the case where we play and – make up the rules as we go along? And there is even one where we alter them – as we go along. I said that the application of a word is not everywhere bounded by rules'* (1958: 83–84). Here he seems to indicate that rules may be altered, or that they even may be non existent.

34.   Translation from one language to another seems to be a special case of this. On a high scale the slow transfer in academia from Latin to national languages illustrates this. Because many Latin words and concepts simply could not be directly translated, given their very strict linguistic rules, many new words and concepts had to be invented in the national language (Stichweh, 1990).

35.   For more on the SWOT technique, see for example Ansoff (1965) and Andrews (1970).

36.   'New rules' may here also mean 'lack of rules', in the sense that no fixed rules have yet been established.

37.   Sometimes we hear words used by our parents or by our grandparents that seem completely out of time and place. We may even have difficulty in understanding the precise meaning of these words, for example, exactly what the word is supposed to emphasize or connotate.

38.   Dahl (1991).

39.   Wittgenstein (1953)

40.   In this case involving more than the language system spoken language.

41.   In an ethnography of a computer manufacturer, we identified situations in which the management 'lost face' by asking subordinates about their support for a change proposal. The subordinates' version was something like this: management was supposed to have the natural authority necessary to just direct change, and should not have had to ask for it. Asking for support was a sign of weakness that eventually would lead to problems of lost confidence in management (see Haerem, von Krogh, and Roos, 1993).

42.   Nonaka (1991) describes speculation used by a Japanese automotive engineering team; 'what would a car look like if it was to evolve like a species?'

43.   In our work with a multinational pharmaceutial company we have come to appreciate the stories made up by the owner and CEO. He

actively makes up stories and communicates his thoughts to the rest of the organization by them. People retell these stories, discuss them, and reinterpret them at many times and under various circumstances.

44. See Luhmann (1990b) on meaning as a basic concept in sociology.

45. Language game as a method has for example been employed by Lyotard (1984) in studying contemporary discourses on the state of knowledge. Lyotard has applied at least three types of utterances (denotative, evaluative, prescriptive) associated with the range of language games that Wittgenstein proposes (see Wittgenstein, 1953).

46. A possible variation on the theme: the rules belong to the tacit knowledge of the organization (cf. Polanyi, 1958).

47. See Huff (1990) and von Krogh and Roos (1992).

48. See Fletcher and Huff (1990) for an example. In this chapter the authors explore strategic reorientations at AT&T by mapping and describing the arguments presented in annual reports over an 11-year period. In line with the cognitivist tradition of accurate representations of a pre-given world the authors claim that argument mapping fulfills a kind of double-representational function: '... our focus is on cognitive reorientation, and our method of analysis is dependent upon argument mapping. Argument mapping is particularly well-suited for a longitudinal study of strategy reformulation, since it can capture the substance of changes in the way the organization presents its understanding of itself and its environment' (Fletcher and Huff, 1990: 166). Nevertheless, if we take as a starting point, the philosophy of language proposed by Ludwig Wittgenstein we find that he, like Maturana and Varela, essentially takes an anti-representationist stance. Wittgenstein has through his work shown us how to avoid a representationist stand to language (Rorty, 1992).

49. Toulmin (1958: 254).

50. Toulmin, in fact, suggests that the analysis of the cognizing subject and the associated psychological and physiological issues, are irrelevant for his own inquiries. In a way, his task is very much to contribute to a 'system of philosophy' which can exist by itself, irrespective of the individual actors contributing to that system. In this respect, his suggestion seems to be aligned with the basic trait of an autopoiesis theory. It should, however, be noted that if we scale our observations to the level of the individual actor, the 'speaker' and the 'listener' we would find additional rules or other types of rules at play, like 'trust' and 'truth'. The listener may trust the speaker to tell the truth about what he knows (see Lewis, 1990).

51. Toulmin (1958: 255).

52. Toulmin (1958), Toulmin, Rieke and Janik (1979). This is similar to what Latour (1987: 23) called 'modalities': 'we will call *positive modalities* those sentences that lead a statement away from its conditions of production, making it solid enough to render some other consequences necessary. We will call *negative modalities* those sentences that lead a statement in the other direction towards its conditions of production and that explain in detail why it is solid or weak instead of using it to render some other consequences more necessary'.

53. Varela (1979: 64) provides insight here. A purpose is assigned to a system by an observer of that system and 'reflect our considering the ... system in some encompassing context'. And this should be followed with Maturana (1988: 30): '*An observer has no operational basis to make any statements or claim about objects, entities or relations as if they existed independently of what he or she does*'. So, intentionality ascribed to certain functions is the doing of an observer of the system, who of course, in ascribing this intentionality, has its own functions and intentions.

54. This was also observed by Fletcher and Huff (1990) who went on to suggest that arguments provide starting points for new arguments. This is not surprising, given the observational scheme developed in this book, where conversations as processes, *reproduce themselves autopoietically on all scales*.

55. Here it should be remembered that our discussion so far deals with conversations and not with historically recorded arguments.

56. We here refer to what Luhmann (1993) would call the 'present future' rather than the 'future present'.

57. Luhmann (1990b).

58. An idiom in Swedish illustrates, ironically the potential paradox in disussing future present and present future: 'Det var bättre förr, ju förr dess bättre ...'.

59. Schutz (1970).

60. Fletcher and Huff (1990) based on the work by Brockriede and Ehninger (1960) suggest that some arguments have 'evaluative claims' without extending this to encompass a whole class of arguments. We believe that the concept of 'value argument', being more encompassing than evaluative claim, is more adequate here given the type of conversations that organizations foster. Much of popular management literature advocates effective discussions of the basic values of an organization, arranged so as to encourage wide participation from management and employees (Senge, 1990). Hence, we imagine instances where whole conversations revolve around the 'values' or 'ideologies' of the organization. These being the issues, full-blown arguments may appear where claims about values are made, the grounds and warrants are grounded in values, and the qualifiers limit the range of the claim.

61. This line of argument is informed by the so called resource-based perspective of the firm (Barney, 1991). One possible implication of this perspective is that the personnel function should redefine its task from primarily employment issues, to develop human resources in such a way that they contribute to the competitive advantages of the firm. See also Roos and von Krogh (1992).

62. This can be compared to a generic argument in figure 6.2.

63. Gioia and Chittipendi (1991) have done an ethnography of a university undergoing a strategic change process. The study reveals the dynamics of the change process and shows the need to apply longitudinal, rather than cross-sectional methodologies for studies of organizational processes.

64. von Foerster (1972).

65. See von Foerster's (1981) idea that cognition results from recursive computation (computation of computation of computation of..).
66. Luhmann (1992; 1990b). See also Quinn and Cameron (1988) on the role of paradox and tautology in organization theory. *Paradox* normally arises when a type is of a type, like the famous Cretan paradox: 'Everything a Cretan says is a lie'. A *tautology*, on the other hand, is a distinction that does not distinguish, like for example: 'this car is a car'.
67. See John Wisdom's (1992) essay on philosophical perplexity. Wisdom shows how perpetual disqualification of statements of observation and knowledge is difficult, if not impossible, in everyday language.
68. See Argyris and Schon (1978).
69. Maturana (1991).
70. Hedberg (1981).
71. The questions we have asked are only a small portion of those that could be asked about organizational knowledge. In order to get an idea of the many diverse questions that have been asked about organizational learning, see Huber (1991).
72. At least temporally distinct from previous statements, arguments or conversations. This holds even in the case of a 'copy-cat' boring its listeners.
73. See Becker (1991) o n the role of silence in language.
74. Mason and Mitroff's (1982) term 'hidden strategic assumptions' is analogous to the concealed warrant found here. The difference, however, is that concealed warrants not only confine themselves to strategic planning activities, but to everyday conversations in organizations, and that any attempt to find them through posing why questions, does not necessarily lead to a final resolution (in terms of attaining the best representation (assumptions) of the world). 'Why' questions in everyday conversations may result in a recursive posing of new why questions.
75. These classes are not substitutes, but additions to the types of arguments outlined above.
76. See also Fletcher and Huff (1990).
77. These classes have been inspired by the phenomenology of Alfred Schutz (Schutz, 1970; Schutz and Luckman, 1989, 1985), and the sociological theories of Peter Berger and Thomas Luckman (Berger, 1981; Berger and Luckman, 1966). In Berger and Luckman's work four levels of legitimation are conceptualized. Knowledge objectivated in a society may be legitimate on all the four levels, that of legitimate language (words), legitimate stories and rudimentary propositions, legitimate theories, and finally legitimate paradigms. Here we should however make the reader aware of some of the controversies between pure phenomenology a la Husserl and autopoiesis theory as it has been conceived of by Niklas Luhmann (1984). For more on this, see for example Luhmann (1984; 1986).
78. See the example reported in Whyte (1991) of a redefinition of the term 'fixed costs' at the Xerox Corporation. This redefinition was accomplished through a project where consultants, management, and

workers studied the implications of using various definitions and the diferent aspects of the operations that these definitions uncovered.

79. See examples of modern business jargon.

80. The word 'rudimentary' here is used as it is used by Berger and Luckman (1966). They distinguish between 'formal theories' and 'rudimentary propositions'.

81. We will return to the issue of 'undiscussability' later. In organization behaviour literature, undiscussability has mainly been framed as a problematic depriving the organization of possibilities to learn (i.e. Argyris and Schön, 1978). As will be seen by our argument, we believe that 'undiscussability' in addition to presenting itself as problematic, may be a necessary facet of the coherent development of socialized organizational knowledge. In many instances, however, e.g. when a team is formed to solve a particular task, it will be beneficial to investigate and uncover/reveal warrants, or in the words of David Bohm, 'suspend assumptions' (Senge, 1990).

82. See for example Dutton and Dukerich (1991) for a definition of organizational identity.

83. Hedberg Nystrom and Starbuck (1976), Hedberg (1981)

84. See von Krogh, Sinatra, and Singh (1994).

85. Here we see an interesting parallel in the philosophy of science. Feyerabend (1972) has tried to show that as new theories are formulated and new phenomena are discovered, 'old' theories do not resist by having an 'invariant meaning'. Rather progress forces new interpretations of old theories.

86. Chapter 8 contains a discussion of impediments to organizational knowledge. Here barriers of agreement are proposed as possible impediments to knowledge development.

7 Languaging and Beyond

TEXTS AND SOCIALIZED ORGANIZATIONAL KNOWLEDGE

So far we have chosen to focus on conversations in organizations, as they unfold over time. Languaging provides a way for organizational members to realise their autopoiesis in a coordinated way, across scale. Another important knowledge-based activity of organizations is writing, which can be seen as a language system along with spoken language.

It has been argued that there is a progression from oral-language statements to written statements, both culturally and developmentally, implying increasing explicitness.[1] An important part of organised activity is to produce texts, for purposes of recording, directing, informing, inviting, entertaining, etc. The texts produced in organizations are many, and vary in style, form and content: reports, memos, letters, procedures, vision and mission statements, value statements, strategic plans, job descriptions, contracts, etc. Clearly, these texts result from the knowledge of an individual, or a team of organizational members in many instances. Being signs and marks, they are objectivations[2] that lend themselves to further study and inquiry by organizational members. Does this mean that they, like conversations, attain an autonomous status of their own, and that they can be analyzed in terms of their forms and functions? For example, does an organizational routine become a statement of socialized organizational knowledge?

Cognitivist epistemologies with representationism frequently presuppose that information equals knowledge. Writings of organizations, hence, are just another representation of organizational knowledge.[3] This information in turn is seen as 'stored' in an organization - wide 'memory' including archives and datafiles. At any time, these representations of knowledge can be evoked by organizational action.[4]

According to the trait of autopoiesis theory, information does not equal knowledge. Information is a process that enables knowledge creation. In effect, the autopoietic system, whether on the social or individual scale, does not import information.[5]

It continuously creates information based on input data. Hence the concept of knowledge and information in the theory of autopoietic systems raises an intriguing question: in this theoretical perspective, what is text? To attempt an answer, text belongs to the environment of the organization as the organization is a knowledge system. It follows from the discussions of the relationship between languaging and socialized organizational knowledge, that text also belongs to the environment of conversations. Texts, produced by the organization, can be read at various times (observed) by the organizational members, groups, and so on, and can be subject to conversations. As such, they become an input to the cognitive processes of individual organizational members, stimulating the creation of individualized organizational knowledge. Texts can also stimulate the creation of new socialized organizational knowledge.[6]

Texts, at the moment of inscription, are made by a cognizing author or authors. An easy assumption to make, then, is that the text 'represents' the knowledge of the writer at a certain point in time, at least the author's 'codifiable' knowledge about a particular topic.[7] But sharing the assumptions of autopoiesis theory, text does not, however, give an adequate representation of what the author knows,[8] not even to an observer of the processes of writing and reading. The two processes, writing and reading are distinct and belong to, at least in the case of textual dissemination, two different cognitive domains. This duality of writing and reading, in traditional morphology referred to as the double articulation property of language, has been excellently captured in this statement by Becker.[9]

> *The state of my consciousness as I write need to have no identities with the state of yours as you read. Our memories are different, and so this languaging is orienting us separately. Languaging is orienting, within our separate, autopoietic domains of distinctions. An observer within his or her own domain of distinctions, may see regularities and explain what happens in terms of a transfer of information, but that will be a third orientation, with no necessary correspondence to what you or I experience.* [10]

When a new procedure is written, a new strategy document inscribed, or a new communication to shareholders is formulated and issued, these texts acquire their own autonomy, or 'begin to live their own life'. Each time the text is read, the process of reading determines the meaning of the text. The possible effects of letting someone else read a text can never be fully predicted, since all cognitive processes essentially are autonomous.[11] This, of course, should make the reader careful to make inferences about the knowledge that was presented by the writer at the time the text was written.

The text presents itself as a unity for observation by organizational members. The text may be observed in 'one single ray', or *monothetically*,[12] in its totality. The reader can track back and forth in the text, discovering new combinations (creating new information and knowledge). A conversation, on the other hand, does not present itself to an observer as a unity, but as a process. It has to be observed *polythetically*,[13] as a sequence of steps following each other in time, statement by statement, argument by argument, warrant by warrant. In retrospect, however, generalizations and conclusions can be made about what is said. Conclusions will always be affected by inadequate memories, effects pertaining to stabilizing languaging, and the perceived need to 'post-rationalize'[14] what has already been said. Organizational members, however, have a great advantage in their participation in a system of socialized knowledge and languaging they and patterns of conversations, even if they have to be observed polythetically, or reoccur. They may predict, for themselves, the development of a particular conversation based on what they are able to remember from the development of previous conversations. Thus, the gap between people's experience with text and conversations need not necessarily be so great in practice. In some instances, perhaps, memory may allow organizational members to observe conversations (based on extrapolations of what they have heard and what they remember) increasingly monothetically.

A particular type of text that is central to the organizational epistemology based on autopoiesis theory, is 'self-descriptions'. Luhmann defines self-description as '*fix(ing) a structure or a 'text' for possible observations which can now be made more systematically, remembered, and handed down more easily, and which can now be connected better to each other*'.[15] Elements of self-descriptions are covered in many organizational texts that result from self-observation of the organization. Here are some common ones in organizations:

(1) descriptions of organizational structure: the way the organization conceives of itself in terms of relations between tasks, people, positions, titles, etc.

(2) procedures and manuals: the way the organization proposes guidelines for the execution of functions within the organization.

(3) policies: the various functions to be covered by the organization, and the possible products and markets it serves.

(4) letters to stakeholders: the organization's way to describe important issues and events.[16]

(5) historical accounts: show the organization's conception of its own evolution into what it can currently describe as itself.

Such organizational texts give, like this book, an observational scheme that can help the organization to systematically observe itself. They provide, like some forms of languaging, a stabilizing effect on organizational self-observation. The texts endure in the face of highly dynamic, event based, self-observations, conversations, and creation of socialized organizational knowledge. They endure in the face of, for example, new definitions of concepts and the relationships suggested between concepts. As mentioned, this may be mistaken for adequate descriptions of how the organization presently functions.

It should be clear to the reader by now, that the enduring organizational texts only provide data to the processes of organizational self-observation and knowledge development. Thus, their endurance does not refer to the conservation of meaning or knowledge, but rather to a 'solid point' to which the organization 'glimpses' in striving to continue its autopoiesis, on all scales. The meanings of texts, however, are enduringly produced anew each time they are read or discussed. The text, like a strategic plan, is contained in conversations of strategy in an organization over a year. But each time a group of managers meets to discuss the strategic plan, their viewpoints, their arguments, their concealed and revealed warrants etc., will have changed. In short, the socialized organizational knowledge is highly dynamic. In the language of general process theory, we may say that the reference to the strategic plan is *recurrent* but not *cumulative.*[17] New knowledge of the strategic plan developed under a management meeting does not add cumulatively to previous knowledge of the plan. Each time the management team meets they develop new knowledge of the plan referring to their previous knowledge, forgetting parts of the conversations, including new experiences, or innovating new interpretations of the strategic plan. This perspective is very different from most normative strategic planning models in literature. Here knowledge accumulation is assumed as management work through different phases of a strategy process; from goal setting, via analysis of opportunities and threats, strengths and weaknesses, formulation of alternative strategies, choice of a strategy, to follow-up activities like implementation and control of deviations from a plan.[18]

Most organizations are not designed or in other ways developed to account for the differences between monothetical and polythetical experiences. In some organizations, newcomers learn how to write short (one page only), effective, lucid, convincing memos, that can be circulated around. In other organizations, newcomers learn how to 'express their thoughts and experiences' in electronic mail systems. Yet in other organizations, conversations are kept to the minimum, the idea being that 'you should not take up to much of your boss's time'. In some organizations, large storage banks are created for internal corporate documentation, the idea being that of accountability: 'if something happens we'd better have our backs covered'. Some organizations pride themselves on developing effective standard reports in which the background material for decisions at the corporate level can effectively be assembled at the divisional level, by the division´s own staff members.

The examples are many, but the point is one: organizations are mostly not designed according to textual - meaning creation and knowledge development. Questions of importance to socialized organizational knowledge development are seldom asked: What is the meaning of this text? What is the argument here? Why was this text written? Why were other messages not included? Are there any concealed warrants here? What does this tell us about the state of the organization? How has our understanding of this text changed? Why has it changed? In some practice of organizational life, these questions are likely to appear too cumbersome, too difficult to answer, too time-consuming, or simply irrelevant. Nevertheless, such questions are often asked privately by organizational members in their private attempts to bring forth a world (Why has Joe written this memo? Should I watch myself? How does this memo affect me? Why isn't Liz on the mailing list? Why isn't *my* area mentioned in the strategic plan?).

If we truly want to unbracket socialized organizational knowledge, knowledge development at the individual scale may resemble knowledge development at the organizational scale – it may be self-similar. Organizations may stimulate processes of textual – meaning creation in order to improve the development of socialized organizational knowledge.

ORGANIZATION AND ENVIRONMENT

So far this book has focused on the internal functioning of organizations, how socialized knowledge, languaging and textual production and reading are related. Although the basic distinction environment-organization has been introduced, little has been said this far about the relationship between the organization and its environment. Below we shall make an attempt to discuss this relationship further, but first, it is useful to recapitulate three points about the epistemology of organizations made earlier in this text.

First, organizations observe their environments, and produce descriptions of this, on which they in turn operate.[19] Making these observations they gain socialized organizational knowledge about their *own* descriptions of their environment. This knowledge in turn enables further observation by the organization. Second, languaging processes and textual production have a stabilizing effect on the socialized knowledge of the organization, across scales. Third, the observer, also an autopoetic system, can describe the environment-organization in terms of an output-input, or import-export relation, making its own arguments, and producing its own texts. However, the observer (following this observational scheme) can also describe the relationship between the organization and its environment as closed, simultaneously open and closed, or *open in a closed sort of way* (!).[20]

Because autopoiesis may have self-similar properties, it should be meaningful to study the possibility of structuring the relationship between organization and environment, like in the case of the individual, in terms of self-similar structural couplings. Gunther Teubner suggests that structural coupling at the level of social systems can be defined in the following way: '*A system is structurally coupled to its environment when it uses events in the environment as perturbations in order to build up its own structure.*'[21] The organization is never idle; by observation it distinguishes events in the environment, and it uses energy to discuss these events within the rules of its languaging. The organization uses such events to discover new themes, issues, opportunities, threats, strengths, and weaknesses. Gradually, new arguments are made that construct a description of the environment. Functional arguments suggest functional change to cope with events in the organization. Temporal arguments provide assessements of the expected duration of a particular event or situation. Value arguments highlight the positive or negative values of environmental changes occuring. Self-similar arguments might be used to stimulate or infix strategic processes and/or organizational norms. A combination of the above - mentioned arguments are played out over time, boosting the development of socialized organizational knowledge.

New texts are produced that redescribe and redefine the organization, the relation between organization and environment, and the environment. In a self-referential manner, previous languaging and texts describing events and situations in the environment form the basis for the next languaging and textual production about the environment. The organization's history of structural coupling with its environment, that is, its history of observation, languaging and textual production, in this way ensures the development of a unique socialized organizational knowledge. However, a 'correct' (cognitivistic) representation of an event, corresponding to how it 'really is out there' is never accomplished, nor is this the goal of an organization. *The organization brings forth its own world; it observes, languages, and knows about events – in its own manner – and thereby, it is sustained as a coherent system of knowledge.*

The environment of an organization is composed of (among other things) other organizations, like customers' organizations, suppliers' organization, owners' organizations, competitor organizations, etc. The organization as a knowledge system may also have some regularity in the relationships in its structural coupling with the environment.[22] These relationships are determined by observation and socialized organizational knowledge, the internal languaging and textual production of the organization. The way the organization argues about a particular relationship constitutes that relationship. Consider the following *partial* arguments:

C: There is a need to compete with organization A for the contract with organization B.

C: In the next round, after having competed with them for the B deal, we need to form an alliance with A in order to win a contract with organization C, over organizations D and E.

The language games that are played with respect to organizational relationships are many, varied and highly dynamic. In previous writings we have attempted to contribute to the development of a language in which organizations could structure and observe their own cooperative relationships.[23] The relationships may be described as varying between a loosely formulated 'Texas Handshake' to a full - blown merger. However, in each given instance, such descriptions, as we have made them, can at best only belong to the domain of the observer (us). How the organization meaningfully describes relationships with other organizations, are of their own doing. They may use the same words, like alliance, acquisition, or merger, *but the rules for the usage of these words, and hence their meaning, will vary across the organizations.* Nevertheless, there are certain generic features that characterize the descriptions of the relationships between organizations, although there will be at least three different and generic types of descriptions involved in a relationship, that of each organization as well as that of an external observer.

Each organizational relationship can be described (self-referentially) along at least four different dimensions: values, trust, structure, and temporality. First, in any structural coupling allowing for organizational relationships *value* will be assigned on a temporal basis to the relationship. The organization´s relationship with another organization will be described with (scaleable) value statements like: 'positive', 'negative', 'cooperative', 'competitive', 'challenging', 'boring', 'productive', or 'devastating'. The languaging of the organization, by assigning value to the relationship, influences action and mutual coordination with the other organization. For instance, an organization will treat differently its two alliance partners if one of them is described as an 'old friend', whereas the other is referred to as a 'newcomer'. Each time a new action by the other organization is distinguished and observed, a value is assigned to this observation in languaging. In this way, organizations are 'judgemental instances' in the sense of continuously evaluating their environments.

Second, *trust* is also an important dimension in describing organizational relationships. Trust may be necessary for the success of economic transactions between organizations,[24] manifested in descriptions of relationships in terms of 'good business partner', 'always paying on time', 'reliable deliveries', 'no surprises', and so on. Trust may also be an important dimension in describing the stability of an organizational relationship,[25] producing value arguments including terms like 'reliable', 'dependable', or perhaps 'irresponsible'. A relationship may influence the level of complexity in organizations and trust may reduce the need for control of this complexity[26] as well as influence the inherent uncertainty that exists in relationships,[27] producing arguments like *she is really a competent and nice representative of Smith & Jones. Co. Ltd., so there is no need for us to run her through the usual red-tape procedures.* Thus, although trust as such requires its own book,[28] it is a dimension that strongly influences organizational languaging and socialized organizational knowledge regarding structural couplings.

Third, *structure* is another dimension to describe organizational relationships. By structure here we mean 'structures of expectations'.[29] A relationship involves a set of expectations referring to observations and descriptions of the other organization's behaviour. It is of utmost importance here to distinguish between descriptions of observations, since these often may not be the same in observations of organizational relationships. Structure is found in that one organization expects to observe certain behaviour by the other organization. If the other's behaviour coincides with these expectations, the descriptions of the relationship with respect to the other's behaviour will overlap with the expectations. In a case where the observations of the other deviate to various degrees from the expectations, one alternative for the organization will be to describe the behaviour as being different from the expectations given for the relationship. There is yet another alternative, however. The description will change so as to accomodate the expectations, that is, 'in a nice way describe a troublesome observation'.[30] For example, if the languaging of the organization has produced descriptions of a 'positive, collaborative, interesting productive relationship', and if in one instance the partner makes a strategic ploy[31] that negatively affects the organization, then the organization may still choose to maintain its original description in further languaging.[32] For example, arguments connected to an observation of negative behaviour may be effectively counteracted in the subsequent languaging of the organization. The organization may or may not prefer to maintain a description, but in instances where a description is enduring, the organization has at its disposal a whole array of tactics for stabilizing languaging as seen above.

The final dimension, *temporality,* frequently enters the descriptions of organizational relationships by indicating various temporal horizons. A relationship may last for a certain period of time, there may be specific milestones characterizing the relationship, there may be certain hopes and aspirations that must be expressed in future or past (as lost hopes) tense, there may be a need to redescribe the sustainability of the relationship etc. Again, temporal arguments play an important role in describing and arguing for a particular organizational relationship. Advocates of a relationship that has been negatively described can resort to hopeful arguments that the relationship eventually will bring success to the organization. Opponents may claim the exact opposite, that the relationship has a record of not producing the wanted results. Temporality in descriptions, in this sense, has a stabilizing effect on the organizational relationship. Observing a negative ploy on behalf of the other organization, the organization does not necessarily react immediately by breaking away from the relationship. Rather it may produce temporal arguments suggesting that the future will show better behaviour.

Descriptions of structural couplings derive their significance from guiding the kind of relationships that an organization can enter into. By suggesting the form of cooperation, the values assigned to the possible relationship, the trust it is building on, the structures in the form of expectations about the relationship, and the temporal horizon for the relationship, the descriptions enable the organization to prepare for and set up a relationship. It follows, however, from the above, that descriptions of organizational relationships are never identical across two organizations. For this reason, many cooperative 'would-be relationships' turn out to be fraught with disappointment, shortened time, lack of trust and negative values.[33] Many management theorists would have it that an increased 'information exchange' would remedy these problems, and that joint planning drawing on this information, for example, of a strategic alliance or a corporate acquisition, would make the partners increasingly aware of the motives behind the alliance.[34] *The problem is that descriptions, since they result from organizational languaging, are highly dynamic in all of the four dimensions and can never be entirely fixed.* A relationship can be structured in a plan, written down with milestones, responsibilities, resource allocations, and control philosophies etc., but the plan as text would belong to the environment of the organization as a knowledge system. Hence, the plan would be nothing but data that *might* fuel the never - ending, dynamic conversations that compose the organization as a knowledge system and its structural couplings.

It is not our intention to provide full answers to this problem in the present text. Nevertheless, we can maybe see the contours of some possible solutions. Planning is an exercise that at the corporate level requires some forms of conversations,[35] and hence, planning conversations by people from the collaborating organizations may form their own autonomous units, enabling the development of descriptions of the organizational relationship-to-come. Such 'conversational units' may be (and they often are) formed by members of the top-management team, but since they are not the only units of conversations in the two organizations, they cannot determine the possible structuring of the coupling. Rather, units of conversations – for example, analyzing and planning for joint marketing efforts, joint product development, or

joint manufacturing – should be composed as rapidly as possible, starting the development of joint knowledge between the
two organizations.[36] Moreover, management should monitor
(observe) the conversations revolving around these activities,
in order to better understand the nature of the relationship
between the two organizations.

The reader at this point may be inclined to give a comment
like: 'Why bother to observe conversations? If the management of the two organizations agree on how structure, dura-
tions, and values should be for the relationship and how trust
should be established, it is only a question of communicating
this to the rest of the organization, and let it get the same perspective'. Such a comment would be based on a representationist viewpoint: that a correct representation of the
relationship could be given by management, and that the rest
of the organization, in turn, could get a correct representation
of this representation.

If we, on the other hand, relax this cognitivistic assumption
of representationism, and suggest that a world is constantly
being brought forth on all scales as organizational members
converse about the relationship, we see the inherent problems
of the representationist: A 'correct representation' cannot be
captured and simply handed down to others in the organization, as the ultimate representation of how the world is. While
the representationist manager would strive to collect the best
possible representation (including how the organizational
members themselves should work in the relationship), the conversation would inevitably have moved forward, bringing up
new issues, new opportunities and challenges in the relationship, new values, new observations etc. Moreover, when the
representationist manager felt that he had enough 'power' in
the representation, he would present it, or perhaps 'broadcast'
it, to the rest of the organization as *the* acceptable way of observing the relationship. This communication would make a difference, not by infixing the reality, but by introducing yet another
observation, and yet other themes for further conversation in
the organization. For instance, some conversations and arguments would centre around what can be seen as a misconstrued
situation, or a flawed representation of the relationship.

At this time, we begin to see the really dynamic form that
the organization takes when applying the new organizational

epistemology. It is true that we can view the relationship between the organization and its environment in terms of stable contractual forms.[37] It is also true that we can choose to bracket certain texts or statements as being representations of the reality of the organization. But in doing so, it is also true that *we are acting as observers applying our own observational schemes to the organization.* We should also be prepared to describe, however, the exemplary plasticity and dynamism of the organization as it unfolds as a system of socialized and individualized organizational knowledge. The observational scheme that we have presented so far allows us to observe the environment as a set of descriptions made by the organization, that hinges on the vast, complex, and continuously changing patterns of conversations that make up the organization.

Notes

1. For example Olson (1977).
2. 'Objectivate' here means making an object out of personal experiences for further study and enquiry by other participants of a social system. See Berger and Luckman (1966) and Berger (1981).
3. For example, authors utilizing cognitive mapping techniques frequently map organizational publications, like annual reports, taking them to represent organizational knowledge. See, for example, Huff (1990). See also the seminal work by Nelson and Winter (1982). In this book organizational knowledge is said to be captured in organizational routines. Fiol (1990) gives a particular example of sensitivity to the nature of the text by introducing semiotics into the study of organizational knowledge.
4. Walsh and Ungson (1991) extensively discusses a concept of organizational memory.
5. Luhmann (1986).
6. Please note that we have not in the way of understanding speech in relation to writing, attempted to introduce a hierachy, suggesting primacy of one over the other. The relative weight put on writing is a consequence of limited space and insight on the part of the authors. However, we are well aware of the movement of deconstructionism headed by the French philosopher Jacques Derrida. His major project is to create a 'science of writing' in which text and speech, writing and talking attains the same status in western philosophy. One of his main claims, however, is very similar to the one that follows from our theoretical perspective, that text achieves autonomous qualities, separate from a pre-given reality. To abandon the idea of text as representational, suggests Derrida, poses particular challenges for the reader of text. Derrida, hence, is first and foremost a critical reader of established and

partly famous texts. His project includes finding the hidden meaning of the text through a systematic process of deconstruction. Derrida shows how the author includes and presupposes meaning from which he attempts to depart. For more on the writings of Derrida and the desconstructivistic movement, see Derrida (1978 and 1988) and Taylor (1986). For an example of deconstructionism in organization theory, see Kilduff (1993) who deconstructed March and Simon´s (1958) 'organizations'. Clearly the implications of Derrida´s work for organization theory need to be fully discovered in more works.

7. See Winter (1987).

8. In the field of literature studies, Italo Calvino (1990) has made great contributions to the understanding of the process of inscription, and how detached it might be from what the author (Calvino self-referentially) experiences as his images or ideas for a theme or a story. The following passage serves to illustrate the point: *'In devising a story, the first thing that comes to my mind is an image that for some reason strikes me as charged with meaning, even if I cannot formulate this meaning in discursive or conceptual terms. As soon as the image has become sufficiently clear in my mind, I set about developing it into a story... Around each image others come into being, forming a field of analogies, symmetries, confrontations. Into the organization of this material, which is no longer purely visual but also conceptual, there now enters my deliberate intent to give order and sense to the development of the story... At the same time, the writing, the verbal product, acquires increasing importance. I would say that from the moment I start putting black on white, what really matters is the written word....From now on it will be the writing that guides the story toward the most felicitous verbal expressions, and the visual imagination has no choice but to tag along'* (Calvino, 1992: 89). Writing, thus, might not be a spontaneous process of re-presentation of pre-fabricated thoughts. Rather it is a process that feeds on, gradually replaces and come to dominate imagination. Calvino continues by suggesting that the written word, in turn, once it is being read, produces its own images.

9. Becker (1991: 229).

10. This can also be interpreted as a scaling issue, i.e., both parties need to be on a compatible 'languaging scale'.

11. For this reason, many western thinkers have, as Jacques Derrida (1978; 1988) suggests, assumed primacy of speech over writing. Immediacy has been the solution to possible misunderstandings and unclarities.

12. We borrow the terms in italics from Schutz (1970) to show possible differences between text and speech. See also Luhmann (1990b).

13. Schutz (1970).

14. See March (1988).

15. Luhmann (1990: 253).

16. Please note that these can be issues and events that in a traditional open systems world-view would be ascribed to the environment of the system. Following the ideas of the theory of autopoietic systems, however, a self-description is necessarily involved in all descriptions of observations made by the organization. If further clarification is needed, see Luhmann (1987).

17. For more on general process theory applied to the field of organization theory and the study of strategy processes, see Ven de Ven (1992).
18. See for example Peter Lorange's (1980) work on strategic planning processes.
19. Luhmann (1990b)
20. Teubner quoted in P. Kennealy (1988). See our discussion in Chapter 2.
21. Teubner (1991: 133). Here Teubner also quotes Luhmann at length.
22. See Teubner (1991) for an alternative perspective on what we call 'relationship'.
23. For a fuller discussion regarding cooperative strategies, see Lorange and Roos (1992), von Krogh, Sinatra, and Singh (1994), Wathne, Roos and von Krogh (1994), and the 1994s special issue of *International Business Review* on Cooperative Strategies and Knowledge Transfer.
24. Hirsch (1978).
25. Blau (1964), Rempel, Holmes and Zanna (1985).
26. Luhmann (1979).
27. Heimer (1976).
28. See Huemer (1994) for an academic treatment of trust as strategic choice.
29. The theories of Niklas Luhmann are essentially anti-structuralistic (King, 1993). Hence, Luhmann has suggested his own interpretation of structure as essentially referring to social expectations (Luhmann, 1982,1986; Deggau, 1988)
30. This might be related to March and Olsen's (1975) concept of 'superstitious learning'. It should be remembered, however, that March and Olsen rely on the organization's ability to represent adequately the environment internally. When this ability is weak or absent, a wrong representation will occur, and so superstitious learning will take place. What we are describing here, given the premise that the environment is *brought forth* rather than represented, is a state where the organization 'is aware' that *it alters the description of the relationship to fit with expectations rather than with an observation.*
31. Mintzberg (1989).
32. This may also be related to the 'image' the partner has built up internally over a long time.
33. See studies by Meeks (1977).
34. See, for instance, Lorange and Roos (1992), Hamel, (1991).
35. This argument has been confirmed in several and often very diverse empirical and theoretical works. For example, see the writings of Lorange (1980), Westley (1990), Chakravarthy and Lorange (1991), and Gioia and Chittipendi (1991).
36. This resembles very much the post-acquisition management approach of domestic appliance manufacturer Electrolux in taking over the Italian white goods supplier Zanussi. Electrolux formed task forces involving experts in various areas from the two companies. The goal of these task forces was very often to improve operations of Zanussi,

like infusing new production technology or restructuring the sales activities. For more information on this, see case 'Electroluz-Zanussi' by Sumanthra Goshal and Phillipe Hapseslagh, INSEAD-CEDEP.

37.   For example, in the vocabulary of transaction cost economics and agency theory (Williamson, 1975).

8 Impediments to Organizational Knowledge

SOURCES OF IMPEDIMENTS

This book has dealt with the realm of organizational epistemology: how and why organizations know. In the organizational epistemology developed in this book, knowledge
development is seen as an autopoietic process that is brought
forth in organizations through languaging on all scales in a
self-similar manner. By now the reader may ask himself: what
can inhibit this knowledge development process? In this
chapter we point at three sources of impediments to organizational knowledge development:

- Improbability of communication
- Barriers to agreement
- Self-difference

IMPROBABILITY OF COMMUNICATION

According to most of our current conceptions organizations
seem to be 'robust'.[1] Our conventional views may bluntly be
summarised as follows: Organizations are rigid in terms of
belief, paradigms, or world-views, and they may even persist
with low performance for a long time.[2] Already established
knowledge structures hardly ever change except in cases
where new management comes in or there is a crisis.[3] But are
they really this robust? Perhaps at the level of resource allocation decisions, top management recruitment, and financial
performance organizations do exhibit characteristics of typically robust systems. At the scale of knowledge development in
organizations, however, the conventional view might need to
be supplemented.

As seen in Chapter 6 and 7, for knowledge to develop in organizations, communication is a prerequisite. Communication allows for language games to be played out, new themes to be conveyed and explored, and misunderstandings to be clarified. Unless communication functions, knowledge will cease to develop in the organization. This dependency on communication, however, makes the organization fragile with respect to knowledge development.

In an essay entitled the 'improbability of Communication', Niklas Luhmann suggested that communication in social systems should not be taken for granted, but rather be seen as an exception, a most unlikely event.[4] Even though we experience 'communication' every day in our lives, even to the point where we take it for granted, every communication[5] might be a rare and highly valuable occurrence. There are at least three reasons why communication is rare and valuable. Firstly, given that human cognition is autopoietic, and therefore autonomous, understanding of what another means should not be taken for granted. We may agree but this does not necessarily mean that we have understood.

Secondly, communication, and hence knowledge development, is also bound by time and space. It is unlikely that communication should reach and knowledge should be developed outside the group that is present in each situation. There are also rules for communication applying to the group present, e.g., those of politeness, student–teacher, super-, and subordinate, etc. It should not be assumed that communication could not stop due to a communication about the lack of interest in, or intention to continue the communication. However, beyond the context of the group of those present, such informal or formal rules, are beyond the control of the participants.

Thirdly, even if the communication or knowledge is understood, it might not be agreed to by the recipients. It might even be that the more one understands a message, the more one can prepare the claims, grounds, and warrants necessary for presenting a full counter-argument. It might, of course, be that even if a message is not understood, agreement is conveyed. As a result, knowledge development can be hindered; the recipient will give his consent, but not add to the messages given. This is an ultimate form of 'lip-service' which illustrates the fragility of organizations as knowledge systems.[6] Thus, 'understanding' and 'agreement' should never be confused in the analysis of organizational knowledge development.

BARRIERS TO AGREEMENT

We suggest three classes of barriers to agreement, which are, as such, impediments to organizational knowledge development. These may be seen as warrants on different scales (see Chapter 6).

The first class of barriers to agreement include *formal procedures and formally espoused theories*, like operating procedures, red-tape paperwork, accounting principles, quality control procedures, information systems, and organizational routines. In a large firm in the consumer package goods industry new recruits are trained in writing memos; these should be one-page, have certain fixed margins, a particular font type and size and so on. The tradition is that if messages are not written in this way they are not considered legitimate.

In some organizations formal analytical tools are a major obstacle for knowledge development. For instance, the use of the well known BCG matrix for portfolio management may become a legitimation barrier: SBUs simply *have* to be labelled 'stars', 'question marks', 'cash cows', *or* 'dogs'.

Likewise, experts that are known to embody particularly useful or valuable knowledge and/or skills may constitute legitimation barriers. In a Scandinavian firm in the chemicals industry, a sole chief engineer is responsible for all mathematical calculations relating to a certain production process, which are formal procedures. This person is very secretive in nature, shielding himself and his notes from other organizational members. Everyone admires his mathematical genius but nobody is allowed to take part in, or even observe his work process. In fact, over time this person has become a modern version of a 'witch doctor'; he obviously is knowledgeable, valuable for the firm because he handles the procedures, and is respected for this, but nobody knows what exactly he is doing, and how it is done. In this firm it is inconceivable that someone else could take care of the calculations and the corresponding formal procedures. All in all, individual knowledge may be made legitimate by making reference to or concretely using or supporting these procedures or espoused theories.

The second class of barriers to agreement includes *myths, stories, proverbs, legends, or maxims* in organizations, i.e., rudimentary theories.[7] A typical example of such rudimentary theories would be if the top management of the local newspaper responded to suggestions that they, too, should invest in a television station with the following statement: *We have tried it before and we know that it does not work* (of course, the reader by now can see that such a statement can be explained with autopoiesis and self-reference). Likewise, maxims are great obstacles to knowledge development. A few years ago the board of directors of a large raw materials firm in Europe recruited a new CEO from the fish processing industry. The new CEO refused to accept the maxim of ten-year business cycles, instead, developed strategies for the firm based on five-year business cycles, like in the fishing industry he came from. On the one hand, new ideas that used to be suppressed by the ten-year world view were allowed to surface. On the other hand, the five-year world view became a legitimation barrier to yet other ideas.

In a well known company in the film industry, the legend of the founder is so strong that it often inhibits socialization of new ideas, and therefore knowledge development. Many suggestions among managers are dismissed with the phrase *the founder would turn in his grave if he had heard that*. Similarly, in many business schools there is a widespread rudimentary theory that *managers do not like to theorise*. A manifestation of this is that in most MBA and executive programmes almost all attention is given to tools for 'how-to-solve-daily-problems' relative to discussion of more speculative nature. It is hard to envision that this book, for instance, will be considered legitimate reading on (conventional)executive programmes in (conventional) business schools. Again, we can see that everything said and done is said and done from a tradition, in line with autopoiesis.

A third class of barriers to agreement is '*organizational paradigms or world views, which put everything in its right place*'.[8] Spender's concept of industry-specific recipes as acceptable firm behaviour[9] illustrates this. Such paradigms can also be seen as warrants on the highest scale in the organization.

A typical example of a 'paradigm' being a legitimation barrier is captured in the relationship between market share and return on investment. In some companies managers are convinced that the relationship is a linear one: increased market share results in increased ROI. Managers in other companies and industries confess to a decreasing return on market share type of relationship, others to an increasing return on market share relationship. Regardless of the paradigm, the point is that it tends to function as a source of legitimation, a warrant to claims (see Chapter 7). Thus, new product ideas, for instance, might have to be shown to increase the market share according to the market-share–ROI paradigm in question.

Other organizations and managers subscribe to the idea of 'key success factors' in their industries, being the main determinant of future success. Such factors can be seen as elements of a paradigm explaining 'how things should be done around here'. Any suggestion or idea raised by organizational members needs to pass through this legitimation barrier – thus, a potential impediment to knowledge development.

SELF-DIFFERENCE

An important property of the epistemology developed in this book is self-similarity, i.e., the autopoietic process may be similar across scales. The way the organization develops knowledge is similar to the way an SBU develops knowledge, which in turn is similar to the way groups, and individuals develop knowledge.[10] On the other hand, the conventional unit-of-analysis scale is based on the legacy of cognitivism and connectionism and we might need to develop a new, distinct scale for the new epistemology. Thus, the scales inherent in the research topics needs to be clarified, not only what scales are used, but also the spectrum within those scales

We suggest that organizational knowledge development may be impeded if the process becomes *different* across scales, which we label self-difference.[11] In practice self-difference can be uncovered quite easily, just reflect over the implication on organizational knowledge development stemming from this claim made by a top manager:

*In the new company, the future and present must be better inte-
grated ... 'Duality' does not really go much down the line – nor
should it. Don't give too much chance for people down the line to
think about the future – they should concentrate on running successful operations.*[12]

Traditional perspectives on strategy design processes, for
instance, may illlustrate how self-difference impedes knowledge development. Such design processes often centre around
a rational, analytical approach beginning with vision and
mission formulation, progressing via strategic goals to various
analyses of the environment and internal resources, continuing with selection of alternative strategies towards operational
plans for implementation, including consequences. Designing
strategy can be seen as: a conceptual process; a formal process;
an analytical process; a visionary process, a mental process; an
emergent process; a power process; an ideological process; a
passive process; and an episodic process.[13] Self-similar strategic
design suggests that the same kind of process, e.g., a formal
process, is applied at each level of the organization; for individuals, dyads, groups, departments, SBUs, and for the whole
organization. Self-different design means the opposite. Let us
illustrate this principle.

A vision statement was recently developed by the top management team in a large firm, focusing on three responsibility
dimensions; financial, employee and customer responsibility.
The objective was, obviously, to get all organizational members
to live up to the vision, thus the intention was to create a self-
similar principle: the fundamental principles should be similar
on all levels in the organizations. After a while it became
embarrassingly evident that the vision statement was not only
virtually unknown further down the hierarchy, but also a
source of *ridicule* among organizational members. Thus, the
principles embodied in the vision statement were not similar
across scales, in this case hierarchical levels. Also, because the
vision statement in some instances was intentionally obscured
by some managers, it became *de facto* self-different.

In organizations there are rules for the usage of certain
words that give the words meaning (see Chapter 6). These
rules are dependent on the social context in which the word
appears. For example, in some organizations the formal use of

the word 'strategy' is limited to the discussions and documents produced by the top management team. In another (scientific) organization the usage of the word 'fractal' has been excluded, instead the people use the word 'level'. Rules for the usage of words are dynamic, especially in companies where little formal control is exerted. Managers frequently discard distinctions, introduce new distinctions, use old distinctions on new situ- ations, put words in new contexts, and use distinctions in a metaphorical sense, etc. Individuals and groups develop their own language that, in turn, influences other individuals' and groups' actions. If such rules, that is the linguistic tradition, are different for the individuals, groups, departments and the organization, then organizational knowledge development will be impeded. Similarity across scales, on the other hand, reduces complexity and facilitates organizational knowledge development.

To sum up, the three issues discussed in this chapter prevent issues from being brought up in conversations, prevent languaging in organizations and, therefore, agreement, regardless of understanding. As such, they are impediments to organizational knowledge development.

Notes

1. For example, presentation by Kagono, Gupta, and Bambhri at the Strategic Management Society Conference, Chicago, 1993, 'Robust Organizations'.
2. Meyer and Zucker (1989).
3. See Chapter 2. Also Prahalad and Bettis (1986), and Hedberg (1981).
4. Luhmann (1990b).
5. See Chapter 4 for a discussion of Luhmann's definition of communication.
6. Interested readers should watch the TV series *Yes, Prime Minister* by BBC for a great illustration of this.
7. Berger and Luckman (1966).
8. Berger and Luckman (1966: 116).
9. Spender (1980).
10. The epistemology presented in this book scales further. Given our discussion of the embodiment of knowledge, *distinctions* might be the natural next step down the unit-of-analysis scale (von Krogh, Roos and Slocum, 1994).
11. This argument builds on Anderson (1977).
12. Mr Beks, Finance Director in Heineken, quoted in Abell(1993: 18).
13. Mintzberg (1990).

9 Opening Up

Given the perspective that epistemology and logic are the two sub-branches of methodology, which, in turn, is a grand division of philosophy, what implications surface from the epistemology developed in this book on research methodology within the realms of organizational studies and management? The answer is embodied in the statement: *a new epistemology implies new research methodology on the highest scale.* Because the ways of interpreting knowledge are interrelated with the ways of attaining knowledge, an anti-representationistic, organizational epistemology, like the one in this book, requires rethinking of the basic 'research logic' within the realm of management and organizational studies.

The representationistic research logic in organizational studies and management is, not surprisingly, as widespread as the representationistic view of cognition in these realms. Just think about the use and impact of different logic, such as 'economics based logic' (e.g., country-specific advantages[1]), 'industrial organization based logic' (e.g., generic strategies[2]), 'resource based logic' (e.g., competence configuration[3]), or 'behavioural logic' (e.g., dominant logic[4]). The new organizational epistemology presented in this book is based on theories of autopoiesis, embodiment of knowledge, and scaling. Because they rest on different philosophical assumptions, it follows that it might not be appropriate to apply representationistic logic of management and organization studies, like the ones just mentioned.

A new epistemology implies rethinking sources of beliefs and ideas, which often determine the type of theory used by researchers. Then, what are the sources of belief in 'representationistic' management and organization studies? Is it testimony of managers? Perhaps abstract reasoning from some kind of universal principles? Sensory experience; touch, smell, sound, sight, or taste? Just plain research intuition? Managerial consequences? Or perhaps propositions that can be neither proved or disproved?

In this book we have stressed the embodiment of knowledge and the scaled, autopoietic process of knowledge development. This opens up speculations regarding sources of belief. Testimony of others (e.g., interviews), different sensory experiences (e.g., participant observation), or practical activity (e.g., action research), only produce perturbations in the researcher's autopoietic process. The key question is how strong these perturbations have to be in order to be included by the self-referential knowledge development process of the researcher, and the extent of his/her 'connectability' in self-referencing. The text, often being the output of the research, for instance in the form of a book is, in turn, only a perturbation of the reader's autopoietic process, like this very sentence is a perturbation to you at this very moment. What criteria we shall use to attain knowledge within organizational studies will depend on the nature of the (self-constructed) reality we are investigating. Perhaps it is not logic at all? Perhaps it is some kind of events? Similarly, the ways of interpreting knowledge in management and organizational studies are interrelated with what we see as basic characteristics, or the 'being' of this realm, as well as our theory of value.

WHEN STUDYING ORGANIZATIONAL KNOWLEDGE

When a researcher enters an organization in search of (articulated or tacit) knowledge (or 'competence', or 'capabilities', or 'aptitudes', or 'know-how', etc.), she often carries the two millennium heritage of the harmonious one-, two-, or three-dimensional universes of Euclid. There is a certain Platonic flair about thinking of organizational knowledge and knowledge development in terms of linear functions (lines and planes), or in terms of areas or volumes (circles, spheres, triangles and cones): What are the (spatial) dimensions of knowledge? What size has it? How can knowledge be encircled? How can knowledge be mapped (in two or three dimensions – not more)? How thick is knowledge? How deep is it? How long does knowledge last? How BIG is it? Of course, these are some of the most fundamental questions researchers can ask about something.

In addition, the researcher often uses modern language, (which paradoxically appears to go quite well with the old legacy of Euclid): What knowledge can be *discovered?* What are the *reoccurring patterns* of knowledge? What is an *objective, impartial* view of knowledge? What are the *causal effects* of knowledge (based on temporal priorities of independent variables)? What *general patterns* exist? How can I *observe* knowledge? How can I *map* knowledge? How can I *sort out divergent interpretations* of knowledge? Although these questions represent some of the most 'natural' questions a researcher can ask,[5] what insights surface from the answers? What wisdom has the 'Modern-Euclidean-Paradox'given us, manifested in the cognitivist and connectionist epistemologies, regarding our understanding of 'organizational knowledge'? Our discussion in Chapter 2 provides some indications.

In our everyday experiences we frequently encounter processes which are dynamic and complex in nature, e.g., the weather, bacteria growth, population fluctuations, the stock market, and managerial decisions. Like such complex natural phenomena, we believe that it is difficult to strip down, brush off, and study organizational knowledge (individualized or socialized) under glass in a laboratory, nor do we believe that it can easily be captured in a questionnaire or in case studies. Why? Because knowledge is what brings forth the world and the world is brought forth in knowledge. If we couple this statement with the Wittgensteinian notion that we give meaning to the word 'knowledge' by the way we use it, it is clear that researchers of knowledge and organizational knowledge are up against some tricky challenges.

So, is there *any* hope of being able to study organizational knowledge? Yes! It follows from the organizational epistemology developed in this book that an understanding of organizational knowledge might come from understanding the boundaries of the organization, its identity, its self-reference, and its languaging – on all scales. This perspective contrasts with the ease by which knowledge often is equated with information, lending itself to a multitude of academic studies. A recent example is the 1993 Winter Special Issue of *Strategic Management Journal*, which we have previously referred to, where '*In essence, information and knowledge are used interchangeably.*'[6] The character of information '*...is seen as central to* *organization in determining how the information will be sought, processed, and used to make strategic decisions*.[7] Here prominent cognitivists, like Richard Cyert, James March and Herbert Simon, dwell in problem areas like how the organization functions as an information processing mechanism and what information is strategic. From this perspective research methodology does not appear to be an issue, perhaps not even considered a problem. From our perspective the assumptions embedded in research methodology must be on the same scale as the epistemological, as well as other philosophical assumptions.

CLOSURE

The epistemology brought forth in this book points at the importance of understanding (boundaries of) organizations. Are organizations open systems or are they closed? Or are they open and closed at the same time, depending on scale? Being the 'conventional wisdom' of many organizational studies and much management theory, the input–output perspective has provided considerable insight, at least if we view the number of publications as manifestations of insights. The vast majority of research within these realms rests firmly on these, the cognitivist's assumptions. Not surprisingly, and in line with autopoiesis theory, the cognitivist epistemology has reproduced its belief systems, and its belief system's ability to reproduce itself, over the last decades, and will probably continue to do so.

From an autopoietic perspective organizations are simultaneously closed and open systems: they are open on some scales, like formal structure, and closed on other scales, like norms and beliefs.[8] Interpreting social systems as closed provides many new insights and gives explanations for phenomena that could not be thoroughly understood from the cognitivistic camp. Gomez and Probst (1983) provided an informative example of this closure, drawing on the Catholic church:[9]

> *Maybe the best example of a social institution surviving in an ever-changing environment is the Catholic church. The secret of its*

'success' lies in a strong set of beliefs – the Catholic faith – and in an institution to protect these beliefs from environmental disturbances – ...the curia would block any outside influences threatening the beliefs and only allow evolution from within the system. The curia would allow minor changes based on external demands to provide the impression of openness. But eventual changes will only be cosmetics – as in the case of changing the form of the holy mass – and never touch essentials.[10]

Most readers probably recognise this type of closure in other (their own?) organizations: many organizations may appear very open on the surface whereas they are closed on 'deeper' scales. Organizational closure is a scaling issue that goes beyond the conventional discussion of autonomy *in* organizations, focusing on 'corporate culture', decentralization, 'skunk works', 'internal ventures' and the like. Thus, we suggest that more research can be devoted to better understand the open/closed simultaneity of organizations.

Normally within a realm like management and organizational studies, people share a certain way of looking at things, a certain way of asking questions, or perceiving issues as critical. Perhaps some would like to call it sharing a paradigm. The cognitivist epistemology, discussed throughout this book, is an example of this. Such 'confessions' are not surprising and can easily be explained by autopoiesis; it is self-reference in action. A quick review of the topics addressed by academic journals and business magazines underscores this tendency. In 1994, for instance, many researchers seem to have confessed to 'process re-engineering'. Not long ago, it was total quality management.

It has been argued that it is only when one undertakes a conceptual journey to another cognitive domain, or changing paradigm, that one really encounters/self-constructs a different world. This implies not only being aware that there is a different cognitive domain that might be meaningful, but also daring to immerse oneself in it. The problem is that as far as cognitive journeys are concerned, the very idea that there might be different cognitive traditions seems perverse to many researchers and practising managers. In this book we have shown that there is a different cognitive tradition regarding cognition, namely autopoiesis. Indeed, this has been a journey to a different 'cognitive culture'.[11] Thus, the implication for methodology that we would like to vouch for is for researchers to increasingly be prepared to venture into unknown cognitive cultures, not seeing them as something bizarre, strange, or something not worth while wasting time on. Of course, there are many examples of management and organizational studies scholars testing out unknown cognitive cultures; some can be found in the reference list of this book. One thing is clear, however: *if you make your own observations with your own self-constructed scientific methodologies and if you describe these observations with your self-generated theories, you cannot escape the self-reference of autopoiesis – on any scale!*

Notes

1. Hymer (1966).
2. Porter (1980).
3. Roos and von Krogh (1992).
4. Prahalad and Bettis (1986).
5. This modernistic research approach is what Rosenau (1992: 8) called the '*techno-scientific, corrupting, cultural imperative*'.
6. Cyert and Williams (1993: 7). Although they referred to one contribution in the Special Issue, we feel that this statement covers all contributions.
7. Schendel (1993: 3).
8. This is analogous to the concept of 'emergence' discussed in the sciences of complexity.
9. Gomez and Probst (1983: 10–11).
10. A recent manifestation of this closure was perhaps the extraordinary gathering of 114 of the world's 139 cardinals in June 1994, discussing the blockage of legalized abortion at a world conference on population problems scheduled for Cairo in September 1994 (*International Herald Tribune*, 1994)
11. Coined by Krishna (1989).

10 The New Epistemology in Use: The SENCORP Management Model[1]

INTRODUCTION

In this last chapter of the book we describe a management model used over the past thirteen years in the US-based firm SENCORP. The chapter is divided into three parts: first, a brief look at themes common to conventional management models and theories; second, a description of the model and its development; and third, a discussion of the model speculating on its implications for strategic management. But before this, it seems necessary to know a little about SENCORP and its reasons for creating a new management model.

THE COMPANY: SENCORP

SENCORP is a privately held US firm based in Cincinnati, Ohio. It is the parent of three operating companies totaling some 2,000 employees. SENCO is the oldest of the companies and has its roots in the automotive industry in the late 1940s. SENCO designs, makes and sells pneumatic fastening systems for a multitude of industries on a worldwide basis. Based on advanced forms of stapling technologies, the company moved into medical wound closure, resulting in the formation of SENMED. Today, SENMED is developing a range of technologies and companies in the medical industry. SENSTAR is a finance company and primarily operates in the area of industrial leasing. Despite the apparent disconnectedness and diversity that these companies represent, there is an important consistency to the management processes that are the basis of their evolvement.

Throughout the decade of the 1980s, SENCORP undertook efforts to research and develop appropriate management

163

methods for its increasingly complex businesses. The obvious solution at first was to find answers in the great body of literature within the realm of strategic management. In SENCORP's view, however, this literature (despite its reliance on historical data and observations) concentrated solely on routines, controls and efficiencies. Most of these management processes can be regarded as implementation processes. That is, once a decision is made, these skills and tools are used to implement the decision. But, without overlooking the tremendous improvements that can be made in these areas, the bigger problem appeared to be how to choose better options to implement, not how to implement better. Therefore, as SENCORP evolved from a one-business company to multiple businesses, it moved beyond the standard approaches and began reflecting on its own methods of management. This led to the creation of a simplified Management Model that explained organizational behaviour within a complex environment.

COMMON THEMES IN MANAGEMENT MODELS AND THEORIES

Modelling Human Nature

We see a management model as an organizational heuristic. It gives a sharable and generalized view on the world and how to relate to it. In addition, it has tangible properties and characteristics that allow managers to recognize it when they see it in use. Yet, by defining a management model so, we make assumptions about fundamental issues, especially those concerning human behaviour and cognition. Central to these issues is the desire to understand human nature. A management model attempts to model human nature and create the conditions under which humans perform their best.

Not surprisingly, management theories differ in their descriptions of human nature. We are, for example, lazy and need to be controlled (Taylor), or we are interested in realizing our full potential (Theory Y). Or we are driven by an underlying economic rationality that we have inherited from our Protestant work ethic (Weber). Or we are altruists or opportunists/egotists (e.g., Williamson). Deeper yet is the distinction some make between our mind and body, two separate yet integrated properties (i.e. Weick). It was with the mind–body dichotomy, in fact, that SENCORP foresaw an opportunity to conceptualize human nature in a way left unexamined by other management theories.

Mind and Body Distinctions

Using the mind–body distinction, conventional models and theories have chosen the 'body' as their focus. They measure the time spent on observable actions, such as attention to tasks and problem-solving. They guide bodily movements, defining who can work together, who solves what tasks or who can talk to whom. Moreover, they maintain hierarchies that concentrate on organizational artifacts and human–artifact interaction (e.g., product quality, information systems, workplace layout and production technologies). But by focusing on things that affect the body, these traditional models do not take into account how and why humans and organizations know – that is, what the 'mind' provides. They do not, therefore, give the appropriate guidance to stimulating and directing knowledge development within the organization. This is a considerable oversight, one which drew SENCORP's attention early on in its quest for a better management model. It was here that SENCORP began its search for ideas and heuristics that balance knowledge development with operations. It was here that SENCORP committed itself to understanding how to stimulate, direct and ensure continuous knowledge development in its company as the basis for improving decision making.

By ignoring the intercourse between body and mind, conventional management models and theories sidestep an old problem extensively discussed by Aristotle, Descartes, Leibnitz and their followers. In contrast, SENCORP searches for models and theories that discuss the body and mind and their connectedness. It is interested in not only how they influence each other, but on their joint and apparent instantaneous operation in knowledge development and relating with the environment.

The Process of Knowledge Development

Of the management models and theories that do discuss knowledge, many focus on its contents rather than its development (see the discussion in Chapter 2), e.g., core competence (Hamel and Prahalad), dominant logic (Prahalad and Bettis), knowledge structures (Nisbeth and Ross; Lyles and Schwenk), and espoused theories and theories in use (Argyris and Schön). Understanding knowledge content is useful, of course, if we wish to trace rudimentary changes in knowledge over time, an exercise that might suggest broad guidelines for knowledge development. But a focus on contents faces severe limits because human knowledge is constantly changing, instant by instant, sometimes through conversation, sometimes by observation. We can but briefly 'represent' what we know before it alters.

In addition, autopoiesis theory (see Chapter 3) informs us that as observers, we can only have a limited understanding of how knowledge works in another individual. The individual has 'privileged access' to his own knowledge development. Within a conventional management model, managers are likely to neglect these knowledge dynamics, making judgements about an employee's knowledge according to our own (or someone else's) performance standards. This approach can frequently lead to erroneous perceptions about another's competencies.

Thus, managers following models based on the contents of knowledge face a twofold problem: first, it is virtually impossible for them to keep track of an employee's knowledge development; and second, if they do try (such as mapping the competence of a work group), they run the risk of being too rudimentary with respect to an employee's actual knowledge. To avoid this problem, SENCORP focuses on the process of developing knowledge rather than on its contents. Only by studying this process has SENCORP been able to develop more detailed guidelines for knowledge development within an organization.

In summary, SENCORP's quest for a management model that models human nature requires two things: that it take into account the process of knowledge development; and that it acknowledge the body and mind as distinct but interactive entities.

THE SENCORP MANAGEMENT MODEL AND ITS DEVELOPMENT

Knowledge Conversion

As SENCORP began to define the role of knowledge development in its management model, it uncovered the natural continuum of knowledge – the conversion of knowledge from the unknown to the known. In the continuum, knowledge flows from left to right as it is converted by one entity (be it an individual or an organization) to be of use to some other entity which recognizes its value and is willing to pay money for it. Money flows from right to left as it is converted to knowledge. SENCORP calls this the value conversion process (knowledge for money, money for knowledge), and each of us, to some extent, plays a role in it.

The continuum begins with the universe, the unknown. (See Figure 10.1.) It is also the starting point for the value conversion process. Confronting the frontiers of the universe is science, which converts knowledge about the unknown into technology. We use knowledge from science and technology in business, converting it into something that can be consumed (goods and services). Finally, knowledge is consumed (used) in the marketplace (as goods and services) in exchange for money. This process (taking into account changes in terminology) is timeless. It explains how human beings have behaved individually and as organizations throughout history.

Thus, knowledge moves naturally along the continuum, constantly being converted until it is in the form of goods and services. Money moves in the opposite direction, eventually supporting knowledge development at its earliest stages of experimental science. Business has the unique role of converting new knowledge to goods and services. It is through business that a critical value exchange takes place: knowledge to use – the value of which is represented by money. To succeed in this role as converter, therefore, business must understand

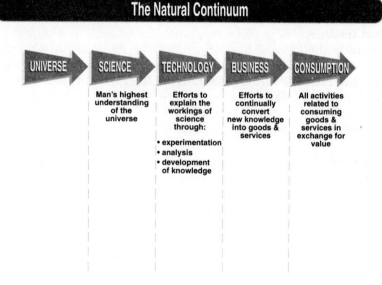

Figure 10.1   The natural continuum (i)

both the science and technology it converts and the consumers and the markets in which it expects to make future value exchanges. And it must know all this in addition to managing its own internal conversion processes (such as producing goods and services).

Management Responsibilities

Against the background of the knowledge continuum, we can identify three distinct responsibilities for business management: (1) to develop knowledge and options for decision making (moving towards the unknown); (2) to make decisions regarding which of these options to implement; and (3) to implement these options (moving towards the known). Rather than being isolated, knowledge development and implementation are connected by a decision-making responsibility which is responsible for allocating resources between the two. In other words, the ultimate balance of resources (like people, time or money) between knowledge development and implementation is always the result of a decision. SENCORP has renamed these three responsibility realms, A, B and C to simplify their use. Thus, we can define all business management activities as three specific, ongoing responsibilities that are interconnected: thinking (B realm), deciding (A realm) and implementing (C realm). These realms of responsibilities are differentiated hierarchically so that the decision responsibility provides separation and balance. (See Figure 10.2.) Over the years, the exploration and description of these responsibilities has formed the foundation of the SENCORP Management Model.

The A realm represents management's responsibility to make decisions. The B realm represents its responsibility to develop new knowledge and options for the A realm to consider. The C realm represents its responsibility to implement decisions made by the A realm, and to manage operations as efficiently as possible.

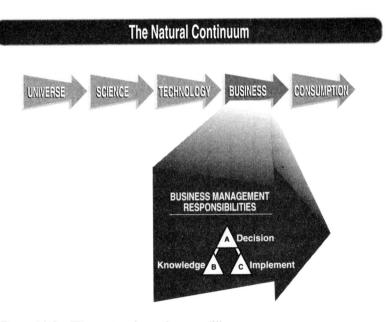

Figure 10.2   The natural continuum (ii)

Fundamental Differences

The B and C realms are managed simultaneously, but in separate ways. Each has its own distinctive management characteristics. The B realm (in order to develop knowledge) is managed as a network of projects, each with a clear beginning and end. The C realm (in order to implement decisions and make them efficient) is managed by synchronizing routines into ongoing, smooth operations. Another difference between the two is the scope of their engagement. The B realm works with information that is greater in scope than the C realm, but considerably less in detail. The B realm is engaged in the ongoing advancement of the organization while the C realm is engaged in its survival.

Advancement and survival are important concepts in the SENCORP Management Model. In the advancement-oriented B realm, resources are more flexibly managed, and gaining understanding is more important than being right or wrong. In the survival-oriented C realm, resources are more specifically allocated, communications are simplified for speed and clarity, and relationships are greater in number, but less in depth. Continuous improvement of survival routines is the focus of the well-structured C realm.

Beyond advancement and survival, a number of other distinctions emerge concerning the B and C realms. These distinctions thematize the differences and complementarity in the ABC model (please see Appendix 'Languaging About Distinctions' at the end of this chapter).

Every decision-maker in the organization manages two types of relationships: those designed specifically for knowledge development and unfettered information flow; and those designed to carry out agreed upon routines. These two relationships need to be managed in distinct ways. The measures, expectations and communications are very different for the A/B and the A/C relationships.

Project versus Operations Management

Project management is the methodology used in the B realm where knowledge is developed through research, experimentation and testing. Here things are being managed for the first time. The only thing that is routine in the B realm is the project management process itself, where each project is unique. Operations management is the methodology used in the C realm where plans are executed and routines are managed. Here things are managed in a way so as to exploit the advantages of repeatability. (Additional distinctions between project and operations management are set out in Figures 10.3 and 10.4.)

One of the most important differences between the two types of management is the way time is used. In operations management, time is used as a measure to gain efficiencies. Because we do not want to stop the operation, and since we want it to run as efficiently as possible, we sub-divide and take snap shots of its process over time. In contrast, project management uses time as a resource. It requires that we set out our objectives and clearly define the necessary start and stop procedures and change our direction as necessary in developing and structuring information into knowledge for the next decision.

Management Characteristics: B vs. C From the A Perspective

	PROJECT MANAGEMENT	OPERATIONS MANAGEMENT
EXPECTATIONS	Expressed as project objectives	Results in accordance to a plan
TIMING	Start-stop	Ongoing (never stops)
MEASUREMENT	Event based measures (periods between accomplishments)	Time-based measures (accomplishments per period)
COMMUNICATIONS	By milestones	By exceptions
SCOPE of CONSIDERATION	Existing operations within a reasonable universe	Existing operations
DEFAULT CULTURE	"Look for ways to change things"	"Getting things running smoothly as possible"
PRIMARY FOCUS	Seek alternatives	Problem avoidance

Figure 10.3   Management characteristics

Management Methodology Comparison: B vs. C

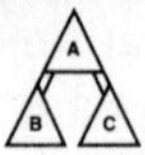

	PROJECT MANAGEMENT			OPERATIONS MANAGEMENT
A REALM OF KNOWLEDGE:	Unknown	Some known	Substantially known	Known
A DIRECTION:	Non-precise	General	Specific	Very specific
RESOURCES: A TIME	Full-time participation	Some participation at planned milestones	Minimal participation as recipient of project results	No participation – communication by routine reports
A MONEY	Low	Higher	May be substantial	Money structured for long-term value exchange
EXAMPLES: NO. 1	Identify interest areas for possible subsidiaries	Subsidiary development and option evaluation	Subsidiary implementation project	Subsidiary operations
NO. 2	Concepts research	Concepts development and structuring	Concepts implementation project	Concepts implementation

MANAGEMENT STRUCTURE:

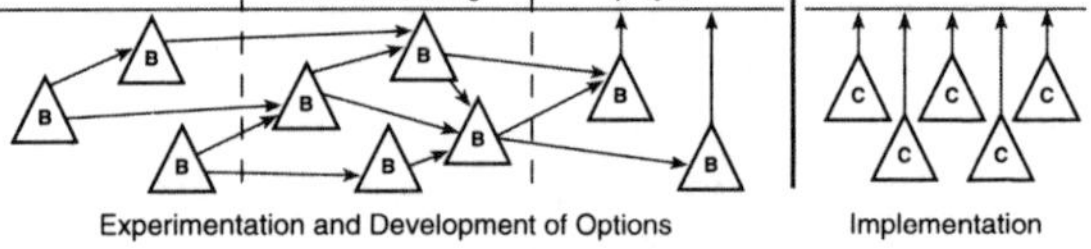

Figure 10.4 Management methodology comparison

Decision making (A realm) and implementation (C realm) represent the more familiar side of the SENCORP Management Model. Their relationship describes how a decision-maker gives direction to have something implemented. That direction is carried out by the routine side of the business, operations management.

For SENCORP, knowledge is developed through self-referencing, distinction-making and through experiments – very much in line with the theory of autopoiesis (see Figure 10.5). Self-referencing means that new knowledge refers to past knowledge. Managers use past knowledge to determine what they see and desire to evaluate in their environment. New knowledge helps managers make finer and finer distinctions. When observations disagree with past knowledge, a boundary is set up where further knowledge development activities and experiments can take place, contributing to the development of new, broader and more rudimentary distinctions.

Processes Internal to the A, B, C

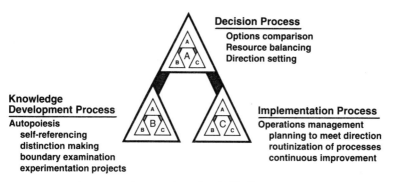

Decision Process
Options comparison
Resource balancing
Direction setting

Knowledge Development Process
Autopoiesis
 self-referencing
 distinction making
 boundary examination
 experimentation projects

Implementation Process
Operations management
 planning to meet direction
 routinization of processes
 continuous improvement

Figure 10.5   Processes internal to the A, B, C

Pursuing Knowledge Development in Practice

One of the most important ways that SENCORP pursues knowledge development processes is through extensive organizational discussions. Consistent with the ABC model, these discussions are targeted at a scale above the scale of implementation. Through these discussions, new terminology is developed for describing the environment and more useful and appropriate definitions for existing terminology (i.e., languaging plays and important role).

Time is spent developing projects that encourage further discussions. These projects, which consider newly developed technologies, current events, scientific theories, geo-political developments, other organizations, etc. help to refine the concepts and its accompanying language.

Individuals within the Organization

As an individual's experience with the concepts advances, further refinement of the definitions, explanations and representations takes place. The environment for discussion and individual learning is that of the B realm – open, exploratory, non-threatening and non-hierarchical. There is also no requirement for closure on any point or issue. The objective is to develop options. This type of environment enables individuals to develop knowledge at more than one scale.

To further understand the role of individuals within the organization, we can use the 'population bulb' concept (see Figure 10.6). The bulb is a figurative plot of any population in the knowledge continuum depending on their position on the continuum from the left side (where knowledge is created) to the right (where knowledge is consumed), as illustrated in Figure 10.7.

The distribution of people across the continuum will follow some sort of exponential function. In other words, for every one person in science, a thousand exist in technology; for every one in technology, a thousand exist in business, and so

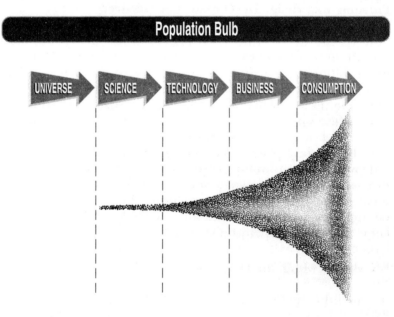

Figure 10.6   Population bulb (i)

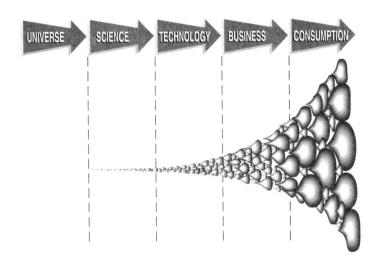

Figure 10.7　Population bulb (ii)

on. Of course, in reality, we each belong simultaneously to many different organizations in different parts of the continuum. We are all certainly consumers. We are all participating in some form of business conversion. And we all seek out new knowledge. Thus, we each have our own personal continuum as one takes on those many responsibilities in an organization, and the shape and location of our bulb is determined by the time we spend consuming, converting or learning.

So it is that an employee can be represented as a single bulb, with his own knowledge continuum, within a larger company bulb (with its knowledge continuum), within a larger industry bulb (with its knowledge continuum), within a larger country bulb, and so on. The layering of bulbs – each like the other, only smaller or larger – reveals the same self-similarity seen in fractals and discussed in chaos theory. It also reveals a fundamental principle of the SENCORP management model: that any model of organizational management should be a replica of individual management.

The responsibilities of knowledge development, decision making and implementation are the same responsibilities that each of us, as individuals, innately use as we manage ourselves. We think, decide and do.

The Fractal Nature of the SENCORP Management Model

The management model is depicted at a single scale, showing the organization as a whole. It's analogous to a single bulb in the knowledge continuum. As we divide routines from knowledge development, however, we see that the C realm is at one scale, where survival of the organization is managed. It is the anchoring scale and is well known and reliable. The B realm is at a higher scale, but includes the scope and scale of the implementation activities in the C realm. The A realm strikes a balance between the two. It establishes a B realm that provides knowledge needed by a decision-maker to take care of (and advance) the C realm. While the B realm operates at a scale above the C realm, it should not be so far out that it produces

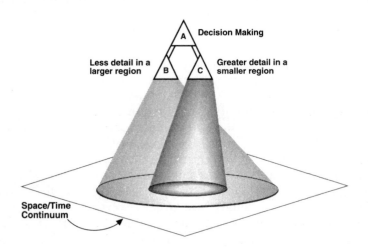

Figure 10.8   Scale of knowledge comparison

options not relevant to the level of decision making in the organization (see Figure 10.8).

Because, in practice, management defines its organization at multiple scales – by level (such as individual, group, business unit and division), by geography or by responsibility – any useful model must likewise be multiple scaled. The principle to follow is that at each successive scale (individual, group, etc.), the responsibilities repeat themselves. Each scale is managed as complete set of responsibilities, just like the original. Thus, each ABC model represents only one entity or organization at one scale. The complete management model encompasses all relevant scales. The model is therefore similar across scale, and, like the population bulb, fractal in nature. In other words, there is no linear way of describing its function. It must be described by scale.

A New View of Organizational Structure

The ABC management model has helped SENCORP change from a hierarchical structure of people, as described in traditional organizational charts, to a network of shifting responsibilities. The traditional chart represents a hierarchy of people (or, more precisely, of bodies). The top is assumed to have all the knowledge, and the people below some fraction of that knowledge. At SENCORP, responsibilities are organized to address areas in the knowledge continuum. We also find in the traditional chart each person is represented by one box. In SENCORP's 'responsibility' chart, this same people will appear in many places simultaneously (see Figure 10.9). Each person will have implementation responsibilities, knowledge development responsibilities and decision-making responsibilities.

The overall value of the SENCORP management model to its organizational members accrues cumulatively. As it is explored and used more extensively, it becomes the basis of the consistent decision-making process throughout the organization. At the same time, the model itself evolves as the company learns more from disciplines outside the organization. Since there is commonality and overlap among the people participating in knowledge development projects at different scales of the organization, there develops an inter-

Comparison of Corporate Structure

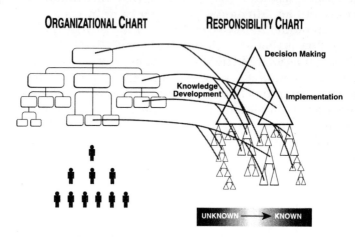

Figure 10.9   Comparison of corporate structure

Corporate Knowledge Base

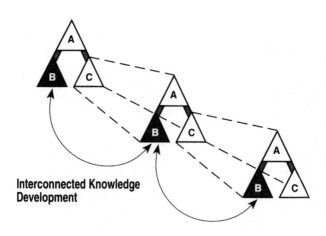

Figure 10.10   Corporate knowledge base

connectedness of knowledge throughout that organization (see Figure 10.10). This means that the organization, as a whole, is guided by management principles and shared knowledge bases that foster change, taking place at all times and all places.

REFLECTIONS ON THE MODEL

The objective of this final section of both this chapter, and the whole book, is to fuel the debate on management models, theories and philosophies. To do this, we have identified some questions we feel are raised by the SENCORP Management Model.

(1) Why do we need new management models?
(2) How can we develop more natural management models?
(3) How can we describe new, natural management models?
(4) What are some of the future challenges for management models?

1. Why Do We Need New Management Models?

Today's management practices are not sufficient to guide business entities and complex organizational relationships of the future because they focus on the contents of knowledge. Changes brought about by such programmes as downsizing, employee empowerment, TQM and re-engineering are incremental, at best. To their credit, any of these programmes could improve service, reduce costs, stimulate functional cooperation and, to some extent, foster greater inner-company communication. But these models, which focus solely on operations-oriented activities, do not address the more critical issues required by management. That is, they do not provide management with the processes and scaled perspective to make complex decisions, decisions that will effect the nature and direction of the organization in future environments.

The most important clue pointing to the need for new methods of organizational management are the technological shifts away from mechanically-based production to information-based production. Likewise, as information is produced, it enables people to gain access and acquire value from seeking out new knowledge. What we find is that value in the organization has shifted away from hard assets and people's bodies to the value of the human mind.

A new management model should describe the nature of the relationships between the individual and the organization and between the organization and the environment. Any new management model must be based on new scientific and technological understanding and new perspectives on human organizations and how they work. It is in this vein that SENCORP has been developing and implementing its new management model.

2.   How Can We Develop More Natural Management Models?

Body and mind are natural components of both individuals and, as demonstrated by the SENCORP Management Model, organizations. Advancement activities (mind) revolve around developing knowledge and options for the firm. Survival activities (body) are necessary for the routine, on-going activities of the organization, i.e. the implementation of selected options and its representations to its environment. Traditional management models focus primarily on the body/survival part.

In contrast, the SENCORP model recognizes and connects the management of knowledge development with the management of operation, (planning, production, sales and marketing, etc.) all through a network of scaled responsibilities. The model is based on organizational management replicating individual management. Thus, the model used to manage oneself is the same model used to manage the organization. Because it is both consistent with the way the human brain works (autopoietic cognition) and allows and stimulates simultaneous survival/advancement activities (complex adaptation), this model satisfies the criteria for being more natural than previous models discussed in literature. In addition, the structure and dynamic characteristics of the model have similarities with fractal geometry (chaos theory) and the science of complexity. These theories seem to capture the way most of nature appears to work.

3.   How Can We Describe New, Natural Management Models?

New management models will need to describe the two major interfaces (or boundaries) of the organization: The People/Organization boundary and Organization/Environment boundary. As these descriptions unfold, it will become evident that a significant change has occurred concerning how we think about organizational management. The description will include new terms and concepts and new definitions of old terms and concepts. Language is key to the model. Because old language will greatly inhibit a new model's potential, new management models must be described with new language.

Crossing the divide from traditional and current management models to new models of management cannot occur as a 'great leap'. The transition will coincide with an organization's ability to develop a scaled knowledge base over time.

4.   What Are Some of the Future Challenges for Management Models?

Drawing on developments in the science of complexity and other natural sciences, we find that the survival and advancement of an organization will depend on its ability to recognize itself as a 'complex adaptive' association of individuals. This, in turn, will make the organization itself a complex and adaptive entity. The large international corporation, for example, embodies a complex system of relationships across a great geographical area. Yet its ability to adapt to changes in the environment or even redefine its environment has been limited.

The complex adaptive organization is simultaneously open and closed. It must have a natural order and structure to embody high scale processes that are defined and understood, while at the same time being open to signals (or data) from the environment (see Figure 10.11). It does not operate in a vacuum, but takes in data, formulates internal information, and percolates it to develop knowledge for decision making. These types of structures and processes will assure the survival of the organization in the present and enable advancement activities that promote the organization's survival in the future.

Data to Information to Knowledge Process

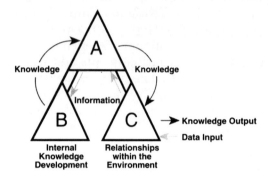

Figure 10.11   Data to information to knowledge process

Appendix: Languaging About Distinctions

This exhibit presents word comparisons for the purpose of conveying meaning. The word pairs (dashed lines) should be considered together in each case in order to provide a comparison that is connected to the understanding of the B realm comparison to the C realm, as a decision-maker (A realm) would see them.

Each word on its own has meaning, but the importance of this exhibit is to relate and compare the meanings of the word pairs (as seen by the A realm) in order to generate another level of meaning constructed from the comparison process.

In addition to comparing word pairs, there is additional meaning to be derived by comparing word sets (solid lines) that are consistent with the B realm comparison to the C realm.

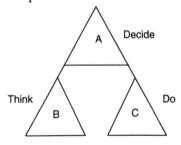

Different concepts in advancement and survival activities

experimentation	implementation
projects	routines
internal	external
knowledge development	data input, knowledge output
competency	capability
multi-scale	single-scale
qualitative	quantitative
analog	digital
network	hierarchy
autopoiesis	signal processing
language development	language use
dialog	negotiation
understanding	agreement

Note

1. This chapter is written by Georg von Krogh, Johan Roos and Ken Slocum.

Postscript: A Final Self-Reference

At this stage some readers may have begun to reflect about the messages in this book. What are the messages? Are we selling you a new solution? Is this the new world view? Will representationism die? In short, are we advocating the new epistemology as the best one? None of these. This book is about knowledge of knowledge. All we have done is to signal to the reader that there is another organizational epistemology. You, the reader, are invited to reflect and to develop your own epistemology. *You decide what is meaningful for you.* If you view this book as one party's languaging in an ongoing dialogue for knowledge development, and yourself as the other party, it becomes clear that you are free to respond to any of the signals. This book is just a brief report from an ongoing knowledge development effort on knowledge in organizations. Because everything said is said from a tradition, and everything you do refers back to what you did, the signals that you respond to will change your life – on different scales. But, as illustrated below, each reader will decide which perturbations this book carries enter into his/her own autopoiesis:

> *Suspicious reader*: If you expect that your new organizational epistemology will be taken seriously within the management and organizational studies realms, you simply must prove to me and my colleagues that you can answer our questions! You must be able to accept or reject hypotheses (or at least show how this would be done) regarding knowledge development. You must tell us how to predict the development of knowledge in organization. You must tell us how knowledge development influences performance of organizations. You must explain the (causal) relationship between power and knowledge development.
>
> *Authors*: But why these questions?
>
> *Suspicious reader*: Because they are the only valid questions for management and organization researchers

Authors: How do you know that they are the only valid questions for researchers in these realms?
Suspicious reader: We know.
Authors: But how do you know that you know?
Suspicious reader: Because we know.[1]

And suddenly the autopoietic process was brought forth...

Note

1.   This dialogue was inspired by King (1993).

References

Abell, D.F. (1993) *Managing With Dual Strategies: Mastering the Present, Preempting the Future* (New York, NY: The Free Press).

Ackoff, R.L. and F.E. Emery (1972) *Purposeful Systems* (London, UK: Tavistock).

Alberts, R.S. and M.A. Runco (eds) (1990) *Theories of Creativity* (Beverly Hills, Calif.: Sage).

Aldrich, H. (1986) *Population Perspectives on Organizations* (Uppsala, Sweden: Acta Universitatis Upsaliensis).

Allison, G.T. (1971) *Essence of Decision* (Boston, Mass.: Little, Brown & Co.).

Anderson, J.R. (1983) *The Architecture of Cognition* (Cambridge, Mass.: Harvard University Press).

Andrew, A.M. (1989) *Self-Organizing Systems* (New York: Gordon & Breach Science Publishers).

Andrews, K.R. (1970) *The Concept of Corporate Strategy* (Homewood, Ill: Dow-Jones-Irwin).

Ansoff, H.I. (1965) *Corporate Strategy: An Analytic Approach to Business Policy for Growth and Expansion* (New York: McGraw-Hill).

Arber, A. (1954) *The Mind and the Eye* (Cambridge, UK: Cambridge University Press).

Argyris, C. and D. Schon (1978) *Organizational Learning* (Reading, Mass.: Addison-Wesley).

Ashby, W. (1960) *An Introduction to Cybernetics* (London, UK: Chapman & Hall).

Astley, W.G. and R.F. Zammuto (1992) 'Organization Science, Managers, and Language Games', *Organization Science*, 3, pp. 443–61.

Bak, P. and K. Chen (1991) 'Self-Organized Criticality', *Scientific American*, January, pp. 26–33.

Ballard, D.H. and S.D. Whitehead (1992) 'Learning Visual Behaviours', in H. Wechsler (ed.), *Neural Networks for Perception*, vols I and II (Boston, Mass.: Academic Press).

Barnard, C. (1938) *The Functions of the Executive* (Boston, Mass.: Harvard University Press).

Barney, J.B. (1991) 'Firm Resources and Sustained Competitive Advantage', *Journal of Management*, 17, pp. 99–120.

Barney, J.B. and W.G. Ouchi (1986) *Organizational Economics* (San Francisco: Jossey-Bass Publishers).

Bartlett, C.A. and S. Goshal (1989) *Managing Across Borders: The Transnational Solution* (Boston, Mass.: Harvard Business School Press).

Bartlett, S.C. (1932) *Remembering: A Study in Experimental and Social Psychology* (Cambridge, UK: Cambridge University Press).

Becker, A. (1991) 'A Short Essay on Languaging', in F. Steier (ed.), *Research and Reflexivity* (Beverly Hills, Calif.: Sage), pp. 226–34.

Beer, S. (1959) *Cybernetics and Management* (London, UK: The English Universities Press).

Berger, P. (1981) *The Sacred Canopy* (Garden City: Doubleday).

Berger, P. and T. Luckman (1966) *The Social Construction of Reality* (New York: Penguin).

Bernstein, R. (1983) *Beyond Objectivism and Relativism: Science, Hermeneutics, and Praxis* (Philadelphia: University of Pennsylvania Press).

von Bertalanffy, L. (1952) *Problems of Life* (London, UK: Watts & Co).

von Bertalanffy, L. (1968) *General System Theory* (New York: George Braziller).

Berthelemy, M. (1971) *L'Ideologie du Hasard et de la Necessité* (Paris: Seuil).

Best, J.B. (1963) 'Protopsychology', *Scientific American*, February, pp. 54–62.

Biederman, I. (1987) 'Recognition-by-Components: A Theory of Human Image Understanding', *Psychological Review*, 94, pp. 115–47.

Bittner, E. (1974) 'The Concept of Organization', in R. Turner (ed.), *Ethnomethodology* (Harmondsworth, UK: Penguin), pp. 267–311.

Blankenburg, E. (1984) 'The Powerty of Evolutionism: A Critique of Teubner's Case for Reflexive Laws', *Law and Society*, vol. 18, pp. 273–89.

Blau, P. (1964) *Exchange and Power in Social Life* (New York: John Wiley).

Bolognesi, T. (1983) 'Automatic Composition: Experiments with Self-Similar Music', *Computer Music Journal*, vol. 7, no. 1 (Spring) pp. 25–36.

Bonner, J.T. (1969) *The Scale of Nature* (New York: Pegasus).

Bourdieu, P. (1977) *Outline of a Theory of Practice* (Cambridge, UK: Cambridge University Press).

Boyatzis, R.E. (1982) *The Competent Manager: A Model for Effective Performance* (New York: Wiley).

Brockriede, W. and D. Ehninger (1960) 'Toulmin on Argument: An Interpretation and Application', *Quarterly Journal of Speech*, 46, pp. 44–53.

Bruner, J.S. (1964) 'Going Beyond the Information Given', in H.E. Gruber, K.R. Hammond and R. Jesser (eds), *Contemporary Approaches to Cognition* (Boston, Mass.: Harvard University Press), pp. 41–69.

Bruner, J.S. and J.M. Anglin (1973) *Beyond the Information Given* (New York: Norton & Co.).

Buckley, W. (1967) *Sociology and Modern Systems Theory* (Englewood Cliffs, NJ: Prentice-Hall).

Cabane, M., P. Rannou, E. Chassefière and G. Israel (1993) 'Fractal Aggregates in Titan's Atmosphere', *Planet. Space. Sci.*, vol. 41, no. 4, pp. 257–67.

Calvino, I. (1990) *Six Memos for the Next Millennium* (London, UK: Cage).

Campbell, D.J. (1988) 'Task Complexity: A Review and Analysis', *Academy of Management Review*, vol. 13, no. 1, pp. 40–52.

Cantril, H. (1963) 'A Study of Aspirations', *Scientific American*, February, pp. 41–5.

Chakravarthy, B.S. and P. Lorange (1991) *Managing in the Strategy Process* (Englewood Cliffs, NJ: Prentice Hall).

Chellam, S. and M.R. Wiesner (1993) 'Fluid Mechanics and Fractal Aggregates', *Water Research*, vol. 27, no. 9, pp. 1493–6.

Cherniak, C. (1986) *Minimal Rationality* (Cambridge, Mass.: MIT Press).

Churchman, C.W. (1968) *The Systems Approach* (New York: Delta Publishing).

Churchman, C.W. and A.H. Schainblatt (1965) 'The Researcher and the Manager: A Dialectic of Implementation', *Management Science*, 11, pp. B69–B87.

Clayton, D.E. (1932) 'A Comparative Study of the Non-Nervous Elements in the Nervous Systems of Invertebrates', *Journal of Entomology and Zoology*, 24, pp. 3–22.

Cookson, C. (1994) 'Is the Quark Hunt Over?', *Financial Times*, 8 May.

Cornford, F.M. (1937) *Plato's Cosmology: The 'Timaens' Translated with a Commentary* (London: Routledge & Kegan Paul).

Crutchfield, J.P., J. Doyne Farmer, N.P. Packard and R.S. Shaw (1986) 'Chaos', *Scientific American*, December, pp. 38–49.

Cyert, R.M. and J.G. March (1963) *A Behavioural Theory of the Firm*. Reprint 1992 (London, UK: Blackwell).

Cyert, R.M. and J.R. Williams (1993) 'Organizations, Decision Making and Strategy: Overview and Comment', *Strategic Management Journal*, Special Issue (Summer) 14, pp. 5–11.

Cyert, R.M., P. Kumar and J.R. Williams (1993) 'Information, Market Imperfections, and Strategy', *Strategic Management Journal*, Special Issue (Summer) 14, pp. 47–59.

Daft, R.L. and K.E. Weick (1984) 'Toward a Model of Organizations as Interpretation Systems', *Academy of Management Review*, 9, pp. 284–95.

Dahl, R. (1991) *The Vicar of Nibbleswicke* (London, UK: Century Random).

Deal, T. and A. Kennedy (1982) *Corporate Cultures: The Rites and Rituals of Corporate Life* (Reading, Mass.: Addison-Wesley Publishing Company).

Deggau, H.G. (1988) 'The Communicative Autonomy of the Legal System', in G. Teubner (ed.), *Autopoietic Law: A New Approach to Law and Society* (Berlin: Walter de Gruyter), pp. 128–51.

Derrida, J. (1978) *Writing and Difference* (Chicago, Ill.: University of Chicago Press).

Derrida, J. (1982) *Margins of Philosophy* (Chicago, Ill.: University of Chicago Press).

Derrida, J. (1988) *Limited Inc.* (Evanston, Ill.: Northwestern University Press).

Dewey, J. (1960) *The Quest for Certainty: (A Study for the Relation of Knowledge and Action)* (New York: G.P. Putnam).

Doedel, E. (1981) 'AUTO — A Program for the Automatic Bifurcation Analysis of Autonomous Systems', *Congressus Numerentium*, vol. 30, pp. 265–84.

Donaldson, T. and T.W. Dunfee (1994) 'Toward a Unified Conception of Business Ethics: Integrative Social Contracts Theory', *Academy of Management Review*, vol. 19, no. 2, pp. 252–84.

Dressler, A. (1987) 'The Large-Scale Streaming of Galaxies', *Scientific American*, September, pp. 38–46.

Dreyfus, H. and S. Dreyfus (1986) *Mind over Machine* (New York: MacMillan Free Press).

Dupeuy, J-P (1988) 'On the Supposed Closure of Normative Systems', in G. Teubner (ed), *Autpoietic Law: A New Approach to Law and Society* (Berlin: Walter de Gruyter), pp. 51–69.

Dutton, G.H. (1981) 'Fractal Enhancement of Cartographic Line Detail', *The American Cartographer*, vol. 8, no. 1, pp. 23–40.

Dutton, J. and J. Dukerich (1991) 'Keeping An Eye in the Mirror: The Role of Image and Identity in Organizational Adaption', *Academy of Management Journal*, 34, pp. 517–54.

Edelman, S. (1992) 'A Network Model of Object Recognition in Human Vision', in H. Wechsler (ed.), *Neural Networks for Perception*, vols I and II (Boston, Mass.: Academic Press).

Edgar, G.A. (ed.) (1993) *Classics on Fractals* (Reading, Mass.: Addison-Wesley).

Eisenberg, E.M. (1984) 'Ambiguity as a Strategy in Organizational Communication', *Communications Monographs*, 51, pp. 227–42.

Eisenberg, E.M. and M.G. Witten (1987) 'Reconsidering in Openness in Organizational Communication', *Academy of Management Review*, 12, pp. 418–26.

Emery, F.E. (1969) *Systems Thinking* (Harmondsworth, UK: Penguin).

Eoyang, E. (1989) 'Chaos Misread: or, There's a Wonton in My Soup!', *Comparative Literature Studies*, vol. 26, no. 3, pp. 271–84.

Fabbri, R. *et al.* (1980) 'Measurement of the Cosmic-Background Large-Scale Anisotrophy in the Millimeteric Region', *Physical Review Letters*, vol. 44, no. 23 (June) pp. 1563–68.

Feder, J. (1988) *Fractals* (New York: Plenum Press).

Feldman, J.A. and D.H. Ballard (1982) 'Connectionist Models and Their Properties', *Cognitive Science*, 6, pp. 206–15.

Feldman, M. (1987) 'Electronic Mail and Weak Ties in Organizations', *Office: Technology and People*, 3, pp. 83–101.

Feyerabend, P. (1972) 'How To Be a Good Empiricist', in H. Morick (ed.), *Challenges to Empiricism* (California: Bellmont).

Fiol, C.M. (1989) 'A Semiotic Analysis of Corporate Language: Organizational Boundaries and Joint venturing', *Administrative Science Quarterly*, 34, 2, pp. 277–303.

Fiol, C.M. (1990) 'Narrative Semiotics: Theory, Procedure, and Illustration', in A. Huff (ed.), *Mapping Strategic Thought* (Chichester, UK: Wiley), pp. 377–402.

Fiol, C.M. (1991) 'Managing Culture as a Competitive Resource: An Identity-Based View of Sustainable Competitive Advantage', *Journal of Management*, 17, pp. 191–211.

Fletcher, K.E. and A.S. Huff (1990). 'Argument Mapping', in A.S. Huff (ed.), *Mapping Strategic Thought* (Chichester: John Wiley & Sons) pp. 355–75.

von Foerster, H. (1962) *Principles of Self-Organization* (New York: Pergamon Press).

von Foerster, H.(1972) 'Responsibilities of Competence', *Journal of Cybernetics*, vol. 2, no. 2, pp. 1–6.

von Foerster, H. (1981) *Observing Systems* (Seaside, Cal.: InterSystems Publications).

Foucault, M. (1980) *Power/Knowledge* (Brighton; Harvester Press).

Frost, P., L.F. Moore, M.R. Louis, C.C. Lundberg and J. Martin (eds) (1991), *Reframing Organizational Culture* (Newburry Park, Calif.: Sage).

Gaines, B.R. (1979) 'General Systems Research: Quo Vadis?', *General Systems Yearbook*, vol. 24, pp. 1–9.

Galbraith, J.R. (1977) *Organization Design* (Reading, Mass.: Addison-Wesley).

Gardner, H. (1985) *The Mind's New Science: A History of the Cognitive Revolution* (New York: Basic Books).

Gardner, H. (1990) *Creating Minds* (New York: Basic Books).

Geertz, C. (1973) *The Interpretation of Cultures* (New York: Basic Books).

Geschwind, N. (1972) 'Language and the Brain', *Scientific American*, April, p. 76.

Geyer, F. (1992) 'Autopoiesis and Social Systems–1', *International Journal of General Systems*, vol. 21, pp. 175–83.

Ghemawat, P. and J.E. Ricart i Costa (1993) 'The organizational Tension Between Static and Dynamic Efficiency', *Strategic Management Journal*, Special Issue, 14 (Summer) pp. 59–76.

Ginsberg, A. (1988) 'Measuring and Modelling Changes in Strategy: Theoretical Foundations and Empirical Directions', *Strategic Management Journal*, 9, pp. 559–75.

Ginsberg, A. (1990) 'Connecting Diversification to Performance: A Socio-Cognitive Approach', *Academy of Management Review*, 15, pp. 514–35.

Gioia, D.A. and C.C. Manz (1985) 'Linking Cognition and Behaviour: A Script Processing Interpretation of Vicarious Learning', *Academy of Management Review*, 10, pp. 527–39.

Gioia, D.A. and K. Chittipendi (1991) 'Sensemaking and Sensegiving in Strategic Change Initiation', *Strategic Management Journal*, 12, pp. 433–48.

Gleick, J. (1987) *Chaos: The Making of a New Science* (New York: Viking Press).

Goguen, J.A. and F.J. Varela (1979). 'Systems and Distinctions; Duality and Complementarity', *International Journal of General Systems*, 5, pp. 31–43.

Goldberger, A.L. and B.J. West (1987) 'Fractals in Physiology and Medicine', *The Yale Journal of Biology and Medicine*, 60, pp. 421–35.

Goldberger, A.L., D.R. Rigney and B.J. West (1990) 'Chaos and Fractals in Human Physiology', *Scientific American*, February, pp. 35–41.

Goldman, A.I. (1986) *Epistemology and Cognition* (Cambridge, Mass.: Harvard University Press).

Goldman, A.I. (1993) *Philosophical Applications of Cognitive Science* (Boulder, Col.: Westview Press).

Gomez, P. and G.J.B. Probst (1983) 'Organizational Closure in Management — a Complementary View to Contingency Approaches', paper presented at the American Society for Cybernations Meeting on Autonomy, Intervention and Dependence, Philadelphia, and Working Paper, University of Geneva, 1992.

Gregersen, H. and L. Sailer (1993) 'Chaos Theory and Its Implications for Social Science Research', *Human Relations*, vol. 46, no. 7, pp. 777–802.

Grinyer, P., D.G. Mayes and P. McKiernan (1988) *Sharpbenders* (Oxford, UK: Blackwell).

Hærem, T. (1993) 'Knowledge Transfer: The Key to Change', MSc thesis, Norwegian School of Management.

Hærem, T., G. von Krogh and J. Roos (1993) 'Knowledge Based Strategic Change', paper presented at the Strategic Management Society Conference, Chicago, 15–17 September.

Hage, J. and C.H. Powers (1992) *Post-Industrial Lives: Roles and Relationships in the 21st Century* (Newsbury Park, Calif.: Sage).

Hall, N. (ed.) (1991) *Exploring Chaos: A Guide to the New Science of Disorder* (New York: W.W. Norton & Co.).

Hamel, G. (1991) 'Competition for Competence and Inter-Partner Learning Within International Strategic Alliances', *Strategic Management Journal*, 12, pp. 83–103.

Handy, C. (1989) *The Age of Unreason* (London, UK: Arrow).

Hannan, M.T. and J. Freeman (1977) 'The Population Ecology of Organizations', *American Journal of Sociology*, vol. 82, pp. 929–64.

Hannan, M.T. and J. Freeman (1989) *Organizational Ecology* (Cambridge, Mass.: Harvard University Press).

Haspeslagh, P. (1982) 'Portfolio Planning: Uses and Limits', *Harvard Business Review*, January–February, pp. 58–73.

Hawking, S.W. and G.F.R. Ellis (1973) *The Large Scale Structure of Space-Time*, 11th edn (Cambridge, UK: The Press Syndicate of the University of Cambridge).

von Hayek, F.A. (1975) 'Kinds of Order in Society', *Studies in Social Theory*, no. 5 (Menlo Parl, Calif.: Institute for Humane Studies).

von Hayek, F.A. (1988) *The Fatal Conceit: The Errors of Socialism* (Chicago, Ill.: University of Chicago Press).

Hayles, N.K. (ed.) (1991) *Chaos and Disorder: Complex Dynamics in Literature and Science* (Chicago, Ill.: The University of Chicago Press).

Hedberg, B. (1981) 'How Organizations Learn and Unlearn', in P.C. Nystrom and W. Starbuck (eds), *Handbook of Organizational Design*, vol. I (New York: Oxford University Press), pp. 3–27.

Hedberg, B., P. Nystrom and W. Starbuck (1976) 'Camping on the Seesaws: Prescriptions for Designing Self-Designing Organizations', *Administrative Science Quarterly*, 21, pp. 41–65.

Hedlund, G. (1986) 'The Hypermodern MNC — a Heterarchy?', *Human Resource Management*, 25, 1, pp. 9–35.

Heimer, C. (1976) *Uncertainty and Vulnerability in Social Relations* (mimeographed: University of Chicago).

Hempill, J.K. (1959) 'Job Descriptions for Executives', *Harvard Business Review*, vol. 37, no. 5.

Henshel, R.L. (1990) 'Credibility and Confidence Loops in Social Prediction', in F. Geyer and J. Van der Zouwen (eds), *Self-Referencing in Social Systems* (Salinsa, Calif.: Intersystems Publications) pp. 31–58.

Herbert, E. (1937) *De Veritate* (Bristol, UK: Thoemmes Press).

Herriot, S.R., D.A. Levinthal and J.G. March (1985) 'Learning from Experience in Organizations', *American Economic Review*, 75, pp. 298–302.

Herrmann, H. (1994) 'Spontaneous Density Waves in Traffic Flow and Related Dissipative Transport', paper presented at the 1994 Gordon Research Conference on Fractals, 1–6 May, San Miniato, Tuscany, Italy.

Hirsch, F. (1978) *Social Limits to Growth* (Cambridge, Mass.: Harvard University Press).

Hergan, J. (1994) 'Profile: Philip W. Anderson', *Scientific American*, November, pp. 19–22.

Hosmer, LaRue (1994) 'Strategic Planning as if Ethics Mattered', *Strategic Management Journal*, Special Issue, Summer, pp. 17–34.

Hout, T., M.E. Porter and E. Rudden (1982) 'How Global Companies Win Out', *Harvard Business Review*, September–October, pp. 98–108.

Huber, G.P. (1991) 'Organizational Learning: The Contributing Processes and the Literatures', *Organizational Science*, 2, pp. 89–115.

Huemer, L. (1994) 'Trust in Interorganizational Relationships: A Conceptual Model', Conference Proceedings from the 10th I.M.P. Conference in Groningen.

Huff, A.S. (1983) 'Industry Influence on Strategy Reformulation', *Strategic Management Journal*, 3, pp. 119–31.

Huff, A.S. (ed.) (1990) *Mapping Strategic Thought* (Chichester, UK: Wiley).

Hymer, S. (1977) *The International Operations of National Firms: A Study of Direct Investment* (Chicago, Ill.: MIT Press).

in 't Veld, R.J., L. Schaap, C.J.A.M. Termeer, and M.J.W. van Twist (1991) *Autopoiesis and Configuration Theory: New Approaches to Social Steering* (Dordrecht: Kluwer Academic Publishers).

International Herald Tribune (1994) 'Cardinals Dive Into the Population Fray: Big Effort on to Block Abortion Issue at World Conference', by Alan Cowell, 15 June, p. 1.

Jantsch, E. (1980) *The Self-Organizing Universe: Scientific and Human Implications of the Emerging Paradigm of Evolution* (Oxford and New York: Pergamon Press).

Jarillo, J.C. (1988) 'On Strategic Networks', *Strategic Management Journal*, 9, pp. 31–43.

Joachim, H.H. (1969) *The Nature of Truth: An Essay* (New York: Greenwood Press), reprint of the 1906 edition.

Joseph, R. (1993) *The Naked Neuron: Evolution and the Language of the Body and Brain* (New York: Plenum Press).

Jurgens, H., H-O. Peitgen and D. Saupe (1990) 'The Language of Fractals', *Scientific American*, August, pp. 40–7.

Jurgens, H., H-O. Peitgen and D. Saupe (1992) *Chaos and Fractals: New Frontiers of Science* (New York: Springer-Verlag).

Kahneman, D. and A. Tversky (1973) 'On the Psychology of Prediction', *Psychological Review*, 80, pp. 237–51.

Kauffman, S.A. (1990) 'Requirements for Evolvability in Complex Systems: Orderly Dynamics and Frozen Components', *Physica D*, vol. 42, pp. 135–52.

Kauffman, S.A. (1991) 'Antichaos and Adaptation', *Scientific American*, August, pp. 64–70.

Kauffman, S.A. (1993) *The Origins of Order: Self-Organizing and Selection in Evolution* (New York/Oxford: Oxford University Press).

Keller, J.M., R.M. Crownover and R.U. Chan (1987) 'Characteristics of Natural Scenes Related to the Fractal Dimension', *IEEE Transactions on Pattern Analysis and Machine Intelligence*, 9, pp. 621–7.

Kellert, S.H. (1993) *In the Wake of Chaos* (Chicago, Ill.: The University of Chicago Press).

Kemp-Smith, N. (ed.) (1947) *Hume's Dialogues Concerning Natural Religion* (London and Edinburgh: Nelson Publishing).

Kennealy, P. (1988) 'Talking About Autopoiesis — Order From Noise?' in G. Teubner, (ed.), *Autopoietic Law: A New Approach to Law and Society* (Berlin: Walter de Gruyter), pp. 349–68.

Kenny, A. (1973) *Wittgenstein* (Harmondsworth, UK: Penguin).

Kiesler, S., J. Siegel and T.W. McGuire (1984) 'Social Psychological Aspects of Computer-Mediated Communication', *American Psychologist*, vol. 39, no. 10, pp. 1123–34.

Kilduff, M. (1993) 'Deconstructing Organizations', *Academy of Management Review*, January, pp. 13–31.

King, A. (1993) 'The "Truth" About Autopoiesis', *Journal of Law and Society*, vol. 20, no. 2 (Summer) pp. 218–36.

Kirsh, A.D. (1979) 'The Spin of the Proton', *Scientific American*, May, pp. 66–80.

Klein, K.J., F. Dansereau and R.J. Hall (1994) 'Levels Issues in Theory Development, Data Collection, and Analysis', *Academy of Management Review*, vol. 19, no. 2, pp. 195–229.

Knoespel, K.J. (1991) 'The Employment of Chaos: Instability and Narrative Order', in N.K. Hayles (ed.), *Chaos and Disorder: Complex Dynamics in Literature and Science* (Chicago, Ill.: University of Chicago Press) pp. 100–22.

Kripke, S. (1982) *On Rules and Private Language* (Cambridge, Mass.: Harvard University Press).

Krishna, D. (1989) 'Thinking vs. Thought: Strategies for Conceptual Creativity', in D.M. Topping, D.C. Crowell and V.N., Kobayashi (eds), *Thinking Across Cultures: The Third International Conference on Thinking* (Hillsdale, NY: Lawrence Erlbaum Associates) pp. 195–204.

von Krogh, G. and J. Roos (1992) 'From Knowledge to Competitive Advantage: An Empirical Study of Strategic Arguments', paper presented at the conference on 'Knowledge Workers in Contemporary Organisations', University of Lancaster, September.

von Krogh, G. and S. Vicari (1993) 'An Autopoiesis Approach to Experimental Strategic Learning', in P. Lorange, B. Chakravarthy, J. Roos and A. Van de Ven, *Implementing Strategic Processes: Change, Learning and Co-operation* (London: Blackwell) pp. 394–410.

von Krogh, G., A. Sinatra and H. Singh (eds) (1994) *The Management of Corporate Acquisitions* (London: Macmillan).

von Krogh, G., J. Roos and K. Slocum (1994) 'An Essay on Corporate Epistemology', *Strategic Management Journal*, Special Issue, Summer, pp. 53–71.

Krohn, W. and G. Kuppers (1989) 'Self-Organization: A New Approach to Evolutionary Epistemology', in K. Hahlweg and C.A. Hooker (eds), *Issues in Evolutionary Epistemology* (Albany, NY: State University of New York Press), pp. 151–70.

Lai, L. (1992) 'Selective Attention in Problem Finding', Doctoral Dissertation, The Norwegian School of Economics and Business Administration, Norway.

Langton, C. (1990) 'Computation at the Edge of Chaos: Phase Transitions and Emergent Computation', *Physica D.*, vol. 42, pp. 12–37.

Lant, T.K. and S.J. Mezias (1990) 'Managing Discontinuous Change: A Simulation Study of Organizational Learning and Entrepreneurship', *Strategic Management Journal*, 11, pp. 147–79.

Lant, T.K., F.J. Milliken and B. Batra (1992) 'The Role of Managerial Learning and Interpretation in Strategic Persistence and Reorientation: An Empirical Exploration', *Strategic Management Journal*, 13, pp. 585–608.

Latour, B. (1987) *Science in Action: How to Follow Scientists and Engineers Through Society* (Cambridge, Mass.: Harvard University Press).

Latour, B. (1991) 'The Politics of Explanation: An Alternative', in S. Woolgar (ed.), *Knowledge and Reflexivity: New Frontiers in the Sociology of Knowledge* (London, UK: Sage).

Leonard-Barton, D. (1992) 'Core Capabilities and Core-Rigidities: A Paradox in Managing New Product Development', *Strategic Management Journal*, 13, pp. 111–25.

Levinthal, D.A. and J.G. March (1993) 'The Myopia of Learning', *Strategic Management Journal*, Special Issue (Summer) 14, pp. 92–112.

Lewis, D. (1990) 'Languages and Language', in A.P. Martinich (ed.), *The Philosophy of Language* (New York: Oxford University Press).

Li, T.Y. and J.A. Yorke (1975) 'Period Three Implies Chaos', *American Mathematics Monthly*, 82, pp. 481–5.

Lorange, P. (1980) *Corporate Planning* (Englewood Cliffs, NJ: Prentice-Hall).

Lorange, P. and J. Roos (1992) *Strategic Alliances: Formation, Implementation and Evolution* (Oxford, UK: Basil Blackwell).

Lorenz, E.N. (1963) 'Deterministic Nonperiodic Flow', *Journal of the Atmospheric Science*, vol. 20, pp. 130–41.

Lorenz, E.N. (1993) *The Essence of Chaos* (Seattle: University of Washington Press).

Luhmann, N. (1979) *Trust and Power* (Chichester, UK: Wiley).

Luhmann, N. (1982) *The Differentiation of Society* (New York: Columbia University Press).

Luhmann, N. (1984) *Soziale Systeme: Grundriss einer Allgemeine Theorie* (Frankfurt: Suhrkamp).

Luhmann, N. (1985) *A Sociological Theory of Law* (London: Routledge & Kegan Paul).

Luhmann N. (1986) 'The Autopoiesis of Social Systems', in F. Geyer and J. Van der Zouwen (eds), *Sociocybernetic Paradoxes — Observation, Control, and Evolution of Self-Steering Systems* (London, UK: SAGE) pp. 172–92.

Luhmann, N. (1987) 'The Representation of Society Within Society', *Current Sociological*, vol. 35, pp. 101–8.

Luhmann, N. (1988) 'The Unity of the Legal System', in G. Teubner (ed.), *Autopoietic Law: A New Approach to Law and Society* (Berlin: de Gruyter), pp. 12–35.

Luhmann, N. (1990a) *Die Wissenschaft der Gesellschaft* (Frankfurt: Suhrkamp).

Luhmann, N. (1990b) *Essays on Self-Reference* (New York: Columbia University Press).

Luhmann, N. (1992) *Ecological Communication* (Cambridge, UK: Polity Press).

Luhmann, N. (1993) *Risk: A Sociological Theory* (Berlin: De Gruyter).

Lyles, M. and C. Schwenk (1992) 'Top Management, Strategy and Organizational Knowledge Structures', *Journal of Management Studies*, 29 (March) pp. 155–74.

Lyotard, J.F. (1984) *The Post-Modern Condition: A Report on Knowledge* (Minneapolis: University of Minnesota Press).

Mahoney, J.T. and J.R. Pandian (1992) 'The Resource-Based View Within the Conversation of Strategic Management', *Strategic Management Journal*, 13, pp. 363–80.

Mandelbrot, B.(1967) 'How Long is the Coast of Britain? Statistical Self-Similarity and Fractional Dimension', *Science*, 156, pp. 636–9.

Mandelbrot, B.B. (1983) *The Fractal Geometry of Nature* (New York: W.H. Freeman & Co.) pp. 71–86.

March, J. (1976) 'The Technology of Foolishness', in J. March and J.P. Olsen (eds), *Ambiguity and Choice in Organizations* (Oslo, Norway: Universitetsforlaget) pp. 69–81.

March, J.G. (1988) *Decision and Organizations* (Oxford: Basil Blackwell).

March, J.G. and H. Simon (1958) *Organizations* (New York: Wiley).

March, J.G. and J.P. Olsen (1975) 'The Uncertainty of the Past: Organizational Learning Under Ambiguity', *European Journal of Political Research*, 3, pp. 141–61.

March, J.G. and J.P. Olsen (1976) *Ambiguity and Choice in Organizations* (Bergen, Norway: Universitetsforlaget).

Martinich, A.P. (ed.) (1990) *The Philosophy of Language* (New York: Oxford University Press).

Mason, R. and I. Mitroff (1982) *Challenging Strategic Planning Assumptions* (New York: Wiley & Sons).

Maturana, H. (1978) 'The Biology of Language: The Epistemology of Reality', in G.A. Miller and E. Lelleberg (eds), *Psychology and Biology of Language and Thought: Essays in Honor of Eric Lenneberg* (New York: Academic Press).

Maturana, H. (1988) 'Reality: The Search for Objectivity or the Quest for a Compelling Argument', *Irish Journal of Psychology*, vol. 9, no. 11, pp. 25–82.

Maturana, H. (1991) 'Science and Daily Life: The Ontology of Scientific Explanations', in F. Steier (ed.), *Research and Reflexivity* (Beverly Hills, Calif.: Sage) pp. 30–52.

Maturana, H. and F.J. Varela (1978) 'Preliminary Remarks', in M. Zeleney (ed.), *Autopoiesis: Theory of the Living Organization* (Amsterdam: North-Holland).

Maturana, H. and F.J. Varela (1980) *Autopoiesis and Cognition: The Realization of the Living* (London: Reidl).

Maturana, H. and F.J. Varela (1987) *The Tree of Knowledge* (Boston, Mass.: Shambhala).

May, R.M. (1976) 'Simple Mathematical Models with Very Complicated Dynamics', *Nature*, vol. 261, pp. 459–69.

McCulloch, W.S. and W. Pitts (1943) 'A Logical Calculus of Immanent in Nervous Activity', *Bulletin of Mathematical Biophysics*, 5. Reprinted in W.S. McCulloch (ed.) (1965) *Embodiments of Mind* (Cambridge, Mass.: The MIT Press).

Medio, G. (1993) *Chaotic Dynamic: Theory and Applications to Economics* (Cambridge, UK: University Press).

Meeks, G. (1977) *Disappointing Marriage: A Study From the Gains of Merger* (London: Cambridge University Press).

Meherabian, A. (1971) *Silent Messages* (Belmount, Calif.: Wadsworth).

Merleau-Ponty, M. (1963) *The Structure of Behaviour* (Boston, Mass.: Beacon Press).

Meyer, A.D. (1984) 'Mingling Decision Making Metaphors', *Academy of Management Review*, 9, pp. 6–17.

Meyer, M.W. and L.G. Zucker (1989) *Permanently Failing Organizations* (London: Sage Publications, Inc.)

Miall, L.C. (1912) *The Early Naturalists: Their Lives and Works (1530–1789)* (London, UK: Macmillan and Co.).

Minsky, M.A. (1975) 'A Framework for Presenting Knowledge', in P.H. Winston (ed.), *The Psychology of Computer Vision* (New York: McGraw-Hill).

Minsky, M.A. (1986) *The Society of Mind* (New York: Simon & Schuster).

Minsky, M.A. and S. Pappert (1987) *Perceptrons* (Cambridge, Mass.: MIT Press).

Mintzberg, H. (1983) *Structures in Five* (Englewood Cliffs, NJ: Prentice-Hall International).

Mintzberg, H. (1989) *Mintzberg on Management* (New York: The Free Press).

Mintzberg, H. (1990) 'Strategy Formation: Schools of Thought', in J.W. Fredrickson (ed.), *Perspectives on Strategic Management* (New York: Harper Business) pp. 105–236.

Mintzberg, H. (1991) 'Five Ps for Strategy', in H. Mintzberg and J.B. Quinn (eds), *The Strategy Process* (London, UK: Prentice-Hall).

Mintzberg, H. and J. Waters (1985) 'Of Strategies, Deliberate and Emergent', *Strategic Management Journal*, pp. 257–72.

Monod, J. (1970) *Le Hasard et la Nécessité* (Paris: Seuil).

Montague, W.P. (1962) *The Ways of Knowing or the Methods of Philosophy*, 6th impression (London: George Allen & Unwin Ltd.).

Moore, E. (1964) 'Mathematics in the Biological Sciences', *Scientific American*, September, pp. 149–64.

Morgan, G. (1986) *Images of Organization* (Beverly Hills, Calif.: Sage).

Morin, E. (1982) 'Can We Conceive of a Science of Autonomy?', *Human Systems Management*, 3, pp. 201–306.

Morrison, P. and P. Morrison (1982) *Powers of Ten: About the Relative Size of Things in the Universe* (New York: Scientific American Library).

Mullin, T. (ed.) (1993) *The Nature of Chaos* (Oxford: Clarendon Press).

Nelson, R.D. and S. Winter (1982) *An Evolutionary Theory of Economic Change* (Cambridge, Mass.: The Bellhop Press).

von Neumann, J. (1966) *Theory of Self-Reproducing Automata* (Urbana, Ill.: University of Illinois Press) (edited and completed by A. Burks).

Newell, A. and H. Simon (1972) *Human Problem Solving* (Englewood Cliffs, NJ: Prentice-Hall).

Newell, A. and H.A. Simon (1956) 'The Logic Theory Machine: A Complex Information Processing System', *Transactions on Information Theory*, vol. IT-2, 3, pp. 61–79.

Nichols, N.A. (1993) 'Efficient? Chaotic? What's the New Finance?', *Harvard Business Review*, March-April, pp. 50–60.

Nisbett, R. and L. Ross (1980) *Human Inference; Strategies and Shortcomings of Social Judgement* (Englewood Cliffs, NJ: Prentice-Hall).

Nonaka, I. (1991) 'The Knowledge Creating Company', *Harvard Business Review* November-December, pp. 96–104.

O'Gorman, D. (1993) 'Chaos Theory: Implications for Strategic Thought', paper presented at the 13th Strategic Management Society conference, Chicago, 12–15 September.

Oldershaw, R.L. (1981) 'Conceptual Foundations of the Self-Similar Hierarchical Cosmology', *International Journal of General Systems*, vol. 7, pp. 151–7.

Oldershaw, R.L. (1982a) 'New Evidence for the Principle of Self-Similarity', *International Journal of General Systems*, vol. 9, pp. 37–42.

Oldershaw, R.L. (1982b) 'Empirical and Theoretical Support for Self-Similarity Between Atomic and Stellar Systems', *International Journal of General Systems*, vol. 8, pp. 1–5.

Olson, D.R. (1977) 'From Utterance to Text: The Bias of Language in Speech and Writing', *Harvard Educational Review*, 47, pp. 257–81.

Onida, P. (1968) *Economia d'azienda* (Torino: Utet).

Osborne, M.J. (1990) 'Financial Chaos', *Management Accounting*, November, pp. 32–3.

Østerberg, T. (1988) *Metasociology* (Oslo: Norwegian University Press).

Penrose, L.S. (1959) Self-Reproducing Machines, *Scientific American*, June, pp. 105–14.

Peters, T.J. and R.H. Waterman jr. (1982) *In Search of Excellence* (New York: Harper & Row Publishers).

Pfeffer, J. (1981) *Power in Organizations* (Cambridge, Mass.: Ballinger Publishing Company).

Pfeffer, J. (1992) *Managing with Power: Politics and Influence in Organizations* (Cambridge, Mass.: Harvard Business School Press).

Pfeffer, J. and G.R. Salancik (1978) *The External Control of Organizations: A Resource Dependency Perspective* (New York: Harper & Row).

Plato/North Fowler (1987) *Plato, Vol. VII Theaetetus Sophist* (Cambridge, Mass.: Harvard University Press).

Poincaré, H. (1880) *Mémoire sur les courbes d'dfinies par les équations différentielles*, I–IV, Oeuvre I (Paris: Gaunthiers-Villars).

Poincaré, H. (1890) 'Sur les équations de la dynamique et le probléme de trois corps', *Acta Mathematica*, 13, pp. 5–270.

Poincaré, H. (1899) *Les Methods Nouvelles de la Mechanique Celeste* (Paris: Gaunthiers-Villars).

Polanyi, M. (1958) *Personal Knowledge* (Chicago, Ill.: University of Chicago Press).

Porter, M.E. (1980). *Competitive Strategy: Techniques for Analyzing Industries and Competitors* (New York: The Free Press).

Porush, D. (191) 'Fictions and Dissipative Structures: Prigogine's Theory and Postmodernism's Roadshow', in N.K. Hayles (ed.), *Chaos and Disorder: Complex Dynamics in Literature and Science* (Chicago, Ill.: University of Chicago Press) pp. 54–84.

Prahalad, C.K. and R. Bettis (1986) 'The Dominant Logic: A New Linkage Between Diversity and Performance', *Strategic Management Journal*, 7, pp. 485–501.

Prigogine, I. and I. Stengers (1984) *Order out of Chaos: Man's New Dialogue with Nature* (London: Heinemann).

Proctor, W.G. (1978) 'Negative Absolute Temperatures', *Scientific American*, August, p. 90.

Quinn, R.E. and K.S. Cameron (eds) (1988) *Paradox and Transformation: Toward a Theory of Change in Organization and Management* (Cambridge, Mass: Ballinger).

Reif, F. (1964) 'Quantized Vortex Rings in Superfluid Helium', *Scientific American*, December, p. 116.

Rempel, J.K., J.G. Holmes and M.P. Zanna (1987) 'Trust in Close Relationships', *Journal of Personality and Social Psychology*, 49, 1, pp. 95–12.

Rittel, H.W. (1972) 'One the Planning Crisis: System Analysis of the First and Second Generation', *Bedriftsøkonomen*, 8, pp. 390–6.

Roos, J., and G. von Krogh (1992) 'Figuring out Your Competence Configuration', *European Management Journal*, 4 (December) pp. 422–7.

Roos, J., G. von Krogh and G. Yip (1994) 'An Epistemology of Globalizing Firms', *International Business Review*, 3, 4.

Rorty, R. (1980) *Philosophy and the Mirror of Nature* (Princeton, NJ: Princeton University Press).

Rorty, R. (1989) *Contingency, Irony, and Solidarity* (New York: Cambridge University Press).

Rorty, R. (ed.) (1992) *The Linguistic Turn: Essays in Philosophical Method* (Chicago, Ill.: University of Chicago Press).

Rosen, R. (1987) 'Some Comments on Systems and Systems Theory', *International Journal of General Systems*, vol. 13, pp. 1–3.

Rosenau, P.M. (1992) *Post-Modernism and the Social Sciences: Insights, Inroads, and Intrusions* (Princeton, NJ: Princeton University Press).

Rousseau, D. (1985) 'Issues of Level in Organizational Research: Multilevel and Cross-Level Perspectives', in L.L. Cummings and B.M. Staw (eds), *Research in Organizational Behaviour*, vol. 7 (Greenwich, CT: JAI Press) pp. 1–37.

Ruelle, D. (1991) *Chance and Chaos* (Princeton, NJ: Princeton University Press).

Sackman, S. (1991) *Cultural Knowledge in Organizations* (Beverly Hills, Calif.: Sage).

Sakaiya, T. (1991) *The Knowledge Value Revolution* (London, UK: Bellew).

Sandelands, L.E. and R.E. Stablein (1987) 'The Concept of Organization Mind Research', in *The Sociology of Organizations*, 5, pp. 135–62.

Sander, L.M. (1987) 'Fractal Growth', *Scientific American*, January, pp. 82–7.

Schank, R. and R.P. Abelson (1977) *Scripts, Plans, Goals, and Understanding: An Inquiry into Human Knowledge Structures* (Hilsdale, NJ: Lawrence Erlbaum).

Schein, E.H. (1985) *Organizational Culture and Leadership: A Dynamic View* (San Francisco: Jossey-Bass Publishers).

Schendel, D. (1993) 'Introduction to the Winter 1993 Special Issue: Organization, Decision Making and Strategy', *Strategic Management Journal*, Special Issue, Winter, pp. 1–4.

Schmuckler, M.A. and D.L. Gilden (1993) 'Auditory Perception of Fractal Countours', *Journal of Experimental Psychology: Human Perception and Performance*, vol. 19, no. 3, pp. 641–60.

Schutz, A. (1970) *On Phenomenology and Social Relations* (Chicago, Ill.: University of Chicago Press).

Schutz, A. and T. Luckman (1985/1989) *The Structures of the Life-World*, vols 1 and 2 (Evanston, Ill.: Northwestern University Press).

Scott, W.R. (1987) *Organizations: Rationale, Natural, and Open Systems* (Englewood Cliffs, Calif: Prentice-Hall).

SENCORP (1992) 'The Sencorp Management Model', paper presented at the 30th Annual Strategic Management Conference, London.

Senge, P. (1990) *The Fifth Discipline* (New York: Doubleday Currency).

Shanon, B. (1991) 'Cognitive Psychology and Modern Physics: Some Analogies', *European Journal of Cognitive Psychology*, 3, pp. 201–34.

Shanon, B. (1993) 'Fractal Patterns in Language', *New Ideas in Psychology*, vol. 11, no. 1, pp. 105–9.

Silver, M. (ed.) (1991) *Competent to Manage: Approaches to Management Training and Development* (London, UK: Routledge).

Simon, H. (1957) *Models of Man* (New York: Wiley).

Simon, H. (1989) *Models of Thought*, vol. 2 (New Haven, Conn.: Yale University Press).

Simon, H. (1993) 'Strategy and Organizational Evolution', *Strategic Management Journal*, Special Issue, Summer, 14, pp. 131–42.

Singh, J. (ed.) (1990) *Organizational Evolution: New Directions* (London, UK: SAGE).

Smale, S. (1967) 'Differentiable Dynamic Systems', *Bulletin of American Mathematics Society*. vol. 73, pp. 747–17.

Smith, K.K. (1982) 'Philosophical Problems in Thinking About Organizational Change', in P.S. Goodman and associates, *Change in Organizations: New Perspectives on Theory, Research, and Practice* (San Francisco: Jossey-Bass) pp. 316–74.

Smith, S. (1991) 'Beyond "Mega-Theory" and "Multiple Sociology": A Reply to Rottleuthner', *International J. Sociology of Law*, vol. 19, pp. 321–40.

Smuts, J. (1926) *Holism and Evolution* (New York: Macmillan).

Sorri, M. and J.H. Gill (1989) *A Post-Modern Epistemology: Language, Truth and Body* (Lewinston, NY: E. Mellen Press).

Spencer, H. (1851) *Social Statics* (London, UK: Johan Chapman).

Spender, J-C. (1989) *Industry Recipes: The Nature of Sources of Managerial Judgement* (London: Blackwell).

Spender, J-C. (1993) 'Workplace Knowledge', paper presented at the conference on 'Distinctive Competences and Tacit Knowledge', IFAP/IRI, Rome, 15 April.

Sproull, L. and S. Kiesler (1991) *Connections: New Ways of Working in the Networked Organization* (Cambridge, Mass.: MIT Press).

Stacey, R.D. (1992) *Managing Chaos* (London: Kogan Page).

Stacey, R.D. (1993) *Organizational Dynamics and Strategic Management* (London, UK: Pitman).

Stauffer, D. (1979) 'Scaling Theory of Percolation Clusters', *Physical Reports*, vol. 54, no. 1, pp. 1–74.

Stein, D.L. (ed.) (1989) *Lectures in the Science of Complexity* (London, UK: Addison-Wesley).

Stern, L.A. (1988) *For All Practical Purposes: Introduction to Contemporary Mathematics* (New York: W.H. Freeman).

Stichweh, R. (1990) 'Self-Organization and Autopoiesis in the Development of Modern Science', *Sociology of the Sciences*, vol. 14, pp. 195–207.

Stinchcombe, A. (1990) *Information and Organizations* (Berkeley, Calif.: University of California Press).

Stoicheff, P. (1991) 'The Chaos of Metafiction', in N.K. Hayles (ed.), *Chaos and Disorder: Complex Dynamics in Literature and Science* (Chicago, Ill.: The University of Chicago Press) pp. 85–99.

Swedenborg, E. (1758) *The Earths In Our Solar Systems Which Are Called Planets And The Earths In The Starry Heavens Their Inhabitants And Spirits And Angels*, first published in Latin, London, 1758 (Rotch Edition: Cambridge, Mass.: Houghton Mifflin, The Riverside Press).

Swenson, R. (1992) 'Autocatakinetics, Yes — Autopoiesis, No: Steps Toward a Unified Theory of Evolutionary Ordering', *International Journal of General Systems*, vol. 21, pp. 207–28.

Swift, J. (1940) *Gulliver's Travels: An Account of the Four Voyages Into Several Remote Nations of the World* (New York: The Heritage Press).

Taylor, F.W. (1911) *The Principles of Scientific Management* (New York: Harper & Row).

Taylor, F.W. (1947) *Scientific Management* (New York: Harper & Brothers).

Taylor, M.C. (1986) *Deconstruction in Context* (Chicago, Ill.: University of Chicago Press).

Teubner, G. (1989) 'How the Law Thinks: Towards a Constructive Epistemology of Law', *Law and Society Review*, vol. 23, pp. 727–57.

Teubner, G. (1991). 'Autopoiesis and Steering: How Politics Profit from the Normative Surplus of Capital', in R.J. in 't Veld, L. Schaap, C.J.A.M. Termeer, and M.J.W. van Twist, *Autopoiesis and Configuration Theory: New Approaches to Social Steering* (Dordrecht: Kluwer Academic Publishers) pp. 127–43.

Thagard, P. (1989) 'Explanatory Coherence', *Behavioural and Brain Sciences*, 12, pp. 435–67.

The Economist (1993) 'Holding a New Mirror to Nature', 6 November, pp. 113–14.

Thompson, J.D. (1967) *Organizations in Action: Social Science Bases of Administration* (New York: McGraw-Hill).

Toulmin, S. (1958) *The Uses of Argument* (Cambridge, Mass.: Cambridge University Press).

Toulmin, S.E., R. Rieke and A. Janik (1979) *An Introduction to Reasoning* (New York: Macmillan).

Tversky, A. and D. Kahneman (1983) 'Extensional Versus Intuitive Reasoning: The Conjunctive Fallacy in Probability Judgement', *Psychological Review*, 90, pp. 292–15.

Uhr, L. (1992) 'Cycling Logarithmically Converging Networks That Flow Information to Behave (Perceive) and Learn', in H. Wechsler (ed.), *Neural Networks for Perception*, vols I and II (Boston, Mass.: Academic Press).

Ulam, S. (1952) 'Random Processes and Transformations', *Proceedings of the International Congress on Mathematics, 1950, vol. 2* (Providence, RI: American Mathematical Society) pp. 264–75.

Ulrich, H. and G.J.B. Probst (eds) (1984) *Self-Organization and Management of Social Systems* (New York: Springer Verlag).

Van de Ven, A. (1992) 'Suggestions for Studying Strategy Process: A Research Note', *Strategic Management Journal*, 13, pp. 169–88.

Van Maanen, J. (1991) 'The Smile-Factory: Work at Disneyland', in P. Frost, L.F. Moore, M.R. Louis, C.C. Lunberg and J. Martin (eds), *Reframing Organizational Culture* (Newsbury Park, Calif.: Sage).

van der Zouwen, J. (1990) 'The Impact of Self-Referentiality of Social Systems on Research Methodology', in F. Geyer and J. Van der Zouwen (eds), *Self-Referencing in Social Systems* (Salinsa, Calif.: Intersystems Publications) pp. 69–84.

van Twist, M.J.W. and L. Schaap (1991). 'Introduction to Autopoiesis Theory and Autopoietic Steering', in R.J. in't Veld, L. Schaap, C.J.A.M. Termeer, and M.J.W. van Twist, *Autopoiesis and Configuration Theory: New Approaches to Social Steering* (Dordrecht: Kluwer Academic Publishers) pp. 31–44.

Varela, F.J. (1979) *Principles of Biological Autonomy* (Amsterdam: North-Holland).

Varela, F.J. (1984) 'Two Principles of Self-Organization', in H. Ulrich and G.J.B. Probst (eds), *Self-Organization and Management of Social System* (New York: Springer Verlag).

Varela, F.J. (1992) 'Whence Perceptual Meaning? A Cartography of Current Ideas', in F.J. Varela and J.P. Dupuy (eds), *Understanding Origins: Contemporary Views on the Origin of Life, Mind and Society* (Dordrecht: Kluwer Academic Publishers), pp. 235–64.

Varela, F.J. and P. Bourgine (eds) (1992) *Toward a Practice of Autonomous Systems* (Cambridge, Mass.: MIT Press).

Varela, F.J., E. Thompson and E. Rosch (1992) *The Embodied Mind* (Cambridge, Mas.: MIT Press).

Varela, F.J., H.R. Maturana and R. Uribe (1974) 'Autopoiesis: The Organization of Living Systems, Its Characterization and a Model', *BioSystems*, vol. 5, pp. 187–96.

Vicari, S. (1991) *The Living Firm* (Milano: EtasLibri) (in Italian).

Voltaire (1985) 'Micromégas', in W. Fowlie (ed.), *Frensch Stories* (New York: Dover Publications) pp. 2–43.

Waldrop, M.M. (1992) *Complexity: The Emerging Science at the Edge of Order and Chaos* (London, UK: Viking).

Wallace, R. (1993) 'A Fractal Model of HIV Transmission on Complex Sociogeographic Networks: Towards Analysis of Large Data Sets', *Environment and Planning*, vol. 25, pp. 137–48.

Walsh, J.P. and G.R. Ungson (1991) 'Organizational Memory', *Academy of Management Review*, 16, pp. 57–91.

Wang, Y.M. and G.J. Wang (1993) 'Self-Similar and Transient Void Growth in Viscoelastic Media at Low Concentration', *International Journal of Fracture*, vol. 61, pp. 1–16.

Wathne, K., J. Roos and G. von Krogh (1994) 'Knowledge Transfer and in a Cooperative Context', paper presented at the 14th Strategic Management Society conference, Jouy-en-Jousas, Paris, 20–23 Sept.

Watson, B. (1968) *The Complete Works of Chuang Tzu* (New York: Columbia University Press).

Weathly, M.J. (1992) *Leadership and the New Science* (San Francisco: Berrett-Koehler Publishers).

Weber, M. (1947) *The Theory of Social Economic Organization*, ed. A. Henderson and T. Parsons (Glencoe, Ill.: Free Press).

Weber, M. (1978) 'Value-Judgements in Social Science', paper presented at the Association for Social Policy, 1913, reprinted in W.G. Runciman (ed.) (1978), *Weber: Selections in Translation* (Cambridge, UK: Cambridge University Press) pp. 69–98.

Wechsler, H. (ed.) (1992) *Neural Networks for Perception*, vols I and II (Boston, Mass.: Academic Press).

Weick, K.E. (1979) *The Social Psychology of Organizing* (New York: Random House).

Weick, K.E. and M. Bougnon (1986) 'Organizations as Cognitive Maps', in H.P. Sims and D.A. Gioia (eds), *The Thinking Organization* (San Francisco, Calif.: Jossey-Bass).

Weick, K.E. and K.H. Roberts (1993) 'Collective Mind in Organizations: Heedful Interrelating on Flight Decks', *Administrative Science Quarterly*, 38, pp. 357–81.

Weiss, G. (1992) 'Chaos Hits Wall Street — The Theory, That Is', *Business Week*, 2 November pp. 58–60.

Weiss, P. (1967) '1 + 1 = 2 (When One Plus One Does Not Equal To Two)', in T. Melnechuk and F. Schnitt (eds), *Neurosciences: A Study Program* (New York: Rockefeller University Press) pp. 801–21.

Weiss, P. (1973) *The Science of Life* (New York: Future Publishing Company).

Weissert, T.P. (1991) 'Representation and Bifurcation: Borge's Garden of Chaos Dynamics', in N.K. Hayles (ed.), *Chaos and Disorder: Complex Dynamics in Literature and Science* (Chicago, Ill. University of Chicago Press) pp. 223–43.

Werner, G. (1987) 'Cognition as Self-Organizing Process', *Behavioral and Brain Science*, vol. 10, no. 2, p. 183.

Westley, F.R. (1990) 'Middle Managers and Strategy: Microdynamics of Inclusion', *Strategic Management Journal*, 11, pp. 337–51.

White, R. and G. Engelen (1993) 'Cellular Automata and Fractal Urban Form: A Cellular Modelling Approach to the Evolution of Urban Land-Use Patterns', *Environment and Planning A*, vol. 25, pp. 1175–99.

Whyte, W.F. (ed.) (1991) *Participatory Action Research* (Beverly Hills, Calif.: Sage).

Wiener, N. (1961) *Cybernetics* (New York: John Wiley).

Wilber, K. (ed.) (1985) *The Holographic Paradigm and Other Paradoxes* (Boston, Mass.: Shambhala).

Williams, D. and B. Julesz (1992) 'Filter versus Textors in Human and Machine Texture Discrimination', in H. Wechsler (ed.), *Neural Networks for Perception*, vols I and II (Boston, Mass.: Academic Press).

Williamson, O.E. (1975) *Markets and Hierarchies: Analysis and Antitrust Implications* (New York: Free Press).

Winograd, T. and F. Flores (1987) *Understanding Computers and Cognition* (Norwood, NJ: Ablex Publishing).

Winter, S. (1987) 'Knowledge and Competence as Strategic Assets', in D.J. Teece (ed.), *The Competitive Challenge* (Cambridge, Mass.: Ballinger).

Wisdom, J. (1992) 'Philosophical Perplexity', in R. Rorty (ed.), *The Linguistic Turn: Essays in Philosophical Method* (Chicago, Ill.: University of Chicago Press).

Witten, T.A. jr. (1993) 'Fractal Growth: A Continuing Mystery', *Current Contents*, no. 18, pp. 8.

Wittgenstein, L. (1953) *Philosophical Investigations* (New York: MacMillan).

Wittgenstein, L. (1958) *The Blue and Brown Books* (London, UK: Blackwell).

Wolf, A. (1910) *Spinoza's Short Treatise on God, Man, and His Well-Being* (London).

Yip, G. (1992) *Total Global Strategy: Managing for World-Wide Competitive Advantage* (Englewood Cliffs, NJ: Prentice-Hall).

Young, T.R. (1991) 'Chaos and Social Change: Metaphysics of the Postmodern', *The Social Science Journal*, vol. 28, no. 2, pp. 289–05.

Zappa, G. (1950) *Il reddito d'impresa*, 2nd edn (Milan: Giuffrè).

Zeleny, M. (ed.) (1980) *Autopoiesis; Dissipative Structures, and Spontaneous Social Order* (Boulder, Co: Westview Press).

Zeleny, M. (1987) 'Cybernetyka', *International Journal of General Systems*, vol. 13, pp. 289–94.

Zeleny, M. (1988) 'Tectology', *International Journal of General Systems*, vol. 14, pp. 331–43.

Zeleny, M. and K.D. Hufford (1992) The Application of Autopoiesis in Systems Analysis: Are Autopoietic Systems Also Social Systems?', *International Journal of General Systems*, vol. 21, pp. 145–60.

Zimmerman, B.J. (1993) 'The Inherent Drive Towards Chaos', in P. Lorange, B. Chakravarthy, J. Roos and A. Van de Ven, *Implementing Strategic Processes: Change, Learning and Co-operation* (London: Blackwell) pp. 373–93.

Zimmerman, B. and D.K. Hurst (1993) 'Breaking the Boundaries: The Fractal Organization', *Journal of Management Inquiry*, vol. 2, no. 4 (December) pp. 334–55.

Zolo, N. (1992) The Epistemological Status of the Theory of Autopoiesis and Its Application to the Social Sciences', in A. Febbrajo and G. Teubner (eds), *State, Law and Economy as Autopoietic Systems: Regulation and Autonomy in a New Perspective* (Milan: Giuffre), pp. 67–124.

Index